GET THE CHILDREN OUT:
UNSUNG HEROES OF THE KINDERTRANSPORT

MIKE LEVY

WITH FOREWORD BY LORD ALF DUBS

This book is dedicated to the countless number of people who helped to rescue and restore the lives of 10,000 children. It is also in memory of the parents left behind and the millions of other Jews who were not saved from the Nazi onslaught.

In support of

LEGAL ROUTES TO SANCTUARY

£1 from the sale of this book will be donated to Safe Passage (charity number 1179608) and used to help child refugees find legal routes to sanctuary. Find out more about Safe Passage by visiting **www.safepassage.org.uk**

Published in the UK by Lemon Soul Ltd
5 Broadbent Close, London, United Kingdom, N6 5JW
Company number 09694095

ISBN 978-1-9993781-4-1

Set in Adobe Caslon Pro

Printed in the UK by Clays Ltd, Elcograf S.p.A.

All views expressed in this book are those of the author and do not
necessarily represent the views of the publisher.

www.lemonsoul.com

Contents

Foreword
By Lord Alf Dubs

I arrived in London in June 1939 on a kindertransport from Prague.

I have no doubt that my place on that train saved my life. The family and friends we left behind in Prague all perished.

Although, at six, I was one of the youngest children on the train I can remember the journey.

I remember my mother putting me on the train with a knapsack of food. I can still clearly see her in my mind standing on the platform waving me off, surrounded by German soldiers in uniforms and swastikas. Of course, for some of the parents waving their children off that day, it was the last time they ever saw them.

We travelled in carriages of 6-8. We had hard wooden seats to sit and sleep on. It was no great hardship for us – we were children and didn't mind sleeping on the benches.

It took one day to get to the Dutch border and two days to get to Liverpool Street. I remember that the journey seemed interminably long to me and that when we reached Holland the older children on the train started cheering – I didn't know why – I was looking out for windmills and wooden shoes. Only afterwards did I understand that they were cheering because we had reached safety from the Nazis.

Foreword

From the border the train took us to the Hook of Holland and from there we took a boat to Harwich and then came via train to Liverpool Street.

I remember that scene too - we children all wore dog tags and were allocated family or foster parents. I was lucky; my father was waiting for me. When I got to London he realised that I hadn't touched the food my mother had packed for me 2 days before.

But what I can't remember, because I never knew them, are the names of all the people involved in that extraordinary effort to save my life and the lives of 10,000 mostly Jewish children like me.

It wasn't until 1988 and a very special edition of That's Life, that I learnt of the central role in that life-saving effort of Sir Nicky Winton. After that TV show we became friends and I was able to thank Nicky personally for saving my life. Nicky's role was undoubtedly remarkable in helping to rescue children from Czechoslovakia but he wasn't alone. There were others who helped him in Prague and also those who organised Kindertransports from Germany and Austria. They were helped by people we hear less about, both in Nazi Europe and the UK, among them volunteers, politicians and activists, who played a part in lobbying, logistics and linking children with families, who also chose to shine light and hope into the lives of children fleeing Nazi horrors. I am very glad that they too will be honoured in this book and that I might learn about another piece of the jigsaw that is my early life and how it was that I was lucky enough to be saved during that dark time in European history.

Prologue

The Chadwick family - Suzie far right, Image 1

On a cold January day in 2009, a 75-year-old woman addressed a 99 year-old man, whom she had never met before, with the words, 'Thank you for bringing my sister into our lives'. The lady was Ann Chadwick, the old man, Sir Nicholas Winton and the setting was the cavernous Guildhall in Cambridge. Another man, Aubrey Chadwick, shook Sir Nicholas' hand with exceptional vigour given that he was then 94 years old. The two nonagenarians smiled nervously at each other while Ann brushed away a tear. There was another person with the Chadwicks and Sir Nicholas on that night in Cambridge. Me.

Seventy years before this meeting, the Chadwicks were a

Prologue

British family who decided to take into their home in Cambridge a complete stranger: a young girl aged five who couldn't speak a word of English. Aubrey and his wife Winifred, with the two-year-old Ann in tow, met the little girl at Cambridge station in early July 1939. The girl with the curly black hair held on tight to the hand of an older chaperone who had travelled with her by train from the city of Prague. The girl was Suzanne Spitzer, born in Vienna to Jewish parents, by that time living as impoverished refugees in the Czech capital. Her mutti and papa, Hansi and Leo, would not survive the Holocaust – two of the six million. Suzie's farewell at the Wilson Station in Prague would be the last time she ever saw her parents. This shattering experience would also be felt by the majority (possibly more than 75 per cent) of the 10,000 Kinder. A new country – Britain – meant in most cases, a new family.

As is pretty well known, Winton is regarded as responsible for bringing 669 mainly Jewish children out of mortal danger in the Czech lands to safety in Britain. Indeed, the Kindertransport programme is often associated in Britain with one name – that of Sir Nicholas Winton. His fame was sealed at a showing in 1989 of the BBC TV series 'That's Life' hosted by Esther Rantzen. Decades on, the programme (still findable on YouTube) packs an incredible emotional punch. Winton, then turning 80, had not been told why he'd been invited to the show. Unbeknown to Sir Nicholas (as he later became), the first few rows of the live audience were populated by middle-aged adults who, it turned out, were saved thanks to the actions of the old man fifty years before. When Rantzen asked the audience to stand if they were here thanks to the rescue work of Nicholas Winton, many of them did. An astonished Winton turned to discover that the adults, whom he imagined were strangers, were there to salute him and give thanks for their lives. The dignified, often unemotional, old man wiped away a tear and so did, I imagine, a myriad of viewers throughout the land.

Since that broadcast and a first reunion of surviving Kinder in the same year as the Rantzen show, public awareness of the role played by Britain in saving around 10,000 mostly Jewish children from the murderous intentions of the Nazis, has grown. Many former Kinder have written their own stories, spoken to schools and other groups, had TV documentaries such as the Oscar winning 'Into the Arms of Strangers' made about them. The Kindertransport has often been portrayed as a triumphant episode in British history – 'one in the eye' for Hitler and his cronies. Successive governments in Westminster have sought to portray the rescue as a 'top-down' initiative, albeit one spearheaded by the iconic Sir Nicholas.

The truth, as with all history, is much more complex and nuanced. For me, the story of how we in Britain dealt with the refugee crises of the mid to late 1930s, and beyond is essentially a 'bottom-up' narrative. Rescuers were overwhelmingly drawn from the massed ranks of British volunteers. Saving and rescuing the children was not done by some benevolent section of the Civil Service (far from it), but by legions of individuals – men and women who responded to the evils of Nazism and its attack on innocent men, women and children, out of altruism; people such as the subjects of this book, volunteers like Win and Aubrey Chadwick.

Uncovering the story of Suzanne and her foster family led me down a long and winding path towards the writing of this book. Suzanne was part of the so-called 'Kindertransport', a rescue programme, unique in many respects, which brought around 10,000 unaccompanied children, mostly Jewish, to safety in the UK during the last month of 1938 up to the outbreak of war in September 1939. The story of the young daughter of Leo and Hansi Spitzer, both Holocaust victims, and the child's subsequent life with her 'new' mummy and daddy, Aubrey and Win - not forgetting 'sister' Ann - became a bit of an obsession for me.

The Chadwick/Spitzer story stimulated my interest in the Kindertransport and the whole issue of unaccompanied children, especially the young Jewish refugees from Nazi Germany, Austria, Poland and occupied Czechoslovakia. I wasn't starting from scratch. As a former history teacher and current Holocaust educator, I knew the basics of the Kindertransport, but admit to falling under the spell of many inaccurate generalisations.

These included the myth that Nicholas Winton was alone in saving the children and that the actions of British foster families were usually motivated by a desire to convert the unfortunate Jewish children in their care or exploit them as unpaid servants (or worse). There is no doubt, however, that Sir Nicholas was involved in organising Suzie's flight from Prague, her journey by train through Germany, Holland, across the seas to England then by train to London and finally a steam locomotive pulling its LNER carriages from London King's Cross Station to the dreamy spires of Cambridge and its historic colleges. It is also more than possible that Winton answered a reply from the Chadwicks to a nationwide call for foster families. Names and photographs of children were posted around the country and some time in early 1939, Win and Aubrey Chadwick answered the call by offering their home to this Suzanne Spitzer, a child they only knew from her photograph. In this sense Sir Nicholas really did bring Ann a new sister – one that would remain with her for the rest of Suzie's life.

I love finding things out. Maybe I should have had a career as a sleuth but sniffing around in archives, finding living witnesses to historical events, putting two and two together (sometimes to make three) – that's my pleasure. Suzie was the tip of a very large but melting iceberg. Melting because the living witnesses to the rescue and care for so many child refugees, shorn from their families, bereft of motherly comforts or fatherly reassurance, were disappearing under the rising tide of mortality.

The events of the Kindertransport took place more than eighty years ago. Anyone with memories, either as a refugee or foster family member, would have to be in their late eighties or nineties. Foster parents – those who volunteered to care for children like Suzie – would have to be over 100. I was lucky to track down Aubrey Chadwick who remained cogent and brimful of memories until his death at the grand age of 102. So far, other foster parents from that time have remained elusive. My dream is that a reader of this book will have a centenarian grandparent who can tell me more about their German Jewish wartime foster child; or failing that, there is a cache of documents and letters waiting to be prised open. Is there a tomb of Tutankhamun of the Kindertransport still out there?

Thinking about the Chadwicks and what they did to try to alleviate the utter tragedy of the deaths of Suzie's parents (both in Nazi death camps), made me wonder about the whole national effort to be in loco parentis for these unfortunate exiles. There are many excellent books about the Kindertransport – memoirs of Kinder themselves abound and learned tomes about the programme have mushroomed in the last thirty years or more. But rarely do these works focus on the organisation of the children's escape from Nazi tyranny.

Who liaised with the desperate parents - isolated, terrorised, locked up and beaten in Berlin, Vienna, Frankfurt or Cologne? Who lobbied the government here to let the children go? Who were the MPs, activists and benign 'troublemakers' who pressurised Neville Chamberlain's government into opening the doors to at least some of the benighted youngsters in peril of their lives? Once the UK government lifted visa restrictions on the children at risk in Nazi lands, who organised their escape? Who selected the children, liaised with desperate parents, arranged the transports, found foster parents in Britain and a thousand other roles?

The answers – some of them – are the subject of this book. Though there is still much digging to be done in the archaeology of obscurely collected documents and living memory, I want this book to be a kind of belated 'thank you' to the men and women who did what they could to resist the onslaught on children, to be a kind hand in a bitterly cruel world, to stand up for humanity and in selfless acts to achieve what must be one of the highest accolades that any human can achieve – to be called 'a rescuer'. A hero no longer forgotten.

Historical Background
Descent into Darkness

The 1930s saw something both extraordinary and deeply tragic: a mass of young refugees, some no more than babies, with no family to support them. Cast adrift in a foreign country with no language, no parents, no money, the world had to learn how to deal with such desperate need. These dispossessed children were those of Jewish ancestry in Hitler's new "German empire". War, persecution and refugees were part of a toxic mix that characterised the world between the rise of Hitler in 1933 and the end of the Second World War in 1945. Of course, every refugee needs a refuge, a place of safety. Britain, or more accurately the United Kingdom, certainly played its part in providing a safe haven for the benighted children who were victims of hate and war.

With the accession of Hitler as Germany's leader in January 1933, that country was led by a party, the National Socialists or Nazi party, which was virulently antisemitic and viciously racist. It was not enough to scapegoat Germany's Jews, a tiny minority in the land (less than 1% of the population) for all of the country's post First World War ills. Relentless propaganda blamed the Jews for Germany's defeat in that war, for the rise of communism, for the evils of capitalism (yes, both), for the nation's economic woes. But overriding all was a deep-rooted belief in racial theories: the Jewish 'race', said the Nazis, were of tainted stock thus threatening the racial 'purity' of those with Aryan blood in their veins. You cannot comprehend the Nazi obsession with eliminating Jews from their society without understanding that behind their beliefs (surely stronger than any religion) was the threat posed by the 'malevolent', 'subhuman' Jew to the future body politick of the Aryan master race. This is why children, even new born babies, were not immune from the Nazi attack on the Jewish people. This is why one and a half million children were murdered in the Holocaust between 1941 and 1945. This is why children of Jewish 'racial origin' were in mortal danger if they stayed in Nazi controlled lands. This is why 10,000 managed to escape to Britain on the Kindertransport. They were Jews or those with a Jewish grandparent. The latter could be practising and baptised Christians. To the Nazis, it mattered not. This was not about religion. It was about race – as defined not by Jews themselves, but by the Nazis.

Though the bulk of this book is about the rescue of Jewish children from Nazi Germany and other countries subjugated by Hitler's forces, the context of the rescue of the 10,000 children should be seen against other attempts to 'get the children out'. This includes the nearly 4,000 children brought to Britain from the Basque country of northern Spain in May 1937 and the 1,000 or so, barely surviving youngsters languishing in refugee camps in war demolished Europe between 1945 and 1948. Attempts were made during the war to get out some of the children trapped inside the wall of steel created by Nazi rule and invasion. They came to nothing. Jewish children in Nazi lands had very little chance of survival once the policy of mass genocide was put in motion (arguably from the summer of 1941).

The position of the Jewish population (and those deemed to

be Jewish 'by blood') gradually deteriorated during the Nazi era. Following on from the so-called Nuremburg Laws of 1935, Jews (as Nazi defined) lost their German citizenship, were forbidden to marry or have relations with 'Aryans' and a string of decrees ensured that they were excluded from wider society. They were barred from dealing with non-Jewish customers, patients and clients, they were forbidden to use parks, skating rinks, swimming pools, beaches, hotels, restaurants... the list grew with every passing month of the mid to late 1930s. Children were not exempt from this policy of pariah status for Jews.

The writing was on the wall from the German annexation of Austria (the Anschluss) in March 1938, and within hours of Nazi troops marching into Vienna, amid cheering crowds, assaults on the city's Jews began in a public way that had not been seen before. Gangs of emboldened young Nazis, often in brown shirt uniforms, thought nothing of beating up and even murdering Jews in the streets.

What was the reaction of the British government? To impose new visa restrictions on anyone trying to enter the UK from the new German Reich. An international conference on the refugee crisis held at Evian-les-Bains in France resulted in next to nothing. Hopes raised and dashed.

The infamous Munich Agreement signed at the end of September that year between Britain, Germany and others in effect gave Hitler the go-ahead to march his troops into German-speaking regions of Czechoslovakia, known as the Sudetenland. This led to the imposition of anti-Jewish actions and the subsequent mass emigration of Jews from these areas to cities such as Prague which remained unoccupied until March 1939. Within weeks of Munich, Czech cities were surrounded by miserably equipped and hastily erected refugee camps.

The pressure on German and Austrian Jewish organisations to help get the most vulnerable Jews out of harm's way dramatically intensified during the night of 9-10 November 1938. The Nazis had been waiting for any excuse to unleash violence on German and Austrian Jews and their moment came in the shooting of a German official at the Paris embassy by a disgruntled Polish Jew, Herschel Grynszpan. Carefully stage-managed outrage was whipped up by Nazi supporters who were prepped to go on the rampage against innocent men, women and children. The signal went out from the Nazi hierarchy to begin a state-wide attack on Jews, their businesses and property.

This was so-called 'Kristallnacht', an ironic Nazi reference to the shattering of glass heard throughout that fateful night. More aptly described as the 'November Pogroms', the attack on Jews throughout Germany and Austria was the largest assault yet by Nazis and their supporters in the five-year history of Hitler's regime. Well-organised and led from the very top of the Nazi hierarchy, the scale of destruction was beyond the worst fears of the Jewish community. Up to 1,000 synagogues were destroyed by fire and local fire brigades were called out, but only to protect adjacent buildings owned by Aryans. During the night Jewish businesses were smashed and looted and while this act of mass theft did not perturb the Nazi regime, they issued orders for that to stop lest the state might be deprived of these Jewish-owned assets. The official death toll that night alone was nearly 100 and there were so many suicides that in one German city the authorities turned off gas supplies to their Jewish users. In most German and Austrian cities, towns and villages the screams of women and children were heard by passive neighbours as their homes were attacked in the middle of the night.

In addition to the assault on buildings some 30,000 Jewish

men – fathers, grandfathers, uncles and brothers were arrested, physically abused and packed off to concentration camps such as Dachau where many perished at the hands of brutal tormentors. Enforced roll calls lasting hours, starvation diets, beatings and public hangings were the order of the day in these terrible camps.

The November Pogrom changed everything; a night that sent shock waves of revulsion throughout the world not least in Britain. The public called for action. It was only now that the British Home Secretary agreed to allow unaccompanied children up to the age of 17 to enter Britain, albeit temporarily, and on the grounds that they would not be a burden on the taxpayer. This was the genesis of the Kindertransport. With mass immigration decidedly not an option, the cry went up, **'WE MUST GET THE CHILDREN OUT.'**

The Times Newspaper, Image 2

This notice appeared in The Times newspaper in January 1939. It was part of a nationwide fundraising appeal led by former prime minister Stanley Baldwin to help bring thousands of Jewish children away from Nazi persecution. The response to the 'Baldwin Fund' was unprecedented - but was it enough?

PART I:

BRITAIN - A COUNTRY OF REFUGE

Chapter 1

The Spy and the Diplomats
Frank Foley and Robert T. Smallbones

Frank Foley, Image 3   Inge and Robert T. Smallbones, Image 4

Tearing up the rulebook is something we usually associate with fictional secret agents such as James Bond. Less expected perhaps was the destruction of regulations staged in the heart of Hitler's Reich by Captain Frank Foley, former soldier turned passport official and British spy who has been dubbed 'The British Schindler'.

In 1961 at the trial of Adolph Eichmann in Israel, a key witness, Benno Cohn who had been in pre-war Berlin as

1

head of the German Zionist Organisation, said this of the British official who had granted desperate German Jews entry certificates to Palestine: 'That was thanks to a man who is to my mind to be counted among the Righteous Gentiles [...] One may say that he saved thousands of Jews from death.'

Francis (Frank) Foley was born in Highbridge, Somerset in 1884. A devout Roman Catholic, he considered a calling to the priesthood and attended a seminary in France. Casting aside a life in the clergy, he entered a French university and subsequently took up a variety of teaching roles around Europe. His travels came to an abrupt end with the outbreak of war in August 1914. Frank volunteered for the army and signed up for the Bedford and Herts Regiment where he became a second lieutenant. Seconded to the North Staffordshire Regiment he was sent with his men to France in January 1917.

Just over a year later in March 1918, Captain Frank Foley was engaged in defending the village of Ecoust against a ferocious German onslaught that culminated in the use of poison gas and hand-to-hand fighting. Foley was shot in the chest and had to be carried back by his men to relative safety.

Though Frank's wounds made him unfit for frontline duty, Foley, a talented linguist, was able to fulfil a personal wish – to work for British military intelligence. It was in this role that he was posted in 1922 to the British Embassy in Berlin. His official role at the Passport Control Office (PCO) was, however, a cover for his intelligence duties, which, in the aftermath of the October Revolution of 1917, included surveillance of refugee Russians in the German capital some of whom were suspected of communist sympathies. A year before his posting to Berlin, Foley married his lifelong partner Kay, with whom he had a daughter, Ursula. They continued to live in Berlin, where Foley reported back to his British handlers on Hitler's rise to power, writing in 1935 an insightful assessment of Nazi racial policies:

"It is becoming increasingly apparent that the (Nazi) Party has not departed from its original intentions and that its ultimate aim remains the disappearance of the Jews from Germany or, failing that, their relegation to a position of powerlessness and inferiority. Indications of this recrudescence of anti-Semitism are apparent in recent legislative measures, in regulations governing admission to the liberal professions, in the boycotting of Jewish concerns and in the increasing virulence of speeches of leading members of the Party."

After the First World War, Britain agreed to waive visa restrictions on citizens of Germany and Austria. However, these were reintroduced a few weeks after Hitler's annexation of Austria in March 1938, when it became clear to the British government that large-scale immigration by persecuted Jews from the German Reich was likely. There was a fear that uncontrolled numbers of refugees, most of them near destitute, would be arriving at British ports, and to avoid unpleasant scenes in Harwich, Dover, Southampton and other points of entry, the government decided to apply visa restrictions on all German and Austrian citizens wishing to enter the country. Advice sent by the British Home Office to the PCOs in the German Reich warned that persons of 'Jewish origin,' or 'Non Aryans' seeking a temporary visitor's visa, were most likely to be potential refugees. It was, they said, the duty of the PCO to judge the veracity of each application – put bluntly, was a Jewish applicant telling the truth when he or she applied for temporary entry into the UK?

These new regulations left Jewish families in the German Reich feeling increasingly vulnerable. After the November

Pogrom events on 9-10 November 1938, Foley's office in Berlin's Tiergartenstrasse was surrounded by ever-lengthening queues of Jewish men, women and children desperate to receive the correct papers that would mean they could leave Germany. Not only did they need a stamp of approval on their British visa, but they were additionally required to have paperwork showing that they had complied with exit procedures enforced by the Nazi authorities: payment of punishing taxes or 'fines', timed exit visas given by the Gestapo and even, for the young, the requirement for an exemption certificate from the Hitler Youth.

With tightening immigration controls and a British Foreign Office almost at breaking point with the sheer scale of applications, the official processes could take two or three months. By late 1938 and the first eight months of 1939, it was clear that time was not on the side of German Jews. Captain Foley knew that and took it upon himself to stamp visa application forms without waiting for London to say 'yes'.

Throughout the tense period leading up to the outbreak of war, Foley worked tirelessly to grant entry documents to as many Jews as he could. His offices were scenes of chaos, and sometimes tragedy, as harassed officials sought to process the crowds of would-be emigrants. 'Families were often represented only by their womenfolk, many of them in tears,' noted one observer on a morning visit to the PCO, 'while the men of the family waited in a concentration camp until some evidence of likelihood of emigration could be shown to the Secret Police'. Racial tensions added to the atmosphere of gathering panic, the same witness reporting that doors to the inner offices were kept closed and guarded, "much to the annoyance of Germans seeking visas, some of whom complained angrily of being forced to wait among Jews and demanded preferential treatment, though without success".

Foley's wife Kay describes the scene in pitiful detail:

Jews trying to find a way out of Germany queued in their hundreds outside the British Consulate, clinging to the hope that they would get a passport or a visa. Day after day we saw them standing along the corridors, down the steps and across the large courtyard, waiting their turn to fill in the forms that might lead to freedom.

In the end, that queue grew to be a mile long. Some were hysterical. Many wept. All were desperate. With them came a flood of cables and letters from other parts of the country, all pleading for visas and begging for help. For them, Frank's 'yes' or 'no' really meant the difference between a new life and the concentration camps. But there were many difficulties. How could so many people be interviewed before their turn came for that dreaded knock on the door.'

Not content with creating what amounted to false papers, Foley also hid a number of Jews on the run from the Nazis in his own home. Foley also allowed Rabbi Leo Baeck, the Chairman of the Association of German Rabbis and a leading thinker in Reform Judaism, to use his apartment to brief the British and other foreign media. Despite offers of a British visa, Baeck decided to stay with his congregation. He was deported to Theresienstadt concentration camp in 1943 but survived the Holocaust.

Frank Foley quietly built up close contacts with many leading German Jews, one of whom was Wilfrid Israel, the owner of a then famous Berlin department store. Israel had joint British citizenship which gave him a measure of protection against summary arrest by the Gestapo. He also had excellent contacts with leading Jewish figures in Britain (such as Lord Samuel and Chaim Weizmann) and is credited as the architect of the

Kindertransport programme.

As leader of the Jewish self-help body, the Hilfsverein, Wilfrid Israel certainly led the German-end of the scheme and is recognised for saving thousands of Jewish children. Foley was also in close touch with a colleague of Wilfrid Israel, Hubert Pollack, a German Jew whom Frank had recruited as a secret service agent. Pollack, an ardent Zionist, was in close touch with many leading Nazis and knew his way around the web of bribery and corruption that underpinned much of Hitler's Reich. Releasing Jewish men from the brutal concentration camps such as Dachau and Sachsenhausen became a priority for men like Israel and Pollack. The way it often worked went as follows: desperate relatives pleaded for help from Wilfrid Israel who gave funds to Pollack which enabled him to secure release documents. Foley completed the triumvirate of rescue by issuing British visas to those vouched for by Israel and Pollack.

Foley's compassion may have become well-known among the desperate but he remained determined to do things in an orderly way. An eyewitness said of Foley and his work: 'The winter of 1938 was a harsh one and elderly men and women waited from six in the morning, queuing up in the snow and biting wind. Captain Foley saw to it that a uniformed commissionaire trundled a tea-urn on a trolley along the line of frozen misery [...] Others pleaded, offered bribes, threatened, flattered, wept, and threw fits. Capt. Foley always maintained his composure [...] he would not allow himself to be upset by the traumatised herd stampeding across his desk.'

Foley was also well aware of the activities of Zionist organisations to get Jews out of Germany and into Palestine. At the beginning of 1936, he sent a memorandum to the Foreign Office in London urging that the bulk of emigrating

Jews in Germany be sent to Palestine and quotas on labour certificates be extended. As the official mandated power in Palestine, Britain was becoming increasingly hostile to further Jewish immigration and strict quotas of 75,000 over a five-year period were signalled by the Government White Paper of 1939. Despite these restrictions, Foley signed blank visa certificates and issued thousands of special papers allowing young Jews to enter Palestine under the aegis of Youth Aliyah and other Zionist organisations still based in the Reich.

Observers noted that Foley worked from 7am to 10pm without a break. He urged his staff to ensure they were being as speedy as possible in approving applications and pestered the authorities in London to send more certificates to sign. As soon as Foley could, he visited prisoners in concentration camps such as Sachsenhausen to secure their release, and from January 1939 he oversaw the speedy release of young Jewish men to a safe haven in the newly established Kitchener Camp in Kent.

Foley used a variety of loopholes to get around the regulations imposed by his masters in London. As an example, the rules for being allowed a 'capitalist visa' into Palestine required the deposit of £1000. Few German Jews had access to this kind of sum as most bank accounts had been frozen by the Nazis. In one of many examples, Elsbeth Kahn had only £10 to her name yet Foley issued her a visa for Palestine on his belief that the remaining £990 would 'somehow be available' as soon as she landed at the port of Haifa. In another case, a similarly penniless Wolfgang Meyer-Michael was advised by Foley to ask a cousin in Holland to authorise a letter of promise for a loan of £1000. Foley told a bewildered Wolfgang, 'Just get a promise; you don't have to use it.' A Jewish mother also approached Foley as all other efforts to leave Germany had failed by 1938. Foley granted her a visa with the words, 'for the sake of the child.'

Despite his role as an intelligence officer, Foley was never given diplomatic immunity. His work therefore placed him at continuous personal risk of arrest. In what must have been a time of huge anguish for the remaining Jews of the Reich, Captain Foley and his team were called back to Britain on 25 August 1939. His last act, on the very day of his departure from Berlin, was to leave a bundle of signed certificates for eighty young Jews, who were consequently able to leave for Scandinavia and travel onward to Palestine.

Frank Foley's post-Berlin career was, if anything, even more dramatic. His next job was to set up an MI6 station in Norway, from which he recruited and directed trusted agents who were free to enter and leave Nazi Germany. Among the first to hear of Hitler's imminent plans to invade Norway in April 1940, Foley and his team managed to get out of Oslo and link up with the free Norwegian forces led by Major-General Ruge. By early May, however, the situation in Norway had become too dangerous for him to remain and he was evacuated to London by the Royal Navy. Back on British soil one of his first acts was to write a letter of support to the wife of a Jewish exile from Berlin who had been interned on the Isle of Man.

A year later Foley, by now a Major, was charged with the interrogation of Hitler's deputy Rudolf Hess, who, in one of the most bizarre episodes of the war on the home front, had flown a German plane to Scotland, parachuted into a field and been apprehended by two members of the Home Guard. Over the course of a year Foley built a trusting relationship with Hess – dining with him, listening to his paranoid ramblings about how the British establishment prevented him gaining access to the King and his fears of assassination by MI6 – before reaching the conclusion that Hess was insane.

Foley's subsequent work for MI6 included managing German double agents, one of whom provided vital information about the development of the V2 missile system which was used against British cities with such devastating effects from September 1944. He also worked on the strategy to deceive the Germans about the location and timing of the D-Day landings.

Frank Foley retired from his intelligence role in 1949 and spent his last years in the Worcestershire town of Stourbridge. He rarely, if ever, spoke about his work in pre-war Berlin, and it remains unclear how many people were saved by his circumvention of the official rules, though a conservative estimate is that he was responsible for the escape and survival of some 10,000 Jews. Writing just as the war was ending and with his customary self-effacement, Foley commented on the revelations about the Nazi's systematic murder of Europe's Jews.

'Now the people here really and finally believe that the stories of 1938–39 were not exaggerated. Looking back, I feel grateful that our little office in Tiergartenstrasse was able to assist some – far too few – to escape in time.'

To his neighbours in the Worcestershire town of Stourbridge, where he died in 1958 at the age of seventy-four, he was just another unremarkable, if not rather dull, retired Englishman living out his remaining years quietly with his family. Decades after his death, his adopted town of Stourbridge commemorated the quiet spy and rescuer in two ways. A statue unveiled in 2018 by the Duke of Cambridge depicts Frank Foley sitting on a bench feeding a bird, a symbol of freedom. It is perched on his briefcase representing, perhaps, his clandestine work in Berlin. An earlier tribute to the local man is embodied in a memorial plaque at the entrance to the town park. It reads

A TRIBUTE TO A STOURBRIDGE MAN WHO SAVED MANY THOUSANDS OF OPPRESSED PEOPLE FROM THE HOLOCAUST FRANK EDWARD FOLEY 1884-1958 HONOURED BY ISRAEL AT YAD VASHEM JERUSALEM OCTOBER 1999 AS RIGHTEOUS AMONG THE NATIONS

In January 2019, a bronze bust of Frank Foley was unveiled in the Foreign Office building in London. Speaking at the ceremony, the then UK Foreign Secretary Jeremy Hunt said, 'We should reflect that it was not the state as a whole but remarkable individuals like Frank Foley who did the right thing, made the correct moral choice, often in defiance of the rules.'

Frank Foley was not the only British diplomat credited with helping to save Jewish lives in Nazi Germany. In Vienna, the passport control officer there also had the dual role of British MI6 officer and rescuer of hundreds if not many thousands of Jewish families. From Hitler's annexation of Austria in March 1938 to his arrest by the Gestapo, Colonel Thomas Kendrick worked day and night to hand out visas to more than 175 Austrian Jews each day. He would ensure that many families with children got out of danger.

According to his recent biographer, Dr Helen Fry, Kendrick pleaded with colonial masters in India and Rhodesia to allow Jewish migrants to enter their territories. Sadly he had little success in this. Kendrick was not averse to bending more rules by, for instance, issuing false passports and on one occasion, stamping 1,000 temporary visas to Palestine for young German Jewish men to take part in a 'sports camp'. After his arrest in August 1938, Kendrick and his wife were allowed to leave Germany. During the war he set up secret listening stations bugging the conversations of high ranking Nazi captives held in Britain.

Robert T. Smallbones was an equally remarkable figure who, like Foley and Kendrick has recently been recognised in Britain and Frankfurt in Germany with plaques in his honour, including the award of the 'British Hero of the Holocaust'.

Known to his friends and colleagues in the Foreign Office as 'Bones', he was, at the time of the November Pogroms, serving as Consul-General in Frankfurt but happened to be on a visit to London when the rampaging Nazi mobs were unleashed that November night. He received a phone call from Inga, his wife, that the Frankfurt Consulate-General was being besieged by hundreds of terrified Jews. Inga reported that she let as many as she could take refuge in the consular building overnight and that she, their daughter Irene and the servants had been up all night helping serve food to the hungry Jews. Inga urged Robert to try and do something to help.

Next morning Robert Smallbones immediately went to the British Home Office to discuss what could be done to help the desperate men and women in Frankfurt. The senior official he met there shrugged his shoulders and said that little could be done to accept an influx of German immigrants at a time of high unemployment in the country. That said, he asked if Smallbones had a plan. Luckily for those many thousands who were eventually saved, Robert Smallbones did indeed have a lifesaving plan. In his own words:

[...] my idea was based on the fact that under American Law quotas for immigrants had been established for every country, according to the number admitted in 1892, which could not be readily expanded to meet this emergency. We however could give

some relief by allowing German refugees, bound eventually under the quota system for the United States of America to spend a waiting period of a year or more in the United Kingdom on condition that they did not seek employment or were liable to become destitute.

Smallbones was asked to draw up the details of procedure that would be acceptable to the Home Office. Wasting no time, he invited Otto Schiff and some of his colleagues to lunch at the Savoy Hotel. Smallbones and Schiff drafted an undertaking that a potential emigrant from Germany would be asked to sign. They then worked out details of the procedure with the American consular authorities in Germany. Smallbones submitted this at once to the Home Office and was authorised the same afternoon to introduce this system in his consular district. The Foreign Office was then asked to send corresponding instructions to the Passport Control Officer at Berlin (Foley) and to all his consular colleagues in Germany.

Smallbones returned to Frankfurt that same night and went to see the local head of the Gestapo. Smallbones later described the purpose of his visit, which in his own words was to, 'arrange that Jews would be released from the concentration camps if they produced the promise of a British visa and if they had only been interned because they were Jews and if no charge was to be proffered against them'.

However, he was told that they could only be released if, in addition, they had all their 22 German emigration papers in order: passports, exit visas, certificates from the tax authorities that they had paid income and other taxes and so on. Smallbones replied that this was an impossible condition as they could not themselves attend to these formalities while locked up. Also as the Jewish lawyers who could act for them were also interned, few Aryan lawyers would risk importuning the authorities on their behalf. Smallbones, not a man to be intimidated, later described how this meeting ended:

We had a fierce argument and I started shouting in the proper German manner. When I jumped up and said that my proposal to help Germany to be rid of some of their Jews was off, and that I would report by telegram to my Government, the Gestapo bully collapsed and we made an agreement in the sense desired by me. I know of no case in which a promise of a visa given by me did not lead to the immediate release of the interned.

One should step back and weigh up the words of that fearless consular official whose Visa Scheme saved so many incarcerated in the hell of Dachau, Sachenhausen or other notorious concentration camps. The task now facing the consulate-general involved proved formidable and Smallbones described how he worked day and night to secure the release from concentration camps. He had said in the Home Office that he would be personally responsible for the ultimate decision in each case in his own district and usually worked around 18 hours a day, once even falling asleep at his desk.

Again the words from his unpublished memoirs are incredibly telling

I went to bed…. After two hours sleep my conscience pricked me. The feeling was horrible that there were people in concentration camp whom I could get out and that I was comfortable in bed…. I returned to my desk and stayed there until the next midnight. I had a nervous breakdown after a few months…. The last straw that broke my back was the case of a person who died in a concentration camp because one of my staff had failed to get my signature and to dispatch the promise of a visa which was in order.

Get the children out!

Robert Smallbones was helped in his rescue missions by his vice-consul, Arthur Dowden. The two men and a fairly large staff churned out 'Smallbones visas' as fast as they could and there is a wonderful story of Dowden touring the streets of Frankfurt in his car personally handing out food to those in need. It is estimated that over 47,000 people were rescued by Smallbones and his team. Among them were the grandparents of British rabbis Jonathan Wittenberg and Julia Neuberger. A question hangs in the air – what motivated Robert Smallbones to do all that he had done? According to his granddaughter he told her that by using his personal initiative and doing what he saw as his humanitarian duty, it made him feel as if he had done his good deed like a boy scout.

Chapter 2

The Parliamentarian
Josiah Wedgwood

Josiah Wedgwood, Image 5

Josiah Clement Wedgwood, the great-great-grandson of the founder of the famous pottery dynasty, was closely related to the family of Charles Darwin and Ralph Vaughan Williams. A radical member of parliament and noted campaigner for the rights of refugees, over a long political career he earned a reputation as a fighter for justice and was often at odds with the ruling elites.

Born in Staffordshire in 1872, young Wedgwood gained a scholarship to the Royal Naval College in Greenwich, but a short-lived career in ship design was interrupted by the outbreak of the Boer War. He volunteered to become a soldier and after a spell in active service became a magistrate in Transvaal, South Africa. Upon his return to England, he won a seat as a Liberal member of parliament in the 1906 election and rapidly gained a reputation as a powerful orator and defender of civil liberties. He publicly criticised the government for prosecuting left-wing writers who had urged troops not to fire on striking workers.

Wedgwood volunteered again in the First World War and was wounded at Gallipoli in 1915. He was awarded the DSO for his bravery and Churchill sent him on official business to Russia to contact Menshevik revolutionaries; he was given the rank of Colonel, a title he used for the rest of his life. In 1924, after the war, and a messy, all too public divorce, Wedgwood defected from the Liberal to the Labour Party, serving as Chancellor of the Duchy of Lancaster in its inaugural government. However, during the 1930s, he was increasingly perceived as a rebellious MP who was at odds with the Labour leader, Ramsay MacDonald, and he often refused to obey the party whip. During a parliamentary career that lasted right up to his death in January 1943, he espoused a variety of causes, including Indian independence, the taxation of land values and a national home for the Jews in Palestine, on which question he advocated the creation of a new 'Jewish dominion' as part of the British Empire.

A frequent visitor to Germany in the 1920s, Wedgwood was quick to identify the threats posed by Hitler and his followers and railed against British establishment figures sympathetic to the Nazi leader. Convinced from the moment Hitler came to power that Britain should prepare for war, he was a fierce opponent of the government's policy of appeasement. He struck up a lasting friendship with Churchill and formed part of a vocal parliamentary lobby, urging the country to rearm and resist any rapprochement with Nazi Germany. As early as April 1933 he turned his attention to the plight of refugees from Hitler's territories, advocating in Parliament the opening of Britain's doors to the Jews of Germany. Every day his mailbox overflowed with letters from desperate Social Democrats and Jews trying to escape before the borders were closed. Wedgwood's response was both personal and political. A more liberal policy towards refugees would, he said, be in the UK's self-interest:

I would beg the Government not to miss this opportunity of so benefiting England to-day and in the future. There we have, driven out of Germany, [...] the thinkers, the intellectually-independent people, scientists, doctors, civil servants, artists and musicians [...] I do not speak from the obvious humanitarian point of view, but from the point of view of the material advantage of this country. Get those people in.

In the same speech to Parliament on 13 April 1933, he berated Britain for lagging behind others in admitting refugees. He cited the British welcome given to Belgians fleeing from war in 1914 and urged parliament and people not to leave the Jews to their fate:

Let English people see whether they, too, cannot receive these people into their family to make a home here, and to show that whatever the Prussian Aryan may feel about the Jews, or the peace-mongers or even the Socialists, we in this country realise the value of brains and the duty of hospitality to the oppressed [...] I wish that we might welcome those men, the free spirits of a free people, who decline to live in a land where liberty is no longer allowed, and get them here to strengthen our home and our love of liberty.

Wedgwood later reflected on his stance in support of the refugees:

Between then [1933] and open war in 1939, I did my duty by England in personally helping to this country, and often thence overseas, two hundred and twenty two of the victims of persecution. I did it in the teeth of every obstruction from Government, from anti-Semites, and from many English Jews who feared for themselves lest anti-Semitism should increase here.

Many of those Wedgwood helped had appealed to him directly and he personally provided financial guarantees for over a hundred Jewish refugees who were waiting their turn for the quotas imposed by the USA, or the British Mandate in Palestine. He took up individual cases with Home Office ministers, whom he usually found helpful (though at one point he signed so many guarantees that the Home Office refused to take any more and he had to call in favours from his friends to help plug the gap). Josiah penned at least ten letters a day on refugee cases, in one weekend alone dispatching fifty, while complaining to his daughter that 'nothing is done'.

On one of his visits to pre-war Germany, Wedgwood had fallen into conversation with a Jewish couple on a train; they knew the famous pottery name and the three got on well. As they parted, Wedgwood gave the couple his card and told them, 'If you ever need any help, just send it along'. At the time they wondered what kind of help this British MP could provide. But within five years of meeting, their stranger on a train had managed to get them visas to escape Nazi Germany. They wrote to him that they were eternally grateful. Another refugee he assisted was Dr Theresa Steuer, who went on to work for him as his private secretary. Wedgwood's own house, 'Moddershall

Oaks', in Staffordshire, which he described as 'The Ark', played host to waves of people cast out of their own societies: not only Jewish refugees, persecuted German Social Democrats and the children of parents sent to concentration camps, but also Indian agitators seeking independence and conscientious objectors.

Wedgwood helped to form the German Refugee Hospitality Committee, which he also chaired. This work brought him back in touch with many of his friends from the Liberal Party days of his youth, among them Charles and Dorothy Buxton (she was the author of the bestselling 1938 study The Economics of the Refugee Problem) and George Peabody Gooch, the historian and president of the National Peace Council, whose house in London had also become a refuge for those escaping Germany.

Four days before Hitler's seizure of Austria, Wedgwood urged parliament to allow in millions of Jews 'with a noose around their necks'. After the Anschluss and the intensification of the refugee crisis which followed, Wedgwood's strategy turned to legislative solutions. In Parliament he advocated granting Austrian refugees (mostly Jewish) British nationality; this he thought would enable and encourage them to play a full part in the nation's development. His proposal was firmly rejected by the Home Office and Foreign Office, but not before Wedgwood had made an impassioned speech to the House of Commons reminding MPs that black slaves who escaped to Britain were then considered to be free: 'If we cannot do for these Austrian exiles what our grandfathers did for the negro slaves, we destroy the traditions of our race and sacrifice to unworthy fears the honour of England.' In the same speech he talked about Britain's long tradition of protecting the defenceless and the 'infamy of throwing back to the wolves those who have managed to escape'.

Though Parliament rejected Wedgwood's ideas, the publication of his powerful speech was read throughout the world. One of those who saw it was a Jewish woman in Vienna, who informed Wedgwood that the British consulate in Vienna was refusing to give visas for Jews desperate to leave in the spring of 1938. Wedgwood wrote to Lord Halifax (with whom he was on first name terms) and ordered a report on the subject; Wedgwood's voice was one that could not easily be ignored. Similarly, a year later, the Home Secretary, Sir Samuel Hoare, tried to reassure Wedgwood that his criticisms of British refugee policy were not valid. Wedgwood had asserted that it was almost impossible for adult refugees to reach Britain, and when Hoare reminded him that 29,000 refugees had arrived in Britain since 1933, Wedgwood replied that this was a very small number compared with the 200,000 admitted to the USA – and that there refugees were allowed to work.

After the declaration of war, Wedgwood became the first MP to join the Local Defence Volunteers, popularly known as the Home Guard and made many parliamentary interventions in support of Jews who had been interned. He described the mass-internment policy as 'insane' and seemingly devised to aid the enemy, arguing that it incarcerated useful people who could add to the war effort. He vociferously criticised the treatment of deported refugees on board the SS Dunera and proposed that Parliament both release those not suspected of being pro-Nazi, as well as grant them a right of asylum and full equality before the law. Jewish refugees should, he urged, be incorporated into a new international brigade working in both military and civilian spheres. He especially advocated a 'Jewish army' brigade for those rejected by the Pioneer Corps; such a force, he believed, would also provide a usefully trained militia for such time as the Jews obtained their own homeland in Palestine. His ideas were again rejected by Parliament, but Wedgwood's criticisms certainly contributed to the phasing out of the internment of refugees. By January 1941, 4,610 'enemy aliens' had been given permission to join the Pioneer Corps and by August 1941 there were only about 1,300 internees still in camps.

In the New Year Honours list of 1942, Wedgwood was promoted by Churchill to the peerage. He relinquished his position as MP and set about using the House of Lords as a platform for his radical views. Sadly his new-found arena was not to last long. After a heart attack, Wedgwood's health rapidly deteriorated and he died in July 1943 just a few days before the fall of Mussolini.

According to his niece and biographer, Dame Veronica Wedgwood, one of Josiah Wedgwood's great qualities was his ability to inspire others to fight on behalf of refugees, not least by his sheer tenacity in handling the often obstructive bureaucracies that sought to put stumbling blocks in front of them. He demonstrated persistence, a burning sense of what was right, and a relish for what he saw as a fight for a just cause. It was the same with any issue he felt strongly about: 'Once you had spoken about it to him at all,' she wrote, 'it was impossible to prove unequal to what he regarded as a duty. Thus recruits were made to the cause of humanity.'

Chapter 3

The Trade Unionist and The Duchess

Leah Manning and Katharine Duchess of Atholl

Leah Manning, Image 6

Katharine Duchess of Atholl, Image 7

A forgotten Kindertranport? A year before the arrival of the first child refugees from Germany and Austria, another mass rescue of children took place but this time from northern Spain. Nearly 4,000 children from the Basque region were brought to safety in Britain from the brutal civil war in Spain. It was in many ways a forerunner of the exodus of Jewish children from

Hitler's Europe. It set an important precedent. A key figure in this 'forgotten Kindertransport' was Leah Manning. She was a tall, fiery orator, politician, noted humanitarian and passionate advocate for left-wing causes. She did not act alone – one of her closest colleagues came from the opposite end of the political spectrum: the aristocratic Duchess of Atholl.

Upon the outbreak of the Spanish Civil War in 1936, a group of activists had met at the National Trade Union Club in London to set up the Spanish Medical Aid Committee. Manning was its first Honorary Secretary and worked tirelessly to raise funds for medical equipment, drugs, nurses, doctors and other helpers. The Committee was able to equip an entire hospital for 800 patients in the Spanish village of Uclés on the Madrid to Valencia road.

Manning's engagement with the human consequences of the Spanish Civil War demonstrated physical, as well as moral courage. In late July 1938, for example, visiting medical facilities near the still independent Republican city of Barcelona, she personally nursed a wounded International Brigadier, Harry Dobson, a former Welsh coal miner, through his last hours of life in a front-line hospital housed in a large cave. It is indicative of the reach of Leah's reputation that when Dobson, who had heard her speak at a rally in South Wales, briefly regained consciousness, he stared hard at her and then whispered the words, 'why surely it is comrade Leah Manning?'

Elizabeth Leah Perrett was born in 1886 in Droitwich, Worcestershire. The daughter of Salvation Army officers, she was the eldest of twelve children and, after her parents had emigrated to Canada, Leah moved into her grandfather's family home in Stamford Hill in London. Her early influences included the evangelical Methodism of her grandparents' family and radical Liberal politics. While at school in London, she met the Reverend Stewart Headlam, whose Christian Socialism made a profound impact on her own beliefs.

In 1906 she entered Homerton Teacher Training College in Cambridge, where she was soon introduced to Hugh Dalton, the future Labour Chancellor of the Exchequer, who was then an undergraduate at King's College. As she wrote in her autobiography: 'Without his friendship, I could not have penetrated very far into the life of the University, nor met some of the men he knew.' Dalton certainly opened the door to the University Fabian Society, which would otherwise have been closed to a training college girl before the First World War. She married the astronomer William Manning (1883-1952) in 1914 and they lived for a time in Cambridge by the Solar Physics Observatory, now the Institute of Astronomy.

After the First World War, Leah Manning's socialism and progressive educational views were further shaped by the experience of teaching in New Street School, Cambridge, where, she recalled, the children 'were so poor, so under-nourished, and so apathetic, that it seemed impossible to strike one spark of interest from them'. She was, though, determined to make a good job of her time there. The death of one of her pupils, a young girl who essentially died of starvation, provoked Leah to make a bitter and very public complaint to the local education authority, who had declined to offer free milk to the malnourished child. Undeterred by the rebuke she earned from her employers and by the half-hearted response of her union, Leah decided to stay on at the school, support the children and create an evening play centre, the first of its kind in the UK. She campaigned for free milk for the children and persuaded influential friends such as Florence Ada Keynes, the mother of the economist John Maynard Keynes, to raise funds and attract support from the female students at Girton and Newnham Colleges.

In 1930 Manning was elected president of the National Union of Teachers (NUT), with which she would remain associated for the rest of her life, and in 1931 she succeeded in winning a parliamentary seat in a by-election, though she lost it at the general election later the same year. From 1934 she held a key position as Joint Secretary of the Co-ordinating Committee against War and Fascism. She made her first visit to Spain in the same year and published her account of the uprising of the miners of Asturias, bitterly criticising the repression which followed.

The rapidly deteriorating situation for civilians in Spain encouraged Manning to visit the Basque region; she arrived in Bilbao on 24 April 1937, two days before the bombing of Guernica. Manning informed the British Consul, Ralph Stevenson, who had not expected her, that she would be supervising the evacuation of Basque children. Stevenson had been in post since 1919, a fluent Spanish speaker with a strong humanitarian, if politically conservative leanings and his relations with Manning were not always positive. When he told the Foreign Office in April 1937 that he didn't like women who meddled in politics, there was little doubt he was talking about Manning and her clear sympathies for left-wing causes and opposition to Franco. In later life, Stevenson also slightly resented Manning's assertion that the evacuation of the Basque children had been her idea, and hers alone. All that said, they found a way to work together.

Stevenson himself had proposed an evacuation plan on 8 April but it had been rejected by the government of Stanley Baldwin, fearful of seeming to take sides in a civil war. Britain's official stated policy was one of 'non intervention' (even though Franco's forces were receiving substantial arms and military support from Germany and Italy). There was also a belief in some British government circles that the anti-Franco voices were in some way pro-Soviet or outright communist in sympathy.

Manning, not to be dissuaded by official opposition in London, stayed in Bilbao broadcasting appeals to mothers on local radio urging them to allow their children to leave the conflict zone. She also made passionate broadcasts to be heard in Britain and these undoubtedly stirred public opinion into wanting to support women and children caught up in the conflict. Sympathies in Britain for the Basque civilians shifted dramatically after the events of 26 April 1937, when the German Condor Legion, under the Nationalist command, bombed the market town of Guernica. It is not entirely known how many civilians died that day but estimates suggest somewhere in the hundreds. The aerial attack on civilians was seen at the time as something especially cruel and unacceptable. The event and the suffering of the civilians in the town became headline news for many days in Britain with graphic accounts from correspondents on the ground, such as George Steer of The Times.

The day after the Guernica bombings, Manning's London colleagues stepped up their pressure on the Baldwin government, which had received a telegram from the Basque president describing the bombing as 'acts of real savagery committed against the Basque Country, exterminating our towns [...]' Following a request from the Spanish Republican Ambassador in London and the London-based National Joint Committee for Spanish Relief (NCR), the Foreign Secretary, Anthony Eden, finally approved, in principle, permission for some children to come to Britain from Bilbao. On 29 April 1937, Sir John Simon, the British Home Secretary formally announced that he would be prepared to allow, 'a limited number of Basque children who are, I understand, to be evacuated from Bilbao'. His position, however, came with a number of caveats: that the children had to be wholly financed by the NCR and that the children would be sent back to Spain as soon as conditions allowed. Also there should be no political bias in the selection of vulnerable children. Despite this there was still opposition from some senior Foreign Office officials and, furthermore, Franco made it clear that he was against such an evacuation.

As Manning continued to work in Bilbao to encourage the evacuation, the NCR embarked on a large-scale nationwide fundraising campaign in support of Basque children. Leading the charge was the committee's chairman, a seemingly unlikely figure and poles apart from Manning's left-wing socialist views: Katharine Stewart-Murray, the Duchess of Atholl.

An aristocrat living on a 200,000 acre estate in Scotland, the Duchess was also one of the first female members of parliament, the first to hold a government office (in the 1920s) and a fiery opponent of fascism and Nazism. As an MP she vigorously supported the democratically elected Republican government of Spain. In January 1937, Katharine was elected chairman of the NCR; her committee also consisted of Leah Manning and fellow MPs, David Grenfell (Labour), Wilfred Roberts (Liberal) and Eleanor Rathbone (Independent).

With boundless energy Atholl toured the UK and North America, speaking and making broadcasts in support of the benighted civilians in Spain. One lunch given in her honour in New York City was on behalf of the 'Spanish Milk Fund' and attended by such luminaries as Dorothy Parker and Ernest

Hemingway. Atholl was also the key figure at a fundraising concert at London's Royal Albert Hall, attended by a glittering array of artists, performers and writers including Pablo Picasso, H.G. Wells, E.M. Forster, Virginia Woolf, Sean O'Casey and Dame Sybil Thorndike. The world-famous American bass, Paul Robeson, sang and the whole event raised £11,000 for the Basque emergency appeal – the equivalent of well over half a million pounds by today's values. Atholl was unabashed in drawing on her personal network of influential people to help raise money for the children. This letter to a member of the government's Privy Council illustrates her method:

'Our Committee for the Basque Children also wants to know whether you would be ready to sign an appeal on the children's behalf to be sent to City men. We want names that will carry weight in financial circles'

The Duchess' committee coordinated a huge nationwide effort of local committees, volunteers and philanthropists. Her letter to The Times published on 1 May 1937 following Guernica was a clarion call to the British government and people to support the plight of the children in Spain.

Our one object here is to appeal to give generous support to an effort which the National Joint Committee for Spanish Relief is anxious without a moment's delay [...] to remove to safety the largest possible number of those children who have already been left homeless, many of them orphans, by the destruction of their town, or who are menaced with a similar fate if there is a repetition of this terrible method of warfare.

Like Manning, the Duchess herself visited Spain but just after the Guernica bombings. Against the strong advice from

Eden not to go, she led a fact-finding delegation to the war-torn regions of Madrid and Eastern Spain, including fellow parliamentarian, Rathbone. What she saw and heard further convinced Atholl that urgent action to save the children of the still-unconquered Basque region was imperative. Back in Britain, the Duchess broadcast an appeal on the BBC in support of the children of Madrid. She rapidly wrote a book, 'Searchlight on Spain', cataloguing with forensic journalistic detail, Franco's assault on the democratically elected government and the savage impact on ordinary men, women and children under bombardment and the threat of starvation. The book became an instant best seller and it was at this time, in the late 1930s, that she was given the nickname 'The Red Duchess'. A press agency rang her to offer a large fee for Spanish relief if the Duchess would write an article entitled, 'Why I am a Communist'. The infuriated Atholl replied, 'No, but I'll write one on why I am not a Communist'. The agency rang off.

Meanwhile Leah Manning stayed in Bilbao to help organise the evacuation to Britain, feeling certain that it would eventually be accepted by the British government. She was right. On 15 May, the Home Office finally accepted the evacuation of the Basque children – but only 2000 and with an upper age limit of 12 years. This was not good enough for Leah Manning; she had already asserted on Bilbao Radio that double that number would be going to Britain. Starvation, caused by the war and Franco's naval blockade, constant threats of bombing and fear of reprisals once the Nationalists had taken the Basque region, meant that mothers were desperate to have their children signed up for departure to Britain. Many feared savage reprisals once Franco's army had taken Bilbao. As one former Basque refugee recalled many years later, his mother was especially keen for her two sons to leave Spain:

I'm going to get you out of the country somehow. Lots of other children are going [...] You two, I want you out. I know what's going to happen to you. They didn't get hold of your father, so they're going to get hold of you.'

On 17 May, the Pro Consul in Bilbao also urged the Foreign Office to double the number to be allowed into the country. This was echoed by a similar call from the Duchess of Atholl to Anthony Eden, adding that girls of 15 years would be in especial danger from Nationalist troops entering Bilbao in triumph. The government relented and said it would indeed allow in 4000 refugee children (and their escorts) up the age of 15, but remained adamant that no public funds would be used to support them once in Britain.

Meanwhile in the Basque region, with the support of Stevenson and Manning, the government in Bilbao began rapidly organising a mass evacuation from the region. They kept lists of each child to be sent away and provided health checks and vaccinations, assisted by volunteer doctors from Britain. Manning worked tirelessly with the authorities in Bilbao, publicising the planned exodus and writing articles for local families encouraging them to send their children to safety abroad. Manning maintained a formidable press campaign in the Basque region urging people to flee; she attended rallies and soon became a very familiar face on the streets of the Basque port, 'In a few weeks I was recognised on the streets and mothers of Bilbao began to feel their children were in the charge of someone in whom they could place their trust.' Before the fall of the Basque country in June 1937 more than 100,000 civilians, many of them unaccompanied children, left for Britain, Russia,

France, Belgium and Mexico. Some of these countries (but not Britain) allowed in whole family groups.

On 20 May 1937 the formalities for getting 3,826 children out of Spain to Britain were complete. Each child would be given a six-sided label to be worn around its neck. Along with a unique number, a prominent notice was to be displayed: 'EXPEDICION A INGLATERRA'. Stevenson, the British Consul, supervised the process ensuring at London's insistence - for the sake of apparent even-handiness - that there should be no bar on allowing on board the children of Nationalist sympathisers (in practice the overwhelming majority of the evacuees were the offspring of Republican sympathisers). The ship that would take them to England was the SS Habana, an ageing 10,500 ton transatlantic steamer designed to carry 800 passengers – and not the 4000 who eventually embarked. Early in the morning of 21 May 1937, the dangerously overcrowded ship set sail from Bilbao. On board were the children, as well as 120 female attendants, 99 teachers, 15 Catholic priests and one very determined member of the NCR – Leah Manning. Though a Nationalist cruiser watched menacingly from the bay, SS Habana was escorted by a convoy of Royal Navy vessels including 'HMS Royal Oak' and the aptly named 'Fearless'.

After a storm-tossed voyage in the Bay of Biscay, during which most of the children were violently sick, the ship arrived in Southampton the next day. Waiting for them was a large tented camp at North Stoneham in Eastleigh. Just a few days before their arrival the NCR committee had expected only 2000 children. There were urgent last minute preparations including extra tents (some of which were hired from the British War Office - for a fee), field kitchens and food (much of which was donated by local tradesmen). Even the Duchess of Atholl rolled up her sleeves to dig trenches in preparation for the arrival of the children.

The ship arrived in Southampton harbour in the evening of 23 May 1937. The whole area was decorated with Union Flag bunting, which was later taken down and stitched by volunteers into sleeping bags for the children. The children thought this was in their honour, but in fact the decorations were left over from the Coronation of George VI a week earlier. Upon arrival and after inspections by health officials, the children and their adult carers were welcomed by the Duchess of Atholl, Walter Citrine, Head of the Trades Union Congress and the editor of the Economist, Sir Walter Layton accompanied by his wife. Many well-known companies and organisations had donated money or goods to help the Basque refugees, including Cadbury's, Rowntree's, Woolworth's, Marks and Spencer and Jaeger. A newsreel of the time shows them smiling, waving and looking happy in their new homes which consisted of 500 bell tents and large marquees. Though food was plentiful, the children, who were used to starvation diets, would hoard part of their meals tucked under their clothing. This sight dismayed the many local well-wishers who visited the camp. The children's happiness came to an abrupt end when news of the fall of Bilbao on 19 June 1937 came through – many wept in anguish, others vented their fury on the loudspeakers which had relayed the news – as they believed this to be fascist propaganda.

Leah Manning and others on her committee decided that the children should not be fostered in private homes but kept together in family groups, living in specially commissioned hostels, or 'colonies'. The London Teachers' Association offered a house in Theydon Bois, Essex, which later became known as Leah Manning House. The Salvation Army also offered hostel accommodation and curated a special exhibition in Central London entitled 'Spain – The Child and the War'. Leah wrote the preface to the exhibition guide; she had become, she said, the 'accidental' mother to 4,000 children, a fact which gave her the right to speak on their behalf. After the camp at North Stoneham, the children were dispersed to over 100 separate hostels around Britain. Though living standards varied hugely, local volunteers often did their best to make the children feel safe and secure. The Duchess of Atholl proudly told a local newspaper, 'It is a credit to the true humanity latent in everyone that the Basque children are now here through the concerted efforts of people holding widely divergent views.'

Manning was put in charge of a group of twenty-nine Basque children from socialist families, each of whom had lost at least one parent in the Civil War. They were accommodated in an old vicarage in Pampisford near Cambridge and later in a college-owned house in the city. Manning's group of 29 children, plus three Spanish female support workers, arrived at Cambridge train station; their arrival in the town had brought out crowds of people to welcome them. Two coaches took them from the station to a local YMCA hall where afternoon tea was provided, including a cake iced with an inscription in the Basque language. Speeches of welcome were made to what must have been an exhausted and somewhat bewildered bunch of children. Duly fed, the children were taken to their new home in the large vicarage in Pampisford.

In the weeks before their arrival in Cambridge, volunteers, many of them university students, had been busy making the old place inhabitable. Most of the rooms had not been lived in for a long time and the house appeared to be sadly derelict. There were around fifteen local helpers working each day 'fortified with much beer' and by the time the children arrived, the vicarage was fit and ready for them. One student took charge of the vegetable garden, transforming it from a wilderness to a plot that would substantially help to feed the children. A local volunteer came to teach them football and later brought a boys' club team to play against the Spanish children – who despite not knowing the game, won 1-0. Two brothers went on to become professional footballers in England. On Sundays the children were taken on long walks – partly to get them away from the neighbouring church whose clergyman objected to the shouting of the youngsters as they played in the vicarage garden.

In the summer, a local Basque committee member, Professor Francis Cornford, took all the children to stay for a month by the sea at his mill in Norfolk. The volunteers noticed how quickly the children seemed to have settled into their new English environment and how their artwork, for instance, had changed from depicting scenes of war and destruction to flowers and happy village scenes. The children also produced their own magazine – one edition of which found itself in the hands of Jose Antonio Aguirre, the president of the Basque region. The children, who were all republicans, resented this – for them the Basque Nationalist President Aguirre did not represent the more militant views of their parents and they refused to send any further editions to him. Lessons, including English, were provided by the three 'senoritas' and English volunteers, mostly university students, under the guidance of the foreign language teaching pioneer, Eric Hawkins. Physical exercise was regarded as very important and in the spirit of the times, 'gym' ended with a cool down in a cold shower. The children took part in regional tours of concerts including Basque and Spanish songs and dances – all to raise money for the refugees. Unfortunately, there were complaints from village neighbours, who did not appreciate these noisy and often boisterous children, and a new vicar at Pampisford insisted that the children move out of the village.

In January 1938, the whole party decamped to a large Victorian house in Cambridge, where the children were filmed by a local photographer in the summer going about daily life in their new home. They are shown industriously helping with domestic duties such as beating carpets, sweeping floors or collecting bread deliveries. They are seen studying in the classroom and getting plenty of fresh air in the parks and gardens nearby.

The truth for others in hostels (or 'colonies') around the country was less than idyllic – newspapers of the day reported that a minority of Basque children could be somewhat unruly and there were rare but well publicised cases of minor delinquency. When the Spanish Civil War came to an end in the summer of 1939, most of the Basque children returned to their home region. Just under 500 stayed in Britain fostered by local families or living independent lives; some joined the forces during the war, while many lived their entire lives in the country and brought up families in Britain.

Like the Duchess of Atholl, Manning toured the UK in support of the anti-fascist cause. Unsurprisingly, a strong opponent of appeasement with Hitler, (as was Atholl who resigned her parliamentary seat in protest) she believed that another war was inevitable and when it came in September 1939 she strongly rebuked her communist colleagues for failing to support it. She spent much of the war working for the teachers' union NUT, but once Russia was attacked in June 1941 she turned her attention to providing aid to the USSR and was spokeswoman for the 'Second Front Now' campaign to open up a western attack on Hitler's forces. She also severely criticised the British government for its handling of the evacuation of children. Her role as a trade unionist meant that she played a crucial role in the preparation of the '1944 Education Act' which revolutionised the provision of schooling for all children in the country.

Leah Manning became the Member of Parliament for Epping in 1945, making education and foreign affairs her special interests, while remaining a forceful advocate for the rights of women, especially in the areas of equal pay and birth control. In 1950 she lost her parliamentary seat and returned to teaching, which she pursued into her late eighties. Appointed a Dame of the British Empire in 1966, she died in 1977 aged ninety-one.

Alongside the more predictable memorials to her long and distinguished career in teaching and politics – buildings named after her in Cambridge and Essex – Leah's obituary in The Times described her as, 'Always an individualist. Leah Manning's work was based on humanity rather than dogma.' In his seminal account of Britain and the Spanish Civil War, Sir James Cable, who was not always enamoured of Manning's self-regarding reputation, summarised her contribution to the evacuation of the children: 'Without her flaming zeal, her emotional outbursts, her real organising capabilities, her broadcasts and her telegrams to all and sundry, the obstacles erected in London to the reception of the Basque children might not have been overcome'.

Of the many tributes to Manning's memory, one in particular chimes with the very heart of the territory whose children she helped to rescue from the carnage of the Civil War. In the city of Bilbao, incongruous among the Basque street names commemorating people and events in the region's troubled history, is a square in the Barrio Thurdinaga. It is known since it was inaugurated in 2002, in the presence of some 100, now ageing, former child refugees, as Plaza Mrs Leah Manning.

PART II:
The Kindertransport rescue

Chapter 4

The Kindertransport
A Landscape of Care

Who was the 'British Schindler?' The media are always looking for that solitary hero who, single-handedly, carried the day to help others, a lone rescuer, a giant among humans. Sadly, this is rarely the case and the Kindertransport was no exception. It took a vast number of, often disparate, individuals and organisations to release 10,000 children from the clutches of Hitler's grotesque regime. For those interested in the big picture I have included an additional chapter (The Kindertransport: Who, How and Where) in the appendix which leads you through the complex maze of individuals and organisations responsible for getting the children out.

But this book is principally focused on the stories of the Kinder once they reached the relative safety of the UK. The welfare and care of 10,000 refugee children was a massive nationwide effort. Every child needed at least one guarantor, one foster parent, one committee welfare officer, one employer, one teacher; there must have been tens of thousands of people caring for the refugee children from Nazi Europe. We will look at some of these people in detail but first here is a broad overview of the 'landscape of care' in place from late 1938 to the end of war (and beyond).

From late 1938 up until the outbreak of war, most of the refugee children were found homes, hostels, or boarding accommodation in or around Britain's big cities – often those with significant Jewish populations. From September 1939, a policy of child evacuation was introduced for the whole country, so that children from cities thought vulnerable to bombing could be sent out into the quieter shires in rural England, as well as Scotland, Wales and Northern Ireland. Along with native born East End kids, recently arrived and settled German, Polish and Czech children were swept up in the mass exodus from the British cities. This meant that towns and villages that had never seen or met a Jew nor any foreigner for that matter suddenly found themselves looking after these lonely, often traumatised, parentless kids. Some came with their schools – the Jewish Free School for example was evacuated to Cambridgeshire and with it many of the recently enrolled Jewish refugees. The children were found a hostel at 37 St Mary's Street in Ely; others were sent out to cottages and farmsteads in the countryside.

The central story in this book is that of individuals who for totally altruistic reasons, volunteered to care for the refugee children. They opened their doors, and their hearts, to these lost souls, most of whom would never see their families again. One such family was that of Frederick and Mary Attenborough in Leicester. They were parents of the film director Richard and the celebrated broadcaster and naturalist David Attenborough. Mary, a tireless social activist, had been central in setting up a hostel for the Basque refugee children in the city and both her and husband Frederick (a college principal) were committed to helping the children fleeing from the Nazis. As a family they decided to provide a home for two half-Jewish sisters, Helga and Irene Bejach who had arrived on one of the last Kindertransports. The girls became part of the Attenborough household and were often referred to by Richard as 'our German sisters'. They were with the film director when he received his Oscar for the film, 'Ghandi' in 1983 and remained as close family members until their deaths.

In the small Fenland town of Chatteris, the Reverend Charles Morton and his wife took in two Jewish boys from Austria called Paul Kohn and Eugene Gunz. The Mortons were childless and Charles served as a minister for the Strict Baptist Zion Chapel a few doors away from their home. The two lads had, by all accounts, a very happy time with the Mortons. In 2017, I took the now 80 year-old Paul Kohn to the house in Park Street where the Mortons lived. Paul was there with his children and grandchildren and told us how the Mortons had been very correct but loving in their own special way. They made no attempt whatsoever to convert the Jewish boys – far from it. When Paul reached his thirteenth birthday, Reverend Morton converted the rear of the Zion Chapel (now a printing works), into a 'pop up' synagogue. 'It was just here', said Paul pointing to a large machine, 'that I read from the Torah for my barmitzvah.' The Mortons, keen to encourage the continuation of their Jewish culture, organised kosher food to be brought from London and encouraged the boys to visit relatives for the Passover meal. Paul showed me photographs of Charles playing chess with him, days out at the seaside (including a snap of a somewhat austere looking, behatted Reverend Morton with Paul in a canoe) and building a snowman in the garden. Paul's happiness was only threatened by the visit of some ultra-Orthodox Jews who wanted to take the boys out of this Baptist home where they (wrongly) feared the boys were prey to conversion. Recalling the incident many years later, Paul said,

One day, some ultra-Orthodox Jews arrived at the Mortons' front door. They had come to return me to the fold. They were very insistent that I go with them and I was extremely apprehensive. Mr Morton informed them that only my parents could decide about my future, and until then I would stay put. He wrote to them about the visit, and the answer from Haifa was clear: 'If you will have him, then our son shall stay in your care until the war is over.'

And so, Paul stayed until the war was over and then went to Palestine to be reunited with his parents. It was a rare happy ending but the Kohns stayed in touch with the Mortons until the old couple passed away. Charles lived long enough to send a message of congratulations to Paul on the birth of his first son in 1964.

There was a similar confrontation between foster parents and religious men who came to 'rescue' another Jewish boy. Erich (now Sir Erich) Reich, a Jewish child refugee from Poland was sent to a non-Jewish couple. Joseph and Emily Kreibich were themselves political refugees from Sudetenland who had fled to the Surrey town of Dorking. Like the Mortons, the Kreibichs told the Orthodox men that they had no right to take Erich away without his parents' permission. Erich stayed. Overseeing the Jewish and other refugees in Dorking was the local refugee committee. Its chair and vice-chair were none other than the famed composer, Ralph Vaughan Williams and the Nobel prize-winning author, E.M. Forster. Vaughan Williams took an especially active role in running the refugee committee – rarely if ever missing a meeting. He invited Erich to tea (which the very young boy thought a very boring afternoon). Later Vaughan Williams campaigned vigorously for the release of Jewish internees who had been professional musicians and composers. It is a side of the illustrious musician's life that has seldom been recorded until recent research by my colleague, Neil Wenborn.

Care given by the Kreibichs and Mortons was replicated around the whole country. Local and regional refugee committees did their best to find hospitality for the children. It was not always easy, as the chapters of Mary Hughes, Greta Burkill and Sybil Hutton testify. Local committees were more often than not organised by women, one such being Colette Hassan in Manchester. A stalwart of local support organisations, she ran the B'nai Brith Lodge Hospitality Committee and was a leading light in the Manchester Jewish Refugees Committee. Following the November Pogroms, Hassan chaired a new B'nai Brith initiative to raise money and 'collectively adopt' child refugees from Germany. In January 1939, she set up a hostel for 22 children between the ages of 13 and 16 at Kershaw House, located at 391 Waterloo Road, North Manchester. Initiatives by other groups included a hostel for refugee boys in Stockport and Harris House for girls in Southport, while the Manchester Home for the Aged provided a place for elderly refugees.

Through Dr Menachem Klibansky, headmaster of a Jewish school in Cologne and a friend of Colette, 16 girls from the Yavne School (a Jewish school in Cologne) aged 14 to 15 years, reached the Kershaw House hostel (renamed Myer Kersh House) in Manchester just before the onset of war in summer 1939. Colette and Victor Hassan also took into their home two teenage German girls, Sara and Margot, to live as part of their family. After the war both girls were reunited with surviving family and left Manchester – Sara went to Israel, Margot to the US. They remained in touch with the Hassan family and each other, visiting until Sara and Margot's deaths in recent years.

Other women playing a crucial role in the care of the Kindertransportees included Cissi Rosenfelder, an Orthodox Jewish lady, who with Rabbi Eli Munk set up two successful hostels – one for boys at Tylers Green in Buckinghamshire and a girls' home in a large building with extensive gardens known as 'The White House' in the Essex village of Great Chesterford. Rabbi Bernd Koschland who came on a Kindertransport has written extensively on his time at Tylers Green. Recalling the influence of Mrs Rosenfelder, he says,

Mrs Rosenfelder, the Hon Secretary, gave of herself to the organisation well beyond the remit of her duties, taking care of us not only in the hostel, but even long after its dissolution; she was looked up to as a mother-figure. Cissi Rosenfelder was born in London in 1900 to German-Jewish parents, went to North London Collegiate School and then worked with Rabbi Dr Victor Schonfeld and the Mizrachi [Jewish orthodox] movement. After her marriage she moved to Cologne, returning to London when the Nazis came to power. She was a member of the Golders Green Beth Hamidrash when Rabbi Munk set up the Refugee Committee, and with the outbreak of War became the Hon. Secretary of the Tylers Green Hostel Committee until its dissolution. She was helped by her husband enabling many refugees to build new lives.

There are countless volunteers like the Reverend Morton and Cissi Rosenfelder who can be found throughout the length and breadth of Britain and Northern Ireland. Young German-speaking refugees were billeted with families in deepest central Wales, the glens of Highland Scotland, or moorlands of Devon and the craggy coastline of Cornwall. It was here in the small Cornish town of Camelford that two Jewish children from southern Germany were welcomed by a wonderfully warm local family. Tom and Violet Jago were pillars of their local community. Tom was a bank manager with left-leaning principles and friend of the playwright and social reformer J.B. Priestley.

Violet kept home but was active in charity work including the British Nurses' Association. They had two teenage boys, Tom

(14) and Geoffrey (12). It was into this happy family that Heinz and his sister Hannah Greilsamer (aged 11 and 13 respectively) came to live in the summer of 1939. They did so via Jewish friends of the Jagos who like Priestley, had a house nearby. Charles and Dorothy Singer were authors of distinguished books on the history of science and active supporters of refugee scholars and Kindertransport children. Geoffrey Jago takes up the story:

One evening in 1939, the Singers held a meeting at Camelford Town Hall seeking foster homes for Kindertransport children, explaining the danger they faced. My parents were shown a picture of Heinz and Hannah. They took the picture at once to show my brother and myself seeking our agreement to allow Heinz and Hannah into the family. I am glad to say that my brother and I agreed at once and my parents returned to the meeting.

The Jago home was a few steps away from the Town Hall so that the go-ahead to let the Jewish children into their family was given in minutes. It was a rapid decision that would have lifelong consequences for Geoffrey, his brother and parents.

Heinz did particularly well at the local grammar school which was run by the headteacher Cyril Leese on enlightened principles. School fees were paid by anonymous donors and all four children excelled. Life at the Jago house was happy and lighthearted. Geoffrey cannot recall any arguments between the teenagers.

Mr Jago's modest salary as bank manager enabled him to run a car and take holidays in the idyllic coves of Cornwall in a touring caravan. By all accounts, Heinz and Hannah mastered English quickly and were soon fully integrated in Jago family life. They called Tom and Violet, 'dad and mum'. Though nominally

Church of England, the family was not religious and there was no attempt made to convert the children, who continued Jewish studies by correspondence. During the war, contact with their real parents became increasingly sparse. In their last letter to their worried children, Jacob and Klara Greilsamer wrote that they were being 'sent east' – a euphemism for transport to the death camps of occupied Poland. They did not survive.

At school in Camelford, Heinz (affectionately nicknamed by his schoolfriends as 'beans') did outstandingly well and after joining the British army, went on to university in London and eventually became a science teacher. With Violet's help, Hannah was encouraged in her lifelong profession in nursing. After her marriage to a Canadian she lived in the USA but kept in constant contact with the family in Cornwall. Heinz (who later changed his name to Harry Grenville) and Hannah were always seen as fully part of the Jago family.

Looking back over eighty years, Geoffrey Jago clearly remembers the day when a couple of snapshots were brought from Camelford Town Hall over the road. It was a day that brought two refugee children into his life, a new brother and sister and the beginning of lifelong friendship.

Camelford was not alone in helping young refugees. Even as early as the outbreak of war in September 1939, there were at least 200 local refugee committees spread throughout the UK – from Aberdeen and Belfast to Cardiff, Gloucester and Worthing. Few areas of the country had nothing to do with Jewish refugees. After mass evacuation of all children in September 1939, those who had come, say to London or Glasgow from Nazi-dominated Europe were moved on again into the smaller towns and villages of the UK. Children who had found homes, perhaps Jewish homes, in East and North London, or by coastal towns such as Southend, Clacton, Hastings or Bournemouth, found themselves further uprooted to areas regarded as safe from bombing (or away from sensitive regions that might soon be subject to Nazi invasion). Those that arrived by ship and train from Berlin, Vienna or Prague, found themselves once more carried by rail to Edinburgh, York or County Antrim. Their care, thousands of them some as young as three or four, was now entrusted to members of these rapidly created bodies of local volunteers.

The local refugee committees helped pay for the children's upkeep – food, clothing, medical bills, pocket money, schooling and eventually training for employment. They tried (not always successfully) to do at least some of the things the absent parents were unable to achieve. In the best case scenarios, they found loving homes for the children and also had the responsibility to move a child who was not happy with their 'new' family.

Not all of the children spent the war years in loving foster homes. Some were billeted with cruel or exploitative families; some were physically and sexually abused, some had foster parents who had little idea about bringing up children, let alone traumatised, parentless kids who knew little of the language or local culture. It is very difficult to say what proportion of these refugee children had to endure unhappy surroundings but the surviving records do suggest that by and large, most children fared well with foster parents who did their best in very trying wartime circumstances.

Many refugee children were never placed in families. Some, especially older children, as we have seen, were housed in hostels such as the one run by the Sainsbury family or a local refugee committee. Some were sent straight to training centres or farms where new skills were offered. Such was provided by Viscount

Traprain (the nephew of former prime minister Arthur Balfour who in 1917 had penned the declaration promising a Jewish national home for the Jews). He offered his beautiful estate with its grand country house in Whittingehame near Edinburgh, as a farm school for around 160 Kindertransport children. His offer was enthusiastically taken up by members of the Salisbury Road Synagogue in Edinburgh which was already running a hostel for Jewish refugees in the city. The farm school had an ambitious two-year curriculum offering a wide general education designed by a professor from the College of Agriculture in Edinburgh with the enthusiastic help of Viscount Traprain. Emphasis was placed on self help and the youngsters were encouraged to run the school like a kibbutz (a collective farm) and take responsibility for work and cleaning rotas. Some of the older teenagers worked for local farmers as Land Boys and Girls helping produce food for the wartime effort. From later memoirs it seems that the school which closed in 1941 was a very happy place and something of a model for the whole Zionist movement in Britain.

Similar schemes were set up such as the one at Gwrych Castle in central Wales. It took in 180 teenagers some of whom came from religious communities. Another training farm near Thaxted in Essex run by Bachad, a Jewish religious Zionist organisation, resulted in the German Jewish boys and girls there winning county prizes for their dairy herd.

The care of thousands of refugee children was thus a nationwide effort. At the epicentre of this vast voluntary operation was Bloomsbury House in central London. From 1939 to well beyond the war it was the nerve centre of the entire refugee welfare operation. Child refugees were but one part of the responsibilities within those walls and the Refugee

Children's Movement (RCM) was the most important body. A cross-denominational organisation, it was led by its formidable General Secretary, Dorothy Hardisty. Searching through the many thousands of surviving records of the Kindertransportees, her name is the one that keeps cropping up. She seemed to have a handle on the welfare of each of the children in the care of the RCM. There are few accounts of this remarkable woman, who was middle aged when she joined the RCM and continued to work for them until 1948. In a valuable memoir created by Veronica Gillespie, a worker at Bloomsbury House, there is a quote from Hardisty's journal, which despite great efforts I was not able to locate. The quote however does give us some insight into the mind of Dorothy Hardisty:

The children had endured over a long period of time and in increasing severity such physical and mental suffering as had stolen their childhood from them. They were often old beyond their years, sometimes dreadfully experienced, always troubled and disturbed. It was not only that at short notice they were torn from the people they loved and trusted, and the places they knew: it was not only that they were suddenly bereft of all sense of security; these blows had been preceded by long periods of unhappiness and fear. Young children had seen the persecution of their relatives; men and boys being taken away from their homes: they had heard of the dread concentration camps.

The records often state that 'Mrs Hardisty went to visit the family and found it to be unsatisfactory' or 'Mrs Hardisty reported that Inge is happy and settled in her home or 'Mrs Hardisty suggested that Kurt be helped to find a training place'..... To call her 'tireless' is probably an understatement. Even after she left the RCM in her sixties, she spent the next 20 years running an infant welfare clinic in London – this was after receiving an MBE for her services to children.

Dorothy Hardisty was at the nexus of the welfare organisations and deserves a fuller biography. Though her granddaughter kindly showed me some of her private papers, the 'Hardisty Journal' remains elusive. She is but one of the small number of professionals leading an army of volunteers in every corner of the United Kingdom: a Landscape of Care.

Dorothy Hardisty, Image 8

Chapter 5

The Grocer
Lord Alan Sainsbury

Lord Alan Sainsbury, Image 9

In late 1938, or early '39, Alan Sainsbury, head of the famous grocery chain, was having dinner with friends and family. They were discussing the terrible situation for Jews in Germany. Suddenly Alan banged his fist on the table and said, 'Why don't we do something about it?' Alan Sainsbury, who later pioneered self-service supermarkets in the UK, was a man of action not just words. There and then, he and his brother, Robert, put their heads together and decided to sponsor a group of child refugees from the Reich. Not only this but they would acquire a large house and create a special hostel for the young exiles. This was the beginning of the 'Sainsbury Home' for refugee Jewish children and a commitment that Alan would fulfil for many years, even decades, to come.

Alan John Sainsbury was born in 1902, the grandson of the founder of the famous grocery and supermarket business. The son of a Jewish mother – Mabel van den Bergh – and John B. Sainsbury, Alan had a lifelong interest in social welfare beginning with a spell working in an East End mission. Strongly political, he stood three times as a Liberal candidate and almost succeeded in his bid for Parliament. He joked later in life that had he been elected the Sainsbury name may have disappeared from Britain's high streets.

During the war Alan Sainsbury was chief representative of the grocery trade to the Ministry of Food, seeing his job as helping feed the nation in a fair way to all. He joined the Labour Party in 1945 and in 1981 was a founding member of the Social Democratic Party. He was a keen philanthropist, especially in the area of underprivileged children and supported the furthering of Jewish-Christian relations.

Back in the winter of 1938/9 Alan reacted swiftly to the plight of Jewish children in Germany. He quickly rented a large house at 47 Lytton Grove, Putney not far from Wimbledon Common. It is not clear why they chose this particular house, except according to the 1939 census, it was empty at the time. Also it may be no coincidence that Lytton Grove boasted a branch of Sainsbury's – then still very much a family concern and news would have filtered back to the brothers that a large empty house was available. So, Alan, his future second wife, Babette (herself from a Jewish background) and Robert staffed the house with a cook, maids, housekeepers, matrons and teachers. After some dragging of feet from the Home Office, they directly sponsored the children as a group. The financial guarantees given by the Sainsbury family ensured that the children were given permission to leave their homes in Germany and come to safety in London.

At Lytton Grove they were introduced to traditional English cuisine, such as custard and kippers and were cared for by Matron Sabakin and her two helpers, Miss Turner and Miss Griffith. One of the Kinder remembered, 'We shared a room with two other brothers. I remember that although most of the children were on their own there was another group of two girls and two boys of the same family. We were looked after in the most generous way by Mr Sainsbury and his friends who obviously funded the whole matter.'

There is a story by John Rosen, who was part of the selected Kinder who came to the new 'Sainsbury Home', that he was collected by one of the brothers and bought chocolate and fruit on their way to the hostel. After their treatment in Hitler's Germany, this simple act of kindness was a gesture that they remembered for the rest of their lives. According to one former resident, 'Alan and Robert Sainsbury were not merely the sort of wealthy philanthropists who put up money for a good cause. They took a personal interest in our welfare and I believe that they derived real pleasure from the results of the rescue operation that they had performed.'

The Sainsbury hostel housed at least 22 German Jewish boys and girls. From the few memoirs that exist, life seems to have been happy there though the children of course worried about their families back in Germany. The hostel staff did what they could to make the children feel at home, having to deal with at least one outbreak of German measles when the whole building was put into quarantine by the health authorities. There was a silver lining, however, as it gave the staff a chance to bring in a tutor to help the youngsters with their English. They learned fast.

Once the infection was over the children could play outdoors, but the local boys and girls treated them with some suspicion: Who were these German speaking children? They were exposed to some verbal and physical bullying but nothing too serious. They watched with bafflement a game of cricket on the common, not realising that both batsmen on the field were on the same side. Life in this new world was not easy.

The Sainsburys clearly understood that these traumatised children, so far from home, needed some welcome respite. Some of the children were lucky enough to be invited on holiday to one of the Sainsbury country houses, including Alan's father's hunting stables in Leighton Buzzard. They stayed with the family's groom called Clark and, as one of the children recalled later, 'They were quite Victorian in their outlook [...] we children were not allowed to use knives and I remember running out one day to hold Mr Sainsbury's horse when he came back from a hack. [Mr] Clark, shouted at me not to come out in the yard and to remember my station, but Mr Sainsbury told him to let me be'. The children were also taken in small groups to the zoo and other places of interest in London. In the summer of 1939, the whole group was taken for a seaside holiday to Bexhill-on-Sea where the family had rented a large house. The Sainsburys were regular visitors to the East Sussex resort, always keen to ensure that the children were happy.

Far from being remote philanthropists, Alan and Babette were also regular visitors to the hostel in Putney. They made sure that the children were provided with clothing, medical care and even individual pocket money of tuppence a week (later increased to sixpence). The children were able to write letters to their parents in Germany and of course receive them. Some children saved up their pocket money to help their parents should they arrive in England. Tragically, all but two of the children lost their parents in the Holocaust.

After several months of learning English at the hostel, the youngsters were sent off in a long line to a local school, West Hill Elementary, where they were greeted by the curious children (most of them very poor) with friendly smiles and even little gifts such as rubber bands and empty match boxes. This generous reception was no doubt explained partly by the attitude of Mr Cook, the very sympathetic head teacher who was charged with looking after their interests when the school was later evacuated to Reading in Berkshire. It seems that the Sainsburys acquired another house there to be used as a hostel but some of the refugees were billeted with local families.

The war years certainly did not mean the end of the Sainsbury involvement with the young people. 'Mr Alan' (as he was known) kept in close touch with the children in Reading – visiting, sending birthday cards, asking for regular reports on their welfare and education or employment (once the children were 14 many of them left school to find work). Where the children were able to stay on at school, Mr Alan and his wife arranged for their school fees to be paid, clothing bought, medical bills paid for and much more.

Alan Sainsbury's continuing support for the children, now young adults by the early 1950s, is evident from the surviving records held at the World Jewish Relief archives. They show him involved in attempts to reunite a few of the children whose families had somehow survived the Nazi onslaught. The records show how Alan liaised with the refugee organisations in London keeping their welfare officers informed about the progress of the former refugees.

In 1953 the former children who had kept in close touch with Alan Sainsbury, organised a reunion of the hostel Kinder. The guest of honour was of course, Alan. He was given a special presentation to give thanks for all that he had done for the Jewish children most of whom had lost their parents in the Holocaust. Even after this date, the Sainsbury family kept an eye on 'their' children. At one of the Sainsbury AGMs, a shareholder told the meeting that her husband, who came on the Kindertransport, had been collected from Liverpool Street Station by Lord and Lady Sainsbury in a Rolls-Royce and received a wedding present from the couple twenty years later.

Upon his death aged 96, a former Kind, Erica Plaut, wrote to the Association of Jewish Refugees saying, 'Lord Sainsbury took a great personal interest in our welfare. Even after our wartime evacuation to various homes this support, including financial help, continued.'

Another former Kind recalled 'How lucky we were to be in the Sainsbury home because many of the other children didn't have such good fortune. Needless to say, the idea of people taking in these little Jewish children from another country, who spoke another language, was daunting to many people,' and added, 'They took care of all the costs, some of our emotional needs. They did what they could for the children to make them as comfortable as possible.'

Similar sentiments were expressed by other Kinder 'We shall always remember with gratitude the tremendous part he (Alan Sainsbury) and his Committee played in looking after all of us in those very difficult days for us children.' One former refugee summed up his feelings for the family which did so much for the children – 'They were a blessing'.

Chapter 6

The Dutch Aunt
Geertruida Wijsmuller

Truus Wijsmuller, Image 10

Confronting the senior SS officer, Adolf Eichmann, organising the largest ever Kindertransport and an eleventh hour rescue mission involving a leaky ship and German dive bombers; thousands of children saved. It is no wonder that Geertruida Wijsmuller – known as Truus – was awarded the honour 'Righteous Among Nations'.

Born in the Dutch city of Alkmaar in 1896 Truus became one of a cohort of Dutch rescuers. Her particular interest was in the welfare of children and she was an experienced volunteer social worker with a strong interest in politics. Truus had been committed to the rescue of Jewish children from Germany for many years and, after the November Pogroms, travelled over the Dutch-German border in her small car to smuggle refugee children back to safety, hidden under the folds of her skirt. She repeated this type of rescue mission many times and would often escort frightened children from railway stations on the German border. Sometimes drunken SS men would detain the German Jewish children for no reason other than to upset them. Truus did not leave their side, waiting with groups of 30 or more in cold waiting rooms in the middle of the night.

After the Pogroms, one group of orphans who had witnessed the burning of their children's home waited with Truus for over ten tortuous hours before being allowed to move on. Truus was very much the border escort at this stage, not involving herself with the onward care of the children. That would be dealt with by the Dutch Jewish committee led by another Geertruida, van Tijn (a remarkable rescuer in her own right and one who worked with Truus. It was said though that the two women had many personality clashes and were not compatible).

Truus was not averse to taking risks; danger could even be quite appealing to this strong-minded woman. She would stop at nothing to help children in peril and answered a call on 2 December 1938 to meet Norman Bentwich in Amsterdam. Bentwich, a senior figure in the British refugee movement, had specifically come to ask if someone not Jewish would travel to Vienna to talk to the feared Eichmann. The future architect of mass deportations to the death camps in Poland, then he was head of the Nazis' so-called 'Central Agency for Jewish Emigration' in Austria. Truus' task was to get his permission to allow the children to leave on the first Kindertransport from Vienna. Fearless, boundlessly energetic, German speaking and ready to travel at a moment's notice, Truus was the obvious candidate to go and instantly agreed to be the refugee committee's official emissary. That same evening (coincidentally the very same day as the first arrival of German Jewish children in Harwich), Truus was on a plane to Vienna via Berlin. Her mission was to meet Eichmann and help organise the escape of the city's persecuted children.

The trip to Vienna did not start well. Truus was horrified by the sight of Jewish victims of random violence in the street, against men who had simply been queuing up to apply for emigration papers. She also witnessed the irony of a Nazi-ordered street charity collection for 'The Little Children', and how their smiles had turned to scorn when she told the tin rattlers that she had come to help the Jewish children. There was worse to come. Later she was thrown into jail for entering a forbidden zone. Truus did not go quietly, ordered the guard to bring his chief and said she would see to it that the world's press would find out about what was happening in Vienna. Emphasising that she had an appointment to meet Eichmann, she was released and met the Nazi head of the Jewish emigration department. The Nazi officer at first treated Truus with disdain. He wanted to ensure that Truus was an Aryan and not a Jew. He demanded that she lift her skirt so that he could inspect her Aryan physique. Later he asked her to remove her gloves to inspect her hands – he believed Jews had a special sort of hand. This was the man on whom the fate of Vienna's Jews would depend.

The encounter with Eichmann, recorded in Truus' Dutch biography, is worth quoting. She introduced herself to Eichmann who sat as though a Roman governor behind a huge desk flanked by a large Alsatian dog. She said:

'I am Mrs Wijsmuller from Amsterdam.' He remained silent, he

waited until she would register who he really was.

She said: 'I have come here to talk to you about the transport of ten thousand Jewish children to England.' But now he had had enough and snarled: 'We are not used to negotiating with women.' 'Oh, that's a pity', she said, and sat down. She had to get the hell out of there, he said, but she remained seated [...] He kept looking at her fixedly, but she was patient. He held out his hand and asked: 'Do you actually have papers, madam?' 'What for', she said. 'I have only come to talk.' 'Papers from England', he said wearily, 'schedules for example, authorisation, that you can get the children across the border.' 'Goodness no, Herr Doktor', she said. 'It was all done in such a hurry'. He then rang for an SS man and ordered him: 'have the Jew, Friedmann, come in.'

This is likely to have been Desider Friedmann, sometime President of the IKG (the Jewish cultural organisation) later murdered in Auschwitz. Friedmann had been reduced by his earlier internment in the Dachau concentration camp to a fearful slave of the arrogant, ignorant and race-obsessed Eichmann. 'The Jew Friedmann' is how Eichmann would address the senior members of the community in Vienna – more 'lowly' ones he probably wouldn't address at all. But here he was with this black SS uniform, presiding in a stately palace (stolen from the Rothschild family) with all the power of the Nazi State behind him. According to Truus' recollection, Eichmann looked at Friedmann and said, 'Let's pull a nice prank. You (Friedmann), take her to the station, order a train, and she leaves with 600 children. If she manages to get them to England and leave them there, then she'll get the ten thousand'.

Friedmann and Truus set about organising the first transport out of Vienna with Rosa Schwarz and her team at the Jewish cultural organisation. Eichmann had given the IKG and Truus only a few days to get the first transport together. And in an act of cruel irony, he insisted that the train depart on the Jewish sabbath. Truus used her contacts in London Helen and Norman Bentwich and Lola Hahn-Warburg – to ensure that all travel arrangements and places to stay in England would be ready in days. Hahn-Warburg phoned Truus to tell her that places on the night ferry to Harwich had been booked for 500 children and accommodation found in Dovercourt and Pakefield camps on the East coast. Friedmann and Schwarz organised the list of children to be sent to England, liaised with traumatised mothers and even instructed the youngsters in British table manners so that they would make a good first impression.

Truus worked ceaselessly to arrange reservations on the train carriages and meals for the children when they arrived in Cologne where they needed to change trains. She returned to Amsterdam, ensuring from there that once the children were on their way, the border guards would not detain them. A bit of bribery with drinks and perfume for their wives went a long way. At the first stop in the Netherlands, the Dutch committee – under the leadership of Gertrude van Tijn – had women waiting on the platform to offer the children bars of chocolate, hot cocoa and sandwiches. According to Truus' biographer, and the testimonies of many of the former refugee children, the children now felt safe and were allowed, yes allowed, to be happy again. Around 100 of that first party were cared for in homes in the Netherlands, the remaining 500 went on by train through the Dutch countryside to the Hook of Holland, then (as now) a major passenger ferry port for crossings to England.

Truus met the children at the Hook and stayed rooted to the quayside until the ship run by the LNER railway company was safely steaming ahead, bound for England. It was a night sailing and the children were offered comfortable cabins – even first class ones. She stood waving in the bitter cold of a December night and kept on waving to the ship on which 'her' children were now safe.

Truus continued to help with the evacuation of Jewish children to a country of refuge. In the months leading up to the war, she became increasingly busy motoring over the German border to bring out Jewish children to safety in the Netherlands. Some of them stayed with Truus and her supportive husband, Joop, before going on to the Amsterdam orphanage, known as the Burgerweeshuis, which had become a sanctuary for unaccompanied German and Austrian children of Jewish background. Even after war was declared her rescue efforts did not cease. Boundaries were of little concern to Truus – she travelled with refugee youngsters to Denmark, France and Sweden. She was arrested as a spy in Marseilles and was often hauled before Dutch police and later Gestapo officers. Nothing deterred this consummate rescuer.

Her final rescue of children to Britain took place in a scenario that even Hollywood would find hard to match. On 10 May 1940 Truus was in Paris on her usual child rescue work when she heard that Hitler's military were attacking the Netherlands. Somehow, even with borders closed, she managed to persuade a railway porter to get her on a military train back home. With bombs falling all round, taking taxis and even a ride on a beer cart, Truus managed to get to Amsterdam (though it had taken three days) and was promptly arrested on espionage charges, albeit quickly released. Incredibly, on her way home she managed to reserve a number of buses to take children from the Burgerweeshuis to the port of IJmuiden, part of an inspired plan to get the Jewish children out to England in the few hours left before the Nazis conquered the Dutch people. Truus packed the buses waiting at the orphanage. She ordered the frightened children to wear double layers of clothing but not to delay. Some managed to grab a favourite doll or pair of football boots. One bus, accompanied by a woman from the Dutch committee, went to central Amsterdam to pick up some more children and a few adults; Truus managed to get one child out of a local hospital. With the deafening sounds of gunfire and bomber aircraft overhead, the buses drove on at speed to IJmuiden. There were inevitable roadblocks, but Truus and the committee managed to get the relevant paperwork in order. With the port buildings now ablaze from enemy bombing, Truus got her children off the bus and ran with them to a ship waiting at the docks. Some adults were turned back by Dutch guards. Truus made sure that she was at the front of the line and would scream the name of this high official, or that decorated army commander – she used every method of getting the children on board the ship. It was over a kilometre from the bus park to the ship and holding hands, the adults and children had to run as fast as they could to the vessel. Waiting for them was the SS Bodegraven, a rather battered old boat but the very last to leave free Holland. There were no fancy cabins, only a fetid hold and room on deck. Truus went on board to say farewell to the children who begged her to stay with them. But she refused. She could not abandon the children left in the Netherlands.

As the ship left the harbour, fighter planes from Germany strafed the boat. Amid the pandemonium, somehow the Bodegraven managed to leave the Dutch port. The last one to do so until the end of the war. The children were kept in the ship's hold for safety, the older boys and girls slept outside on deck. Conditions were primitive with no heating, no toilets and very little food. One small child cried as somehow in the melee to get on board, she had lost her doll. Seasick was common especially as the journey to England was a very long one. It took five days to reach a port that would accept this ship. Despite carrying innocent child civilians, the British authorities classed the vessel as one from a now enemy country. It was only when the ship had sailed around southern and western England that the children were allowed to disembark finally arriving at the port of Liverpool. Sick, exhausted and starving the children were nevertheless safe. There were 74 children on the Bodegraven and each one could thank Truus for their subsequent lives.

Working for the Dutch underground resistance, Truus kept up her work to help refugees throughout the war and for many years after. This powerful lady (who surely deserves a full English-language biography) continued on countless committees, helping the poor in former Dutch colonies and uniting those displaced by war.

She died in 1978. The words of Yad Vashem's citation for her 'Righteous Among Nations' award sum up her life's work: 'Resistance worker Geertruida Wijsmuller fought courageously to save thousands of Jews from certain death at the hands of the Nazis.' The children she looked after gave her another title: 'Tante Truus' – Auntie Truus. I suspect this meant more to her than any other accolade.

Chapter 7

The Brigadier General
Sir Wyndham Deedes

Sir Wyndham Deedes, Image 11

Born wealthy in a castle, died poor in a lonely bedsit; once ruled Palestine, devout Christian, ardent Zionist, battler for the East End poor, and a central figure in the Kindertransport. Not a bad CV though it tells only a fraction of the story of the man once called 'Wyndham Bey' by the Ottoman Turks. Described by Norman Bentwich, a close friend, as 'a modern saint', the life of Brigadier General Sir Wyndham Deedes is the more remarkable for the way in which this great figure's name has been lost.

Shy, diffident, modest, spiritually ascetic, fiercely intelligent but passionate about causes that mattered to him – his retiring character may go some way to explaining his absence from the history books. In most photographs of Wyndham Deedes he is lurking in the background. The foreground is where he operated but he never wanted to be seen there. And yet he was without doubt a central figure in the creation of the Kindertransport story.

Deedes was born in Saltwood Castle in 1883, the son of landed gentry in Kent and his early life followed an expected trajectory for an upper middle class Englishman: educated at Eton, a career mapped out in the army, he played the role of the gentleman soldier during the Boer War – cricket and cocktails one day, and a little light hand-to-hand fighting the next. A bookish personality might suggest the wrong kind of persona for a military man, but like a lot of things in the life of Wyndham Deedes, his character was never easy to pin down nor put into neat slots. A voracious reader and exceptional linguist, he mastered Turkish to the extent that locals mistook him for one of theirs. That language became crucial in 1910 when, still a very young chap, he was commissioned to create an efficient new gendarmerie in the Ottoman Empire. That posting which required travels in Turkey, Egypt and Palestine, cemented a lifelong love of the near Middle East.

When the Turks entered the First World War in 1915, Deedes was drafted into British military intelligence (his thorough knowledge of the language was a big driver in getting the job) and it rapidly became clear that he was also a battle strategist of the highest order. Even Churchill consulted him about his plans to open up a front at Gallipoli – a disastrous move that would dog the future prime minister's reputation (he ignored a much more sensible tactic suggested by Deedes). Wyndham himself volunteered to leave the comfort of the senior officer's quarters far away from battle to pitch up in the very midst of the fighting. Those that knew him said that Deedes was the bravest man they ever met – totally fearless but always most concerned for the welfare of his men.

Rapidly promoted to Brigadier General, Wyndham's travels in Palestine further increased his interest, and indeed passion for the cause of the Jews. He became a convinced Zionist, arguing all his life for a permanent home for the Jewish people in Palestine. An ardent reader of the Bible and keen historian of the Jews, he was one of a small band of British Christians, some of them military men like him, who wanted to help found a new state for the dispersed peoples of the Old Testament. During the First World War, he helped found a Zionist military unit – the Mule Corps – which provided recent immigrants to Palestine with the fighting tools first to help beat the Turks who ruled the land, and then help defend a nascent homeland. In the early 1920s, Deedes became second in command to the High Commissioner for Mandate Palestine, Viscount Herbert Samuel. In periods of Samuel's illness, Wyndham Deedes often became the de facto ruler of British Palestine. Even-handed towards Arabs and Jews, his commitment to the Balfour Declaration promising a Jewish home in Palestine, never dimmed.

His stay in Palestine was relatively short-lived. He wanted to return to London to live with his mother in their large house in Bethnal Green, then one of the poorest districts of the capital. It was there that Deedes began to devote the next stage of his colourful life to helping the poor. He would spend most of his life living among the poorest in society, a man with a mission to give service, to devote himself to the needs of others. It was clear by 1936 that the Jews of Germany needed his help.

Glimpse into any of the child rescue archives from this period and Wyndham Deedes' name will appear. As a scholarly non-Jew

He was a tireless campaigner to get the British government to admit more into this country and relax the extremely limited quota allowed into Mandate Palestine. He was one of a group trying to negotiate with the Nazis to allow Austrian Zionist organisations to re-open and to facilitate the transfer of Jewish funds to Palestine. The Nazis were having none of it. Their interest was in terrorising the Jews into emigrating but without any means to support themselves.

After the November Pogroms, Deedes became joint president (with his former boss Sir Herbert Samuel), of the newly founded Movement for the Care of Children from Germany. He was considered as the man for the job – after all, his Inter Aid Committee had provided a role model for bringing refugee children over to Britain.

Deedes' standing in the Jewish community as a 'good man' was never higher than in the late 1930s. He even became patron of the Jewish Maccabi swimming gala. In launching a Liverpool branch of the Jewish sports organisation, Deedes told his packed audience, 'If only countries of the world would realise – and how few did – the value of the contribution that the Jew could, and did, make to civilisation the world would be a much better place to live in today.' He rounded up a rousing defence of physical fitness by stressing the role of Maccabi in the creation of a Jewish home in Palestine. For a man who by this time was something of a pale shadow of the young gallant army man, perhaps Deedes was a strange choice but his commitment to the Jews and Zionism in particular was enough to draw in the crowds.

Almost none of the family papers refer to Deedes' work with Jewish refugees and certainly during wartime, his attention was re-directed to the needs of East End Londoners during the

Blitz. He became Chief Warden of Civil Defence in Bethnal Green doing his best to alleviate the wrecked homes and lives of the victims of the Nazi bombing campaign on the capital. His war years were also spent in the BBC where he became a regular broadcaster to and about the peoples of Turkey.

After the war he resumed his dedication to the East End poor and pursued a typically low-key but important role as Labour politician and ardent Zionist. He was Chair of the London Council of Social Service and he helped set up the Anglo Israel Association, a body also closely associated with Leonard Montefiore.

This brief summary does little to encompass the many activities and passions of this extraordinary man. After the war he still found time to write two books: 'A New Way of Life' about the kibbutz movement and (as editor), 'Religious Aspects of Zionism'.

His last years were spent in a mean bedsit in Hythe in Kent, his health going from bad to worse, his body in constant pain but his spirit and faith never dimmed. Two books have been written about Sir Wyndham Deedes, one with a strange connection to the refugee story. 'Deedes Bey' is an account of his time in Turkey and the First World War. It is written by one John Presland. This in fact was the nom de plume of Gladys Skelton, the co-founder with Sir Wyndham, of the Inter Aid Committee. The second was a book of eulogistic memories written a few years after his death. His former friends and colleagues paint a picture of a much-loved and admired man.

In a moving obituary written by Norman Bentwich, Deedes is described as 'a saint among Christian friends [...] He lived to help everybody he met [...] and for the last 33 years of his life he was concerned only to help his fellow men [...] a noble

example of what our sages call "the righteous of the nations."
We shall not see his like again.'

Chapter 8

The Bishop
George Bell

George Bell, Image 12

Bishop George Bell was a tireless campaigner in support of refugees from Nazi Europe, especially those who had been defined as 'non-Aryan Christians,' and an outspoken critic of the internment of German Jews from 1940. As Bishop of Chichester, he spoke out against persecution of the Jews and called for a more open-door approach to those fleeing from Hitler's Europe. By so doing he made many enemies in the political establishment and was once described by Anthony Eden as 'this pestilent priest'.

Bell was born in 1883 into a comfortable middle-class home within sight of Chichester cathedral and educated at

Westminster School and Christ Church, Oxford. His lifelong interest in ecumenism was nurtured at Wells Theological College, and he was ordained in Ripon cathedral in 1907. Serving as a deacon in industrial Leeds, he came face to face with the effects of urban poverty, an experience which kindled a lifelong passion for social justice. Two years later he was offered a place as a Clerical Student back at Christ Church, Oxford, where he met many of the men who would influence his thinking, including Albert Mansbridge, the founder of the Workers' Educational Association (WEA), where Bell lectured for a time, and William Temple, the future Archbishop of Canterbury.

Bell took up a post as Chaplain to the Archbishop of Canterbury and participated in an enquiry into 'Christianity and Social Problems'. Happiness and tragedy struck in equal measure - firstly the joy of his marriage to Harriet Grace, but then the tragic loss of two brothers in the fighting in France. Bell's reputation for clear thinking, innovative ideas and organisational skills saw him rise rapidly in the Church of England hierarchy. In 1924 he became Dean of Canterbury and continued to lecture and publish works on ecumenism and social justice. He invited preachers from different traditions within Christianity, encouraged the radio broadcasting of services and commissioned works of drama, most notably T.S. Eliot's Murder in the Cathedral. In 1929 he became Bishop of Chichester, a post he held for the rest of his life.

Bell was an early supporter and advocate for the 'Life and Work' movement which promoted collaboration between differing churches collectively involved in helping the poor. His ecumenical interests also took on international dimensions. He was especially interested in contacts with German theologians, promoting dialogue between English and German churchmen and becoming a close friend of the young pastor, Dietrich Bonhoeffer, a key figure in the German Confessional Church which opposed many of the Nazi doctrines imposed after 1933. Bell himself observed the rise of Hitler and his anti-Jewish policies with growing alarm.

The parlous position of non-Aryan Christians was first brought to Bell's attention by Sir Wyndham Deedes in August 1933. Deedes sent Bell a letter received from Helen Bentwich in which she urged the churches in Britain not to be complacent about what was happening in Germany. Hitler's appointed bishop, Ludwig Müller, had pushed through the adoption of the 'Aryan Paragraph' by the Prussian Church Synod, which effectively excluded pastors who had Jewish ancestry, and Bentwich was concerned that these outcast churchmen and women had no community to support them.

Outraged, Bell devoted himself to raising awareness of the issue in Britain and abroad, writing to churches around the world, sending letters to national newspapers and convening a mass meeting at London's Albert Hall. He met the newly appointed League of Nations High Commissioner for Refugees and asked for a new worldwide appeal to be instigated; he also urged action from international bodies such as Inter-Church Aid. Bell drafted a Christmas appeal signed by leading Christian clergy and asked Sir John Reith to put it out on the BBC. All were disappointed by the poor response.

Despite this disappointment, Bell remained busy in the cause of those persecuted because of their Jewish heritage. In November 1935 he moved a resolution in the Church Assembly expressing a hope that:

Christian people in this and other countries will exert their influence and make it plain to the rulers of Germany that the continuance of their present policy will arouse widespread indignation and prove a grave obstacle to the promotion of confidence and good-will between Germany and other nations.

Reaction to the speech in Britain was very positive, Chief Rabbi Hertz commenting that 'Your words will come as a ray of hope to hundreds of thousands whose annihilation seems to have been decided upon by the Nazi rulers.' On 24 September 1936, Bell made a radio broadcast in which he referred to the tragedy of the 12,000 'Christian outcasts' and the 80,000 people who had fled Germany since Hitler's accession to power. Four months later he paid a visit to Berlin to meet the leaders of the non-Aryan Christian groups, including members of the Paulusbund (a self-help group) and the Quakers. He concluded shortly afterwards that, 'There is no future for them in Germany and they are absolutely clear about that.'

In the autumn of 1937, Bell sent his sister-in-law, Laura Livingstone, to Berlin as a representative of the International Christian Committee for Refugees. She had some knowledge of German and was free at that time. She set up an office with three or four staff and worked closely with the Quakers who thought her decisive and courageous, though somewhat disorganised (she often left sensitive correspondence lying around on her desk). Her toughness meant that she was a good person to send to the concentration camps to assist in the release of prisoners.

She was well acquainted with Pastor Heinrich Grüber, one of the leading anti-Nazi churchmen in Germany. Grüber and his team risked their own personal safety in helping Jews and 'non-Aryan Christians' out of the camps and out of the country. He travelled to Britain several times before the outbreak of war to secure visas for persecuted victims of Nazism. Livingstone had worked with Grüber in Berlin and both were part of a complex web of rescuers operating under the Gestapo 'radar'. That said, Livingstone was not averse to directly approaching senior SS officers about helping Jews and others to leave Germany. For instance, as soon as she started work, she requested an interview with SS Oberführer Werner Best who told Livingstone that, 'Since the work which you are undertaking has nothing to do with politics, I have nothing against your project.' Before the November Pogroms, she found that people in Britain didn't know very much about the situation in Germany. As she later recalled, 'We did what we could to help people escape. It was uphill work [...] At home attention seemed concentrated on victims of the Spanish Civil War.' As war approached, Bell urged his sister-in-law to return to England which she did; she went back to Germany as one of the first female relief workers at Bergen-Belsen in 1945.

Despite a continuing poor response in terms of fundraising for the German non-Aryan Christians, fifty refugee migrants, including twelve children, set sail on 16 February 1937 for Colombia in South America. Bell was an enthusiastic supporter of this project, which involved the resettlement of farmland there (but which ended in failure due to the poor quality of land and the refugees' inexperience as farmers).

In the same year Bell formed the Church of England Committee for non-Aryan Christians. Its task was to raise funds to educate children and train young people. This ambition was to be achieved with the help of the Inter-Aid Committee (which evolved from the Save the Children Fund) and the Germany Emergency Committee of the Society of Friends. Bell remained chairman of the Church of England Committee until after the war. Like other such bodies, it located to Bloomsbury House in 1939 and formed part of the coordinated efforts to support refugees from Nazi-dominated Europe. It was responsible for the care and welfare of nearly 200 children who were mostly fostered in British homes.

In April 1938, despite by now being on an official blacklist, Bell visited Berlin once again. The situation for Jews and non-Aryan Christians had become even more perilous following the Anschluss, and on his return to London, Bell addressed the Church Assembly, urging support for bringing out as many refugees as possible from the Reich. In July he was appointed to the House of Lords and made the events in Germany the focus of his maiden speech:

I cannot understand – and I know many Germans – how our own kinsmen of the German race can lower themselves to such a level of dishonour and cowardice as to attack a defenceless people in the way that the National Socialists have attacked the non-Aryans.

He told the listening peers that refugees were an asset, not a liability, and that they could bring new wealth, new work and new manpower to countries where these things were needed. He urged the British government to offer new training places and to open up emigration to the Dominions. Writing in the Chichester Diocesan Gazette, Bell told his flock: 'These non-Aryans can no longer be called "refugees" as they have as yet no countries of refuge.' Given the size of the British Empire and Dominions, Bell noted, 'It seems to us impossible, both on the grounds of charity and on the grounds of statesmanship, that the doors can remain forever shut.'

Following the November Pogroms, Bell went to the

he had excellent contacts with church figures, academia and the British Establishment. His long-held passion for the creation of a Jewish state (and track record in commanding Jewish Palestinian units against the Turks in World War I) meant that he was liked and trusted by Anglo-Jewish figureheads such as Otto Schiff, Lionel Montefiore and Anthony de Rothschild.

Deedes was closely bound up with the issue of Jewish refugees and their escape to Britain and Palestine in particular. He was instrumental in the setting up of the Inter Aid Committee in 1936 and served on the Council for German Jewry – a non-Jew in a largely Jewish organisation set up to help finance emigration, especially to Palestine.

The concept behind the Inter Aid Committee (IAC) grew out of a conference called by Deedes to coordinate relief work for child refugees both Jewish and non-Jewish. Pulling all sorts of high level strings, Deedes was soon off on a fact-finding mission to Nazi Germany. There he saw for himself the traumatic effect of isolating Jewish children from German state schools and understood that the pressure to leave would only grow. His organisational skills were brought to play in ensuring that the many aid agencies in Britain, Jewish, Christian and non-denominational, would have to work more closely to cope with the rising demand from desperate parents.

Whilst many of the men and women on the refugee committees had active social lives, Deedes was regarded somewhat as a workaholic who was driving himself to ill health (which dogged him mercilessly in his latter years). Thin and pale, his colleague Norman Bentwich remarked that there was nothing wrong with Sir Wyndham that couldn't be put right by a square meal. Though totally different personalities, Bentwich and Deedes were united by the plight of the Jews especially those in Vienna.

Home Office and personally guaranteed to support twenty Confessional Church pastors and their families. He worked hard to raise the funds for this scheme, which included using a large house lent and furnished by Canon Griffiths, Rector of St Leonard's in St Leonards-on-Sea. It was also in November 1938 that Bell initiated the inter-denominational Christian Council for Refugees from Germany (CCRG). He was supported in his campaigning by, among others, the Quaker Germany Emergency Committee (GEC), the Reverend Henry Carter of the Methodist Church and by Cardinal Arthur Hinsley, the Catholic Archbishop of Westminster and was instrumental in encouraging the Church Assembly to allocate £50,000 from its central funds to help pay for the welfare of refugees.

In February 1939 Bell gave a crucial speech at the University of London. Entitled 'Humanity and the Refugees', it was chaired by Britain's Chief Rabbi Dr Hertz, and in it Bell set out his beliefs about assisting refugees: 'The problem of the refugee today, though it is in a special sense a problem of Jewish race, concerns not Jewry alone, but mankind. And if there were no non-Jewish refugees in the whole world, it would still be the concern of mankind.' He went on to define the term 'refugee' as meaning, not someone who is a fugitive from the law but:

He is a person who has been banished, or who, though not suffering an actual sentence of banishment, has sought refuge in another country because, owing to religious or political causes, he can no longer live in his own [...] [A] refugee is a person suffering, or fearing oppression, and [...] so far from it being discreditable to be a refugee, the style, "refugee" (other things being equal) is more likely to be a title of honour'.

In this speech, Bell then turned to the 'huge refugee movements

[...] greater in their total bulk than any yet on record', which, he said, represented a 'challenge to humanity. Indeed in some ways I believe that our attitude to the refugees is a test of our attitude to God, as well as our attitude to man.' Rebuffing the view that what was happening in Germany was no business of the people of Britain, he asserted: 'It is our business because we are human beings. If humanity means anything it is impossible to shut our eyes. It is equally impossible to refuse to take action'. Citing the greater per capita numbers being allowed into France and Switzerland, he reminded his audience that many refugees were skilled workers and would in fact create employment and that, 'that which carries with it the true kind of hope and encouragement, is that which is given in countries and in circumstances which allows new scope for creative living'. Bell concluded his speech with a powerful call to action and a vision for the future:

'[...] We must do everything we can to help the victims, of all classes and occupations and creeds. And this "everything we can" means more than philanthropy or private charity [...] Prime Ministers and their cabinets cannot afford to be passive here; for it is an essential part of the whole business of creating a true international order.

The outbreak of war brought new challenges for Bishop Bell, especially during the mass internment of 'enemy aliens' after May 1940. Among those interned under Churchill's policy of 'collaring the lot' were thirty-three 'non-Aryan' pastors of the German Confessional Church whom Bell had helped bring to safety in England, as well as some of their wives. The interned pastors included Franz Hildebrandt, a former curate of Martin Niemöller, a leading opponent of the Hitler regime in Germany, who had taken up a role as pastor to German exiles in Cambridge and of whom, in a testimonial to the tribunal examining his case, Bell had written: 'I count him as an intimate friend. He is a man of the highest honour and integrity. He is utterly opposed to the Nazi regime [...] I would answer for his loyalty to this country anywhere and at any time.' Another was Hans Ehrenberg, a former professor at Heidelberg University who had been imprisoned at Sachsenhausen concentration camp. Bell was appalled that people he had personally rescued from persecution, a group with exemplary anti-fascist credentials, should be treated in this way. Bell's intercessions with the authorities did no good, despite an intense period of letter-writing to the Home Office. However, he successfully urged the Bishop of Sodor and Man, and his sympathetic dean, Ernest Barker, to make visits to the internment camps in the Isle of Man. In a speech to the House of Lords on 12 June 1940, Bell told the assembled peers:

I venture to think – and I have some knowledge in this matter – that internment of aliens of German and Austrian origin irrespective of character, irrespective of their attitudes to the Nazi regime, irrespective of their devotion to the interests and cause of this country and our Allies, is demanded neither by national security nor by justice.

Though Bell's speech was not met with universal approval, it put him firmly at the centre of the opposition to internment policy. At the end of July 1940 he undertook a four-day visit to the camps on the Isle of Man, including the women's camp at Port Erin and Port St Mary, where he preached a sermon assuring the internees that 'Your friends outside this camp are many and they do not forget'. He twice visited the Central Promenade camp in Douglas, where he met Hildebrandt and others. In August he made a second powerful speech in the House of Lords, drawing attention to the 'waste of talent and ability' inherent in mass internment, hailing Britain as 'upholders of freedom,[...] fighters against evil things – brute force, bad faith, injustice, oppression and persecution' and calling for 'justice to the men and the women who have already suffered bitterly from these things in Germany and have fled from them to us'. A telegram followed from the Isle of Man saying, 'Camp immensely cheered by all you did'.

Bell spent the next weeks dealing with an ever-growing file of internment cases, including medical hardships, wives interned in Holloway Prison and students deported to Canada. In September 1940 he visited the camps once more and wrote a detailed report on what he observed were significant areas of complaint, including mixing Nazis and non-Nazis in the same camp. Hildebrandt was released in October and most of the interned pastors followed by February 1941. Bell made a third House of Lords speech in December 1941 which focused on the plight of those still interned in camps in Australia and Canada, who, he said, 'suffer especially from the feeling of inability to give the contribution they want to give to the British cause'.

Again, Bell was not universally praised for his stand. The local newspaper on the Isle of Man described him as 'the self-appointed champion of captive Nazis and Fascists in our midst', while Joanna Cruickshank, commandant of the women's camp, called him a 'highly dangerous man'. Bell also made enemies by taking up the cause of some imprisoned British fascists and was seen by some to be in league with communist factions. Towards the end of the war he was further criticised for his condemnation of the Allied 'carpet bombing' of German cities. Despite such opposition, Bell was fully supported by most of the Church's senior leaders, including Archbishop Lang who in August 1940 had written:

I cannot tell you how grateful I am to you for all the noble work you are doing on behalf both of these Pastors and of refugees generally. I should feel that the Church had been wanting in an obvious duty if you had not been able with your exceptional knowledge and your indefatigable zeal to take it up.'

As Hitler's defeat seemed increasingly inevitable, Bell's thoughts turned to the future of Germany and the continent as a whole. He embarked on his own 'crusade for a new Europe' and was a vocal member of the Churches' Peace Aims Group, which involved church leaders, politicians, academics and civil servants in discussing the post-war settlement. Against the views of other members of the group, who were more concerned with building closer ties with America and the British Empire, Bell advocated a kind of united states of Europe and the rebuilding of German church life.

George Bell died in 1958 at the age of seventy-five. Reflecting on the bishop's legacy, his friend Franz Hildebrandt, whose emigration from Germany and release from internment Bell had helped to secure, wrote of him that 'He never got, or asked for, the measure of public recognition which should have been his due.' Writing of Bell's significance and influence, his biographer Andrew Chandler summed up a life in turbulent times: 'To men and women who lived in other countries, and to many of those who endured the costs of tyranny in other lands he was the most conspicuous English Christian of his generation.'

Chapter 9

The Quaker
Bertha Bracey

Bertha Bracey, Image 13

Bertha Bracey was one of the leading British Quakers involved in the rescue and humanitarian support of refugees, especially those escaping Nazi persecution. She and fellow Quakers were particularly concerned with the plight of Kindertransport children in need of foster care, as well as the rescue and subsequent welfare of women who might come to Britain as domestic servants.

In 1933, Bertha Bracey became Secretary of the Friends' Germany Emergency Committee (GEC), a post she retained until 1945. Within just two years of its foundation under her leadership, the GEC succeeded in bringing more than 600 people out of Germany, many of them in those early days of the rescue, opponents of the Nazis who found themselves in grave danger: socialists, communists and pacifists. A fluent German speaker, Bracey was well-placed to build close contacts with Jewish welfare organisations in Berlin and Vienna. She also coordinated the efforts of German Quakers to help identify those most at risk of Nazi persecution and assist them to flee the country. By 1938 she spearheaded a staff of eighty volunteers at the GEC offices in Friends' House in London and later at Bloomsbury House. Without doubt she was also one of the driving forces behind the Kindertransport.

Bertha Bracey was born in Bourneville near Birmingham in 1893, the daughter of a worker for the Quaker-owned Cadbury confectionery firm. She attended Birmingham University, became a Quaker at the age of nineteen and, after a five-year spell as a teacher, went to live in Vienna, where she worked at the Quaker Centre; there she helped to run youth clubs and support needy children affected by the aftermath of the First World War. Later she moved to Germany, first to Nuremberg to help set up and run a depot where deprived families could buy cheap food and clothes and subsequently to Berlin, where she continued working with children in great need. She was part of the 'Quakerspeisung', a relief programme which undertook to feed over a million children daily. It is somewhat ironic that some of the children she helped in 1920s Weimar Germany went on to become leading Nazi figures in the following decade. However, as it turned out, that fact stood her in good stead in her negotiations with those same Nazi officials, who later remembered their own debt of gratitude to the Quakers.

Bracey's time in Germany enabled her to observe at first hand the rise of Hitler and the Nazi party. She was in no doubt as to the threat they posed to Jews and other opponents, noting: 'If more people had read Mein Kampf they would have seen that the very regulations of National Socialism contained its poison and its deepest poison was of course its anti-Semitism.'

Bracey returned to London in 1929 as administrative secretary of the Germany and Holland Committee of the Friends' Service Council, aiming to develop the network of Quaker centres in those countries as havens of peace and reconciliation; in time both countries would become focal points of the rescue effort for Jews and 'non Aryans'. Life in Germany had helped Bracey make valuable contacts with the German and Austrian Quakers and leaders of Jewish welfare organisations, such as Wilfrid Israel whom she had first met in Nuremberg. Her astute observation of the rise of Nazism was used to good effect when she was called upon to report to the British Quakers on developments in continental Europe. As she wrote in Quaker World Service a few weeks after Hitler assumed power in January 1933:

Anti-Semitism is a terrible canker which has been spreading poison for decades in many Central European countries. It came to a head on April 1st, when Germany dropped back into the cruelty of the 'Ghetto' psychology of the Middle Ages [...] Words are not adequate to tell of the anguish of some of my Jewish friends [...]

Clearly, she was referring to the attempted Nazi mass boycott of Jewish businesses in Germany in April 1933 and the passing of an 'Enabling Act' which allowed Hitler to bypass the Reichstag and in effect to rule by diktat. For instance, in attempting to support the Jews by ignoring the boycott, German Quakers found themselves increasingly threatened, and many were imprisoned and harassed. It was against this background of rising tensions that Bertha assumed responsibility for the

GEC and, with her increased workforce, supported the cases of individuals who were at particular risk in Nazi Germany, and later in Austria and Czechoslovakia too.

As early as June 1933, Bertha's committee sent a circular letter to all Quaker Meeting Houses around the UK. It spoke of the shock felt by the British Friends at the turn of events in Germany and of the need to raise funds to provide aid to the victims of the Nazi regime. Bertha sent the letter under the auspices of the Small Case Committee, whose function was to attend to the needs of individual refugee Germans 'who seem to us to have a claim upon our practical sympathy and guidance'. 'Non-Aryan' refugees who applied to her committee for help would initially be passed to one of the other relief bodies, such as the Jewish Refugee Committee which was originally based in Woburn House. But for those who had connections with the Friends in Germany, the GEC and provincial Meeting Houses could offer help. Many, said Bertha, were students 'cut off in the middle of their professional training on account of being pacifists, Jews or Socialists, and who have no hope for a future career in Germany'. Bertha asked local Friends, such as the community in Manchester, to find temporary hospitality in private homes. She added:

We think that you will share with us a sense of the tragedy of these young lives, uprooted from their environment and set a-drift separated from their families, not wanted anywhere, with no definite prospects for the future and yet firm in their adherence to pacifist principles. Some of them are exceptionally fine characters indeed.

In the case of Manchester, Bertha's letters were dispatched to all members of the Quaker Monthly Meeting. There were apparently precious few replies and no offers of free accommodation – perhaps a reflection of the serious economic crisis faced by people in an industrial city during the early 1930s.

Back at Friends' House in London, a rapidly growing set of case files (14,000 by 1938) placed huge personal pressures on Bertha, despite a commensurate rise in the numbers of her staff. In 1936 she took almost a year off work due to nervous exhaustion, returning thereafter to control the operations for the Kindertransport 'transmigrants' and for Jewish and other 'non-Aryan' women coming into Britain on domestic permits. Throughout this pre-war period, Bertha made frequent visits to friends and colleagues in Germany. She used her influence and considerable powers of persuasion to help secure the release of Jewish men, Quakers and political opponents of Hitler from concentration camps such as Dachau. Once she received a direct response to a query (about some men who had 'disappeared') from Reinhard Heydrich, then head of the Nazi intelligence branch and later the architect of the 'Final Solution'. She was unafraid to write letters direct to Goering and even to Hitler himself. Her inside knowledge of what was happening in Germany was of great interest to the Foreign Office, who kept a file of the information she had gathered there.

Bracey's interest in children's welfare, dating back from her work in 1920s Vienna, came to the fore with her support for child refugees. By 1934 Bertha had helped establish a Quaker School in the Netherlands for 100 German Jewish children and, in that same year, had also assisted in the setting up of the Stoatley Rough School at Haslemere in Surrey. A progressive co-educational boarding school for refugee children from Germany, Stoatley Rough was the brainchild of Dr Hilde Lion, herself a refugee, academic and principal of the school from its inception. It was she who contacted Bertha Bracey and the GEC for help and typically Bertha found a donor for the school building, chaired the board of governors from 1938 to 1945 and took an active role as governor until 1960.

After Kristallnacht, Bracey made contact with her old friend, Wilfrid Israel who had appealed to the Council for German Jewry in London to save Jewish children below the age of eighteen. Bertha and other Quakers travelled to Germany to assess the situation on the ground. Reporting on this trip in later years, Bracey recalled:

It was clearly not possible for a Jewish organisation to undertake the task [of investigation], and at their request, the Germany Emergency Committee selected five persons to go into Berlin, make contact with one of the few Jewish men leaders not in prison or concentration camp [Wilfrid Israel]. Under the direction of this man, the investigators went into various regions[...], gave financial relief where it proved possible and financially necessary, and returned to London to report.

Soon after her return from Berlin on 21 November 1938, Bracey formed part of the high-profile delegation to the Home Office, which heralded the formation of the Kindertransport programme.

Bertha's letter to a friend in 1986 recalled the genesis of the rescue operation:

When the Jewish refugee Committee could not risk sending a Jewish delegation, we sent five Quaker workers to Berlin to confer with Wilfrid Israel, who directed them to different areas to work alongside the Jewish women doing welfare work, and helping the younger people for whom emigration possibilities still existed... Ben

Greene, who was one of the five people in the Quaker mission, came
back to London after a few days, and went with me [and three others]
to talk to Lord [Herbert] Samuel and the Home Secretary [Samuel
Hoare], in the morning of 21 November. Parliament, sitting that
night, authorised emergency permits to admit 10,000 children.

Bracey's recollection wasn't quite correct. Parliament did
not authorise any upper limit of the number of children to be
allowed to come in on these simplified entry permits. It was
a combination of severe shortage of private finance and the
declaration of war in September 1939, that limited the numbers
coming under the Kindertransport scheme to just over 9,300.
Two days after the debate in the House, the Home Office
signalled as a first step that they would be willing to accept an
initial number of 5,000 children. What followed in the months
after the 21 November announcement became an agonisingly
slow process of bureaucratic delay and financial constraints.

Apart from its focus on child refugees, under Bracey's
direction the GEC worked tirelessly to secure domestic permits
for women - mostly Jewish or non-Aryan Christians - seeking
entry to Britain between 1933 and 1939. Her committee
cooperated closely with the Domestic Council for German
Refugees and the merging of interests between Jewish and
non-Jewish organisations led to the formation of the Domestic
Bureau, which was recognised by the British Government as
the official body representing the wellbeing of refugees (mostly
women) who had come to the country to serve as maids, cooks
and servants.

Bracey and others attracted funding for the GEC's work
from the Baldwin Fund, government grants and the Quakers'
own fundraising efforts, such as the 'Quaker Shilling

Appeal' promoted in the national and local press by fellow campaigner, Edith Pye. One such donation by the Baldwin Fund substantially helped finance the move by several refugee-supporting organisations to Bloomsbury House, a former hotel in central London. Bertha and her staff moved into offices on the third floor and were soon inundated with requests from families desperate to get their relatives out of the German Reich, the newly occupied Czech lands and Poland. The bureaucratic challenge to organise the arrival of Kindertransport children and the granting of domestic permits was monumental.

By 1940, Bertha Bracey's overriding concern became the situation of refugees now classed as 'enemy aliens'. Up to 7,000 domestic servants (now officially potential enemies of the state) had been dismissed at the outbreak of war and many had been interned or deported to Australia or Canada. Those former domestic servants who were not interned (as many women were not) soon found work in Britain's wartime factories or the armed forces. The GEC also offered training places for out of work migrants, who were rapidly becoming destitute. During the war, Bracey became Chairwoman of the Central Department for Interned Refugees where, with the MP, Eleanor Rathbone she vigorously lobbied parliament for the release of 'enemy aliens,' or at least an improvement in their living conditions once interned.

As the war drew to a close, Bracey turned her attention to the plight of the young survivors of concentration camps. She later described the most significant of her interventions with the British Government on their behalf:

When the concentration camps were being opened up at the end of the European War, I went with Mr. Leonard Montefiore [Chairman of the Committee for the Care of Children from the Concentration

Camps] to the War Office and persuaded them to put at our disposal 10 large bomber planes, which, with their bomb racks removed, enabled us to bring 300 children from Theresienstadt, Prague, to England.

The youngsters, many of whom were pale, sick and emaciated from their traumatic imprisonment, arrived in the English Lake District on 14 August 1945 and were initially housed in an unused hostel near Windermere, where they were well cared for. Soon after the arrival of the concentration camp survivors, Bertha returned to Germany, where she was appointed by the Allied Control Commission in Germany to assist in the relief operations for the starving civilians of that defeated country. She worked in Germany until her retirement in 1953.

Bertha Bracey died in 1989. A friend who often visited remembered her at ninety-five years old, suffering from Parkinson's disease but still 'in a way formidable, her intellect fantastic and she knew all about philosophy, geology and outer space. But refugees were always her main concern.'

In 1942 Bracey received the OBE in recognition of her outstanding work to support refugees, and in 2010 she was posthumously recognised by the UK government as a 'British Hero of the Holocaust'. She is also one of twenty-one Britons to be awarded the status of 'Righteous Among Nations' by Yad Vashem.

A sculpture in her honour was placed outside Friends' House in London in 2001. The plaque reads: 'To honour Bertha Bracey (1893–1989) who gave practical leadership of Quakers in quietly rescuing and re-settling thousands of Nazi victims and lone children between 1933–1948.'

Chapter 10

The Holiday Camp Manager
Frank Bond

Frank Bond, Image 14

On the morning of 2 December 1938, a party of around 200 German Jewish teenagers arrived in Harwich on the SS Prague, a cross-channel ferry which left each night from the Hook of Holland. Waiting to receive them was a small team from the Refugee Children's Movement (RCM), whose job it was to check that the children's names matched those on their list and to give them a numbered card, which they wore around their necks. After a quick health check to ensure they were not bringing in infectious diseases, the children were free to disembark onto the quayside. There they were met by an immigration official who checked their numbers, and a posse of national and local press keen to capture this first arrival of Jewish refugee children, the vanguard of the 9,354 who came on various Kindertransports.

A newsreel of the time shows one small girl being given a doll to hold while the cameraman takes her picture – one of many to be circulated in the national and regional press in coming days. The party was made up of older boys and girls from various Jewish orphanages in Germany, who were regarded as especially vulnerable after the November Pogroms. Variously bewildered, excited, fearful and apprehensive, the children were led from the dockside onto a double-decker Eastern Counties bus to take them to their first home in Britain: the Dovercourt Bay Holiday Camp. A summer facility offering around 1,000 beds, the camp – one of four such pre-war holiday camps developed by the innovative leisure entrepreneur and former artillery officer, Captain Harry Warner, had been hired to house the first cohorts of Kindertransport children and was conveniently situated less than twenty minutes' drive from the port of Harwich. It was here that they made the acquaintance of Frank Bond – the camp's nattily dressed manager and an associate of Warner's business colleague and rival, Billy Butlin. Frank Bond and his wife welcomed them to England.

A couple of weeks later as more children arrived at the camp, ten year-old Lore Groszmann (later Segal), a Jewish girl from Vienna, remembered being led to the main dining room of the camp and being addressed by, 'a small man with an enormous bald brow [who] stood on a wooden stage, out in front, and talked through a megaphone'. This was most likely to have been Frank Bond. Calling the children by their number (given to them by the RCM staff on board the ship), he divided the youngsters into groups of four: three younger and an older teenager who would serve as 'counsellor'. Each group would be assigned a chalet and having chosen their bunk beds, the children were urged to return to the dining hall for their first hot meal in England. Some of the food on the menu was very strange to these young German Jews. Leslie Brent (born Lothar Baruch), a thirteen-year-old refugee from Köslin in Germany (now Koszalin in Poland), was introduced to kippers and porridge (which he rather enjoyed). Like many of his refugee friends, Brent remembered the bitter cold weather descending in the middle of that December – the coldest of the century it was thought. He recalled frozen hot water bottles and having to huddle round the few warm but smelly stoves in the dining hall. It was all a far cry from the attractions of the summer season such as tennis courts, boating lake and swimming pool which drew busloads of holiday makers to Dovercourt from the East End of London.

Frank Bond had been taken on as Dovercourt's first manager when the camp opened in the summer of 1937. He and his wife lived in Harwich, where they had bought a family house near the new camp and where Frank, a keen amateur painter, soon became a stalwart of the local theatre company and the annual pageant. In the newsreel from 2 December 1938 he can be seen supervising the children's first meal in the dining hall. Three days later he and Mrs Bond led a party of youngsters up the hill from the camp to the town cinema, The Regal, to see the recently released Walt Disney film Snow White and the Seven Dwarfs. Free tickets and ice creams were provided for them by the cinema manager, Mr Bostock.

While Mr Bond and his staff of cooks and cleaners looked after the camp for Captain Warner, the business of looking after the children who were arriving each week from Germany and Austria was delegated to a team provided by the Refugee Children's Movement in London. Coordinated by Major Geoffrey Langdon of the RCM, they appointed a 'camp commandant' to oversee the arrival and departures of the Kindertransport children. There was a Mrs Drew, who was described as 'the children's hostess'. Sophie Friedlaender, herself a German Jewish refugee, was brought in as deputy 'commandant' after there was some unhappiness at the way the camp commandant, a former colonel in the Indian army, was treating his staff and the children; his style was considered too militaristic and he was summarily dismissed. Friedlaender's role was primarily as 'selection officer', a position that involved attempting to allocate foster families to the children. 'I conducted the correspondence with expectant foster parents and tried to get to know the homeless children,' she recalled many years later, admitting that although she understood the children and their backgrounds, she had little idea of the social context of the would-be foster parents. There were some children, often older boys, who were very difficult to place – most prospective families wanted younger children, often girls or older females who could help with domestic chores. 'I still hear as if it were yesterday the voice of a young Jew from Vienna who came into my office every day, asking urgently, "Miss Friedlaender, do you not have a family for me?" It was hard to imagine into what kind of family he would fit.' She also found problems in placing the small group of children from Orthodox Jewish families – there were relatively few offers of homes from observant communities in London, Manchester and Leeds.

The method of finding foster parents – suitable or not – was crude. Families would answer calls in the national and local press, register with the RCM and arrange to come to the camp to inspect likely children. This was usually done at Sunday lunchtime. The children were given haircuts and generally made to look clean and tidy. The families were asked to be discreet as they paced up and down the dining room trying to spot a 'suitable' child to take away with them. As Friedlaender noted, 'It was inevitable that you heard the term "cattle market" amongst the children.' The RCM asked Bunce Court, Anna Essinger's boarding school in Kent to take ten children from Dovercourt. Leslie Brent was one of them and asked directly by Essinger if he would like to come back to the school with her and her staff, he jumped at the chance.

Education at the camp was a major concern for the organisers. The early days were a little chaotic and no one was really sure what to do with the hundreds of children. English language was a top priority, but who could teach them? After an appeal for help in the local press, many Harwich folk volunteered. One was a Mr J. J.Firth of Dovercourt, another a Mrs Tann whose husband Fred, a railway clerk at Parkeston Quay, was one of those who met the children coming off the ships. When Fred told his wife about the children, many of whom he remembered as being very apprehensive, she and a friend turned up at the camp. She recalled: 'We put everyday articles on a table, sat around and taught them to ask, "What is this?" – a spoon, fork, knife, sugar, milk and, later, because they watched the workmen, a saw, hammer, screws, nails. It was all a game but they learned very fast.'

After a week or so the RCM asked Anna Essinger and some of the older pupils from Bunce Court School to come and oversee the education of the youngsters on a more professional basis. Essinger's role was to organise the camp volunteers and sort out the education of the children. With her usual vigour and sense of purpose she immediately got to work assessing the children's abilities and providing daily lessons. These consisted of basic grammar, useful phrases and the words to popular songs of the day. The children were formed into groups, with tutors leading discussions on all kinds of subjects, mostly relating to England and its language and manners. One of the helpers was the artist, Archibald Ziegler, who together with his wife spent the days chatting to the children and creating sketches. Some children were taken to the local school in Hall Lane for a few hours of English lessons.

Hanna Bergas also came from Bunce Court with Anna Essinger to teach the children. Her memories of those weeks paint a stark picture of the state of mind of the young refugees:

Hundreds of children streamed into the camp, children who were strangers to each other, to the adults who accompanied them, strangers who received them in strange surroundings. They had experienced various degrees of bad treatment, even brutality, in the schools of their countries [...] The main thing was to instill in them calm and confidence that people here would be kind to them.

There were paper, pencils and a blackboard at the camp, Bergas remembered, but books were virtually non-existent. She also recalled that while the behaviour of the children was generally good, tensions between older boys from Vienna and Berlin could sometimes erupt into fights which were hard to break up. While David Hughes remembered the 'happy chatter' of the children, fear and anxiety about the fate of their parents were never far away. A local girl remembers going regularly to the camp to play with the refugee girls. Her uncle Alf Wheeler, was the jovial head chef at Dovercourt. One day her father came to the camp to visit his brother Alf. He was wearing a watch chain with a swastika design – a Hindu symbol and nothing to do with the Nazis. The refugee children froze in fear when they saw this. The chef worked hard to reassure them that his brother was no Nazi. The girl, now an old lady, says that she will never forget the look of fear on the faces of those children.

Undergraduates from Oxford and Cambridge were recruited to help teach the refugees, including David Hughes, who was also appointed by Essinger to run the camp post office tucked into a corner of the dining room. Some of the children were given pocket money to help in the post office, others had jobs working on local farms, helping in the kitchen, doing the laundry or assisting in the sick room, which was overseen by Dr Julius Levy, a local physician and himself a German Jewish refugee. In 1940 Dr Levy was arrested as an enemy alien and deported to Canada. Furious locals petitioned Parliament, and their local GP was returned to the town, where he stayed as a doctor and surgeon for the rest of his life.

For many of the volunteers at Dovercourt, this was their first contact with the Jewish world. Hugh Barrett arrived by bus at the camp in December 1938. In contrast to David Hughes' memories of the happy children, Barrett described the camp's atmosphere as 'highly emotional [...] The whole camp was charged with anxiety and fear. It was there I first heard the word angst and appreciated what it meant'. One day, Barrett and fellow volunteers went into Harwich for a meal. Their first course was interrupted by a phone call from the camp:

A rumour was going round that a pogrom was under way in Vienna: we were needed quickly to help. We rushed back to the camp. It was impossible to describe the situation. Imagine seven hundred contagiously frightened, crying, wailing children milling around the huge and echoing dining hall. The Viennese staff, poor souls, were in almost as bad a state, anguished and caught up in total fear.'

Barrett recalled that calm was restored when the rumours were scotched following a phone call to Vienna but also by one of the older Jewish helpers singing a Hebrew hymn which all the children knew and could join in with. It was a moment that Barrett would never forget.

Attempts were made to cheer up the youngsters by inviting entertainers to perform for them; doubtless some of these were known personally to Frank Bond, who had connections in the show business world. One show, captured on a newsreel of the day, drew in top-line acts including Giovanni, a celebrated 'pickpocket' who is seen lifting the watch of a local dignitary, much to the amusement of the onlookers. The same film shows Paul Berny, internationally famous in his day, artfully juggling tennis rackets. Lore Segal remembers a concert hosted by Mr Bond ('the camp leader') who began the entertainment by teaching the refugee children to sing 'Ten Green Bottles', 'Rule Britannia' and 'Boomps-a-daisy'. All this was a prelude to the main act of the show: a muscle man who flexed his biceps to music. 'Afterward, the camp leader went up to thank him. He said the muscle man was very sorry that he could not speak German.' There were visits from the Harwich Town Band and locals offered to take the children on trips in the countryside, as well as inviting them home for afternoon teas. Fish and chips were provided by a local 'chippie', probably free of charge and for many of the refugees their first taste of this English staple and an experience one of them, Harry Baum, would remember for the rest of his life.

When it was not too cold, the volunteer group leaders took the children on walks along the beach, and in the evening there were often dances in the main hall. Residents of the camp made their own entertainment too. There was many a romance, not least among the adult volunteers: one couple, both Jews from Germany, had their wedding in Harwich and the Bonds hosted a party at their home. Some of the older boys who were accommodated for a time at the local Salvation Army hostel (where they remembered with fondness the kind treatment given by the wardens, Colonel and Mrs Parker) got into deep water when they discovered that their neighbourhood of Old Harwich happened to be the town's red light district.

Most memoirs written by former refugee children refer to the freezing cold conditions and how hot water bottles would ice up in the chalets at night. Even the water in the jugs on the dining room table froze over, despite this being the only part of the camp that was properly heated. One volunteer recalled catching pneumonia from carrying children to safety after a flood of freezing sea water entered the camp one night.

When, in mid-December, a BBC outside broadcast crew arrived to make a documentary for radio, the weather was so cold that the radio van had to install an electric radiator, though it produced such an audible hum that it had to be turned off during the recordings. Produced by Robert Kemp, an Orkney-born Scot who had cut his teeth on the Manchester Guardian, the programme aimed to alert the British public to the plight of the children and to help secure more offers of foster homes. The crew interviewed Frank Bond and the other camp managers, as well as several of the children, including Leslie Brent. Remarkably, thirteen minutes of the thirty-five-minute programme still exist, discovered in the BBC archives by the author Barry Turner. In addition to a camp choir and two girls chatting about their dreams for the future, we hear Brent telling the audience about his typical day and how one day he hoped to become a cook. (In fact, he went on to become an eminent professor of immunology). The programme, called 'Children in Flight', was broadcast by the BBC Home Service on 3 January 1939. It had a profound effect on one couple from Leigh-on-Sea, around sixty miles away: 'It was so terribly sad, we felt surely there was something we could do. So we decided at the weekend we would go to Dovercourt to see the children and find out if we could help in any way.' Help came in the form of outings to the nearby seaside town of Clacton and afternoon teas - the couple's first encounter with the Jewish world.

After the programme, parcels of food and clothing started to arrive at the camp, including a large trunk of winter clothing from Johannesburg, where news in the local paper had inspired the Ladies' Circle to start knitting. An Essex butcher offered to provide beef sausages once a week; someone else sent a dozen cases of fruit every week for several months. Nine Jewish barbers gave up their free time and came down on Sundays to cut the children's hair. Marks and Spencer donated free clothing for the children, and a London sports club offered to supply boxing gloves.

On 1 April 1939 Dovercourt Bay reverted to its normal use as a holiday camp for families. By this time only boys were left at the camp – a newsreel from the end of March shows Frank Bond shaking hands with them – the girls having been sent to another holiday camp, owned by Pontins, in Selsey. A farewell party was held for the remaining youngsters, who were destined to move on to a training farm at Barham in Suffolk, about an hour away from Dovercourt. The party was organised by Mr and Mrs Bond and attended by the holiday camp staff and volunteers who had been looking after the children. Civic dignitaries were invited, including the Mayor of Harwich and the vicar of Dovercourt, both of whom had been stalwart supporters of the refugee children during their stay in the seaside town. The mayor told the large gathering in the dining hall:

We will miss you in many ways. We shall miss seeing you about the town, on the front, and on our main streets but I sincerely hope that wherever you go you will be happy and take pleasant memories of Dovercourt with you. I sincerely hope that the worst of your troubles are over. We in England have an old saying that 'every cloud has a silver lining'. I hope that the silver lining to your very black cloud if not already here is not very far distant. In whatever part of the world in which you finally pitch your tent be of good courage. Do not lose heart.

Dr Levy paid tribute to the volunteers who ran the camp. Reminding the audience that he was 'from the other side' (Germany) and thus in a special position to understand what the boys must be feeling, he said:

I have seen these people working in the early hours of the morning and late hours of the night. Nothing was too much trouble. I think that all the children who have passed through this camp are healthier in spirit and bodily condition. I think that the fresh air of the East Coast coupled with the excellent food they served in the camp have helped to keep up bodily condition and I am sure they will never forget these days at Dovercourt in their lifetime.

In fact, of course, not all the memories would be happy ones. The children were already becoming increasingly anxious about the fate of their families back in the Reich, and in later years, while most praised the care they received at Dovercourt, many would also remember the harsh conditions in the chalets, the humiliation of the 'cattle market' selections, and their sense of being alone and fearful.

As the culmination of the thanksgiving evening, Frank Bond himself was called to the stage. He was handed an illuminated address signed by all the boys in the camp. Acknowledging the gift, Bond said that what he had done was a labour of love. For him, Mrs Bond and Captain Warner, it had been no different from the way one would respond to an individual case of suffering: 'If one saw a child run over in the middle of the road one did not stop to wonder whose child it was, where it came from, what its parents' religion was, one just rushed to help.'

The Forties and Fifties were Dovercourt's heyday for family holidays and a long decline set in as foreign vacations became affordable competition, and it closed in 1989. In those last few years, however, it achieved a new and unlikely fame: the traces of its time as a refugee camp had long disappeared, but its original 1930s chalets and dining hall can still be seen in the popular BBC comedy series, Hi-de-Hi, which was filmed there in the 1980s. Riding the tide of the holiday camp heyday, Frank Bond worked for the rest of his life for Warner's rival Billy Butlin. He assisted in finding new locations for the business and set up home near the gates of the Butlin's camp at Pwllheli in North Wales. According to his granddaughter Mandy, it was a very happy home. Years after the events in the harsh winter just before the war, Frank would regale his family with the stories of the Jewish children who sought refuge in an English holiday camp.

It was in the 1990s, that Mandy received a call from the Jewish Museum in London. A lady searching her attic in Dovercourt had found a huge postcard signed by many foreign names. Not knowing what to do with it, she offered it to the museum. Staff then traced Mandy who identified the object as the thank-you card given to her grandfather and grandmother back in late March 1939. The words on the postcard brought a tear to Mandy's eyes: 'A token of appreciation for Mr and Mrs Bond for all that they have done for us during our stay in the Holiday Camp. From the German refugee children.'

Chapter 11

The Farmers
Harry and Emily Moye

Emily and Harry Moye, Image 15

Keith Lawson, Image 16

So far we have looked at the people responsible for organising the Kindertransport. But beneath the surface are thousands of individual stories of good Samaritans who welcomed weary Jewish children into their homes. This chapter focuses on one family, the Moyes, but it pays homage to the thousands of unsung heroes who opened their homes and their hearts to the Kinder. Harry and Emily Moye were Suffolk farmers, who tended 200 acres in the heart of Constable country, and they helped to transform the life of a German Jewish refugee.

In March 1940 they employed Kurt Lazarus, who had arrived on the Kindertransport a few months earlier (and who later changed his name to Keith Lawson). It was soon apparent that Keith had moved into a generous and welcoming home. The Moyes treated him as much more than a farm worker and, for the rest of his life, the former refugee regarded them as a second family – especially important, as the Holocaust had claimed his first.

Keith was born in Berlin in 1925, the son of Siegfried and Erna Lazarus; his father owned a drapery shop and his mother worked as a secretary. Siegfried had long been an enthusiast for British education and, after the November Pogroms, the boy's parents encouraged him to join a Kindertransport to Britain.

Keith arrived in London in July 1939 and was sent to a training farm run by the Refugee Children's Movement at Barham House, near Claydon and just north of Ipswich in Suffolk. Several hundred refugee boys were housed in a disused Victorian workhouse which had been rapidly converted into suitable accommodation and classrooms by the Refugee Children's Movement. The 18th century buildings were arranged in a quadrangle and there was a peacefully derelict chapel in the grounds. The place had long been used as a government training centre for would-be builders and so there were a number of bungalows ready to be renovated.

Barham House had the dual use of serving as a transit camp for teenage German-speaking boys for whom finding foster homes was a challenge, and a genuine effort to equip the lads with agricultural skills that would stand them in good stead being employed in Britain or overseas (and for many, that would include Palestine). Though the diet was apparently not of the highest order – hard boiled eggs and fish cakes were regularly on the menu – it gave the boys a taste of feeling free from persecution. They were able to play football, roam the countryside and build rafts on the river. They collected firewood and when war broke out, helped to blackout the windows against bombing raids from their erstwhile country.

The youngsters were also drafted in to help repair the rundown fabric of the old workhouse thus earning valuable building skills for good measure. They repaired broken floorboards, stopped up gaps in the walls and even made their own cupboards.

In an echo of the public school system, Barham House was organised in a series of 'houses', each named after someone connected to the RCM's work. These included Viscount Samuel, Lord Baldwin, Dennis M. Cohen and a Mr Brentnall, a retired headmaster who was the Movement's man in charge of hostels and camps. Teachers were recruited to develop not only technical skills, but also vital subjects such as English language. One photograph kept by Keith into old age, was of a blazered gentleman reclining on a summer lawn at Barham; he was one of the teaching staff and fondly regarded. Keith recalls learning how to handle animals and there is a photograph of him leading a horse and cart; another shows two lads in jackets untangling a length of rope presumably as a tether.

As part of their training, the youngsters were encouraged to obtain work experience on local farms. Among them was the one owned by Harry and Emily Moye at Stratford St Mary, around twelve miles from Barham House. Here Keith's hard work in picking sugar beet – which he regarded as important war work – came to Harry Moye's attention.

Harry found Keith's English good enough to start a conversation with him while working in the fields, and one afternoon suggested he must meet his wife, come for tea and sample her homemade cake in their farmhouse kitchen. On Keith's third visit to the farm, Harry invited him to work on a more permanent basis: the farm would need extra help because Harry's nephew was due to be called up.

Mr Haybrook, the Barham House manager, accompanied Keith to finalise details; the boy was pleased to leave, since many of his close friends had already gone and he was keen to start earning some money for himself. So, at the age of fifteen, and with no farming background, Keith joined the Moyes as a farm labourer, earning eleven shillings a week. Out of this he would pay Mrs Moye six shillings a week for his board and lodging with the family. He had his own bedroom and although there was no running water, or electricity he led a comfortable life, with good food and the knowledge that he was welcome.

Emily and Harry were born in the 1880s. Emily went into domestic service in London, but at some point came to work in Suffolk, where she met her future husband. A forthright person with a keen sense of moral duty, she is remembered by her former lodger as combining 'great kindness with a Victorian attitude towards behaviour and manners'. As Keith recalled, 'Even twenty years later she would still criticise me for badly combed hair or wearing the wrong type of shirt on a Sunday'.

Harry shared his wife's sense of duty, but was a more reticent personality, a hardworking farmer always keen to do the right thing. The couple also had a strong sense of community – they organised local village dances and Harry was a stalwart churchwarden. The arrival of a stranger in the village was not universally welcomed by local folk and some of the Moyes' neighbours were suspicious of this German-speaking foreigner. Emily was shocked by their attitude but determined to keep her home open to the refugee boy.

The Moyes had one daughter, Marjorie, who had two children of her own. Widowed early in the war, she came to live first at the farm and shortly afterwards at the lockkeeper's cottage at Dedham Mill (immortalised in the painting by Constable). Both Marjorie's children, Edward and Dianne, formed a close lifelong bond with Keith, whom they regarded as an uncle figure.

Keith didn't stay with the Moyes for very long. Their nephew was not in fact called up – he was designated as being in a 'reserved occupation' – and the couple realised that there simply wasn't enough work for Keith to do on the farm. Harry therefore arranged for him to work for another family: the Moyes' good friends, Mr and Mrs Abbott, who owned a small farm at Ardleigh near Colchester. That post, too, only lasted for a short time, so Keith applied for a farming job in Wiltshire. There he found the welcome far from generous and even somewhat hostile. Keen to get away and also to 'do his bit' for the war effort against the Nazis, he was determined to join a fighting regiment and signed up for the Royal Engineers. After initial training Keith was sent out to the Far East. He survived the war unscathed.

As years went by, the relationship between Keith, his wife Olive and the Moye family grew ever closer. The Moyes attended his wedding, were witnesses to his naturalisation and shared many family events together. Keith and Olive visited them whenever they could, and a close relationship also developed between their own children and the descendants of Mr and Mrs Moye.

Harry died in 1962, his wife Emily in 1977. Remembering Emily, Keith later wrote. 'I loved Mrs Moye[…] She became the nearest substitute to a mother I was to know.' Keith Lawson sadly passed away on 4 October 2017 aged 92.

Chapter 12

The Shopkeeper
Alan Overton

Alan Overton (right middle)
with some of the boys from his hostel, Image 17

'Overton, Rugby, England.' So many letters from desperate Jewish parents in Germany were addressed in this way that the postal services knew exactly where to deliver them. Robert Alan Overton was a shopkeeper from Rugby and a devout Christadelphian who dedicated his considerable energies to helping Jewish children fleeing from Nazi persecution. As the founder and honorary secretary of the Rugby Refugee Committee, he organised foster homes for up to 250 Jewish refugee children and, where homes were not forthcoming, set up two hostels: Elpis Lodge in Edgbaston (a suburb of

Birmingham) and Little Thorn in Rugby. These two hostels ran throughout the war, providing a safe and happy home for many teenage refugee boys.

Overton's faith as a Christadelphian was integral to his refugee work. Christadelphians – the name derives from the Greek for brethren in Christ – are a millennialist Christian community who ground their beliefs exclusively in a literal understanding of the Old and New Testaments. Non-Trinitarian in theology and apolitical in civil life, they do not recognise priesthood in their churches (or 'ecclesia') and base their practice on what they see as that of the earliest Christian communities. Christadelphians feel a special affinity to Jews and, since their foundation in the 1840s, have stayed true to their conviction that the establishment of a Jewish state in Palestine was part of a divine promise.

Alan Overton galvanised the entire Christadelphian movement around Britain, estimated at around 25,000 people, to support Jewish refugees. A tireless campaigner, he was active in urging parliament to have a more tolerant policy towards the plight of the Jewish people. He attended parliamentary debates on Palestine and was present in the House of Commons for the important debate on refugees on 21 November 1938. The Christadelphians made a substantial contribution to the Baldwin Fund, sending a cheque for £1,000 (equivalent to £64,000 today).

He volunteered his services to the Movement for the Care of Children from Germany and regularly drove to Liverpool Street station to collect children from the Kindertransport trains, taking them to join his wife and four children at his own home if no place was immediately available for them. He and others ensured that there was transport arranged to take the children to their new homes. According to his son Bruce,

Overton remembered, 'Heartrending scenes which even brought hardened London 'bobbies' to tears [...] Very young children, as young as two years old, crying for their mothers, were herded together until separated, some to England, some to Wales and Scotland.' Overton's home became a virtual transit house for children arriving from Nazi Europe. Overton's daughter recalled as a young girl hearing her father's car draw up in the middle of the night, the crunch of footsteps on the gravel path, the voices of young children and later when tucked into bed, the soft cries of 'mutti, mutti,' as the lost mites yearned for their mothers.

According to Bruce Overton,

He would often arrive home, in the night, with a car full of frightened, exhausted children unable to communicate their most basic needs or fears. Mr and Mrs Overton, with their own growing family of four children, worked ceaselessly to provide for their new wards until they could be picked up by the Christadelphian families taking them in. If the host families could not make arrangements to transport the children, Mr Overton would drive them himself to their new homes.

Faced with such a huge challenge, Overton set about raising funds from his local Christadelphian community, his fellow shopkeepers and the many readers who saw his letters and articles in journals and newspapers. He toured the British Isles urging his fellow Christadelphians to offer homes to the refugee children, referring to himself in a 1939 report on the workings of the Rugby hostel, as one who 'felt compelled, whenever he could make opportunity, and at every ecclesia he visited, to spread the news of their unhappy plight and urge all who heard his appeal to offer hospitality and loving care to these little ones whose sorrow was so poignant [...]'.

With a small group of helpers he vetted applications from potential foster parents and did his utmost to keep siblings together. In a letter to one foster mother, who had already taken in a Jewish girl from Germany, he urged her to take the girl's brother too: 'They have enough parting to suffer without that and a little extra sacrifice will not kill us – when we work for Him that gave his life for us.' One former refugee child remembered being met by Overton: 'Mr. Overton was very kind, and he took me to Lyons Corner House, and he said, "You might want something to eat", and I was very shy... He said, "Just eat whatever you think." He made me very welcome, and I had tea.'

Little Thorn Lodge opened in Rugby from July 1939. The hostel provided a home to about a dozen boys but acted as a temporary transit home for many others. Its warden was a Czechoslovakian Jewish refugee, Mrs Sperber, who had been sponsored by Alan Overton along with her two teenage sons. Though the boys arrived in Rugby, their mother was still held by the Nazis. Undaunted, Overton made an overseas telephone call to the camp officials. With one of her sons standing by as interpreter, he explained that Mrs Sperber had all the papers she needed to leave. The bureaucrat agreed to check his files to see if the woman was in fact detained in the camp. He returned saying that there was no record of her. Persistence was one of Alan Overton's great qualities. He told the Nazi, 'I know that when I am filing a name, I sometimes place the papers in the wrong place, often on either side of where it should be in the cabinet. Could you please check again?' The camp official did as he was asked and came back saying that he had indeed misfiled Mrs Sperber's card. She was duly allowed to leave the camp and came to Rugby on Overton's guarantee of work. That telephone call had saved her life, the life of the warden, the life of a mother.

Mrs Sperber settled into daily life at Little Thorn, where part of her role was to teach the boys the Torah, and to enable them to retain their Jewish identity and roots. A former resident of the hostel, who was offered a part-time job by a friend of Overton's and continued his studies at night school, recalled many years later: 'It was a good atmosphere of course, we were about a dozen boys...most of them were Czech, some were German, and Alan Overton was very much involved [...] We were a close-knit community.'

Brother Overton, as he was known in the Christadelphian community, took a leading role in the hostel, entertaining the boys with film shows and organising sporting activities and other events. In his own inimitable way he attended to the spiritual needs of the boys (even though most had come from liberal, non-Orthodox families). It is clear that some conversions in families did take place, although for Alan Overton this was by no means the central purpose of providing aid to refugee children. His devotion to the children was exemplary. In the words of one of the boys, Hanush Snarbl, who lived at Little Thorn throughout the war, 'We grew to love him, he was like a father to us'.

The Elpis Lodge hostel in Edgbaston, funded by the Birmingham and Coventry Christadelphians, opened its doors on 21 April 1940 and continued to offer a home to refugees until 1948. The residence was a large Victorian villa set among lawns and although it had been modernised with new bathrooms and a kitchen, the bedrooms were often freezing cold in winter. As with each of the hostels, Overton was determined that the day-to-day running of the home should be in Jewish hands and he personally took more of a backseat role. As they worked closely with the Birmingham Jewish community, former German refugees Dr Albert Hirsch and his wife were appointed as wardens.

The regime at the hostel was reportedly frugal but buzzing with energy. In an address to mark the closing of the hostel, Hirsch painted a vivid picture of life in the house during wartime. It depicted a colourful scene of Friday night fish meals, games of Monopoly, visits to the ballet and theatre, card games and discussions about work opportunities. Overton, Hirsch and their colleagues were keen to see that the boys were trained in practical trades that would ensure future employment, such as tailoring, engineering, upholstery or jewellery. The warden taught Hebrew and Jewish history and the boys were encouraged to join sports clubs and play musical instruments. The older boys who worked contributed half of their earnings to the upkeep of the hostel and everyone took responsibility for daily chores.

Alan Overton died in 1974 at the age of seventy-four. Vera Gissing, in her memoir, Pearls of Childhood, remembered his contribution to the refugee cause. He was, she said, a remarkable man who had 'striven tirelessly, even prior to the occupation of Czechoslovakia, to convince the British government that Jews in occupied territories were in great danger and that something must be done to save the children.'

She recalled the story of one of her friends, a fellow refugee, who visited Overton many years after the war had ended. Overton brought down from his loft what he said was his proudest possession - a cardboard box with over two hundred labels. These were name tags that the children had worn around their necks when they arrived in England and came into his care. As Gissing notes, 'each tag represented a life that he had saved.'

Chapter 13

One Household – Two Rescuers
Sybil and Robert Hutton

Sybil and Robert Hutton, Imagees 18 & 19

'My whole house here is working night and day on refugee problems, mainly for children with which my wife is concerned, and for academic people. Professional, commercial and industrial cases come in between and in many ways the most difficult of all'. Thus wrote Robert Salmon Hutton, Goldsmith Professor of Metallurgy, Fellow of Clare College, Cambridge, in a letter of 17th June 1939. Robert and his wife, Sybil Hutton were exemplary rescuers, passionately concerned for the welfare of those fleeing persecution.

Sybil's concern for refugees can be seen in a letter to Walter Michel, a German Jewish refugee student then studying at

Cambridge University. 'Tell your sister to come to us for Christmas and if we think she is worth educating we will send her to school'.

Walter's younger sister, Lore, had come to England on the Kindertransport from their home town of Cologne in June 1939. She was fifteen years old. Alone and friendless, Lore was sent to lodge with a family of strangers living in Devon. The family had promised Lore's desperate parents that they would care for her, give her a good home and education. Their words turned out to be hollow.

The stipulations of the Refugee Children's Movement (RCM) were that no refugee child should be treated as a domestic servant and given every opportunity to continue their education. The family flouted these strictures on both counts: Lore was made to work as an unpaid servant from morning till night, six and half days a week. Education was out of the question for this bright girl who had previously flourished at the Jawne Jewish School in Cologne.

Walter, aggrieved at hearing about his sister's plight, shared his concerns with his Cambridge landlady, Miss Kathleen Wood-Legh, who lived in the leafy borough of Newnham. With the siblings' parents still trapped in Nazi Germany, here at last is where good fortune smiled on Lore. It transpired that Walter's landlady was a founding member of the Cambridge Refugee Committee. Canadian-born 'Kay' Wood-Legh, a blind academic historian known later for her studies of medieval chantries, was a key player in one of the country's most active (and successful) local refugee committees. Her fellow committee members included Greta Burkill (of whom more later) and Mrs Sybil Hutton. Sybil and Robert were to become what Lore's future children would call 'granny and granddad'.

Facts about Sybil's life are hard to ascertain. Born in 1891, she was the daughter of Sir Arthur Schuster, a German émigré with a Jewish background (Arthur was baptised) whose own parents had come to Manchester to develop their textile business in the mid 19th century. Her mother, Cary, was active in the women's suffrage movement and her father a professor of Physics at Manchester University. One of his many pupils was Robert Hutton who saw Sir Arthur as mentor, guide and future father-in-law. Sybil and Robert were married in 1912 and set up house in Sheffield where he worked in the family silversmith business. During World War One the Schusters suffered anti-German prejudice, a painful experience that did not go unnoticed by Robert. In 1921 Robert helped found the British Non-Ferrous Metals Research Association and became its first director. This position allowed Hutton to travel widely and his name gained rapid respect among the world's select cohort of material scientists. It was these Pan-European connections that would be brought into play in the later rescue of Jewish scholars. Hutton's reputation and standing was boosted even further by his elevation to the Chair in Metallurgy at Cambridge and his election as a Fellow of Clare College in 1936. Robert was also a founding member of the Society for the Protection of Learning (SPSL), a body set up in 1933 to provide support for the benighted students, teachers and researchers in Germany.

In between bringing up her children, Sybil became active on the National Council of Women (NCW) which she joined in 1932. It is here that she probably made the acquaintance of Eva Hartree, the first woman mayor of Cambridge, a fiercely independent thinker who was to become the national president of the NCW and a close colleague on the CRC. Hartree lived five minutes away from the Huttons and in the same street, just a few doors down, lived Professor Charles and Mrs Greta Burkill, the mainstay and founder of the Cambridge Refugee Committee. The area not far from the leafy banks of the gentle River Cam was a hotbed of rescue and refugee care. We will be returning to the central powerhouse of refugee activity at No. 20 Chaucer Road, a neat detached house with a veritable menagerie in the garden. The home of the Burkills.

Sybil Hutton took on the case files for the CRC – at least 100 children in the town of Cambridge and many hundreds more in the wider region. High on her list of charges was Lore Michel from Cologne. Sybil Hutton, hearing of how Lore was being exploited, was determined to help rescue the child and if necessary look after her personally. Walter must have been reassured. But before this could happen, Sybil had to contend with the RCM administration at Bloomsbury House. Her dealings with 'Head Office for Refugees' show clearly that a local committee such as the one in Cambridge was not seen as inferior to the London organisations. If Bloomsbury House got in the way of doing its best for a refugee child, staunch local volunteers like Sybil Hutton were more than willing to take them on.

Sybil's concern for Lore's position in the Devonshire house was not shared by Laura Gaster, the Movement's provincial after-care officer. Gaster told Sybil that she felt that for Lore, 'her guarantors [...] are very fond of her and she of them.' Gaster did not feel that she was being overworked and concluded that Lore's unhappiness was due to feelings of loneliness living in the heart of Devon. That said, she felt that Lore should be given more free time and receive some payment for her work. If the family agreed with these conditions then, 'there is no reason why she should not stay on.' Gaster communicated her thoughts to

Lore's host family but the response was not positive. Her foster parent told Lore that, 'I should think you've got enough free-time. I wish they'd mind their own business.' Pocket money was definitely not on offer.

Sybil Hutton was unhappy with Gaster's handling of the case. She was particularly concerned that the foster mother had been alerted to Lore's complaints and that this would sour relations between her and the refugee girl. She told Gaster, '[I] asked that nothing should be done which would make [her] think that Lore had been complaining as she is very afraid that if it appeared that any complaint had been made, that it would make the relationship between herself and the foster mother very awkward and it was thought that the best method of dealing with the case was for someone to visit the girl as this would appear to be the usual routine visit which always is made to the home where refugee children are placed.'

Hutton was thinking that Lore's exploitative situation would be 'revealed' not by a complaint from the girl herself but by the eagle eye of a local Movement inspector. The fact that Lore was placed with a family in far-off Devon, probably explains why the inspection regime there was so poor. It was definitely the case that levels of support and care dwindled the farther away the child lived from a local refugee committee, whose remit included being effectively in loco parentis. Even for the super efficient Cambridge team some of the young people on its books, like those that were looked after in remote Suffolk villages, had little contact with anyone from the refugee committee. One refugee said that in all the years he lived on a farm in a tiny village miles from Ipswich, no one ever came to check on him. Lore was doubly fortunate to have her brother as an advocate and then Sybil Hutton as a rescuer.

Before Lore arrived in Cambridge, Sybil battled it out with the RCM's Mrs Gaster. Hutton was concerned that the Movement's after-care officer paid scant regard to the stated policy that such child refugees were not to be put to work as domestic servants. 'I am very surprised to see that you do not consider it wrong for Lore to be employed as a domestic in her hostess' household.' Hutton, clearly furious at Gaster's actions, fired off a letter to Mrs Brust, Gaster's predecessor: 'I very emphatically disagree with Mrs. Gaster's point of view not only re the working hours of Lore, but to the irregularity of employing Lore at all as a domestic as this is entirely against the principle of the [RCM].' Hutton told Brust that she felt very strongly about 'cases such as this' and was trying to get a new home for Lore in Cambridge, 'but up to the present have not been successful.' That Mrs Hutton eventually offered her own home to Lore was not untypical. Of the other main players on the CRC, Greta Burkill and Eva Hartree each took in at least one refugee child once it was clear no suitable homes in the town could be found for them. Finding such desirable billets was a constant issue for members of these local refugee committees.

Finance was another constant threat. In Lore's case, Hutton informed the former welfare officer at Bloomsbury House that, 'My Committee is quite ready to pay for Lore's education for one year' but that the Huttons would need financial help with her weekly expenses. Through her network of friends and neighbours she managed to raise enough funds to pay for Lore's schooling. As Lore noted years later, 'She didn't have to do this but thought it was the right thing to do'.

At the end of her tether with the RCM's inability to help Lore, Sybil took action. She invited Lore up to Cambridge to spend Christmas 1939 at their home in Chaucer Road. As Sybil

Hutton observed, 'I could not possibly allow her to return to [the foster family] and my husband and I are prepared to give a home to her.' The records for Lore Michel held by the World Jewish Relief (WJR) show that on the 10 January 1940, the foster family's care for Lore was 'suspended because of exploitation.' Sybil went further and secured a place for Lore at the County School for Girls in Long Road, Cambridge observing that, 'She is an intelligent and bright girl doing very well at school and is a most delightful child in every way. We feel we have done a useful service in providing her into (sic) educational facilities.'

If Hutton had expected the erstwhile foster family to be supportive of Lore's new opportunities, she was to be sadly disappointed: 'The fact that they are indignant proves to me that they had not got her welfare at heart, and only wanted to make use of her.' That said, Hutton still emphasised Walter and Lore's gratitude to the family noting: 'it was only through them that Lore was able to leave Germany.' Walter had even travelled to Bournemouth (where the family had moved from Devon) to explain that Lore was staying in Cambridge, at least in term time, to be educated. Their reply was emphatic – they sent a trunk of Lore's clothes to the Huttons and washed their hands of her. But the acrimony between the foster family and the refugee committees continued into the early months of 1940. In a reply to Lore's former host family, a Mr O'Brien from the RCM regretted the 'intemperance' of the former foster mother's letter sent on the 25 February 1940. He reminds her that the Movement as the guardian of the refugee children is required to ensure that guarantors carry out their obligations, 'One of the most important of these is that the guarantor should arrange to provide the child with a specific training to befit her/him to earn a living with the least possible delay.' He goes on to comment on what must have been a very negative description of the guarantors' lately formed view of the work of the RCM. Says O'Brien to the foster mother:

'I greatly deplore your statement that you regret all your efforts on behalf of refugees from Germany. My own view – and I am not of the Jewish race – is that it was, and is, the bounden duty of every person to do everything in their power to endeavour to alleviate the lot of those who have been persecuted merely because of their race, and you have no justification for your mention of "misguided enthusiasm".'

Clearly annoyed at losing Lore as a domestic servant, the foster family's regret over their 'misguided enthusiasm' may not have been so unusual. Looking at the local committee records and reading the memoirs of Kindertransportees, there are many instances of British foster families becoming disillusioned with their charges. This could be on the grounds of what they saw as bad behaviour (which could be as mild as 'answering back' or 'Germanic pride'), or a sense that the child was 'ungrateful' for all the family was doing for him or her. In Lore Michel's case, the family's disappointment seemed to be focused on her reluctance to act as an unpaid skivvy.

Sybil Hutton's intervention to help Lore was not unusual and certainly not for the members of the Cambridge Refugee Committee. Sybil was an 'academic wife' as were many others in that team, a role which was highly conducive for helping the refugee children who came alone, penniless and without a home. Women like Sybil Hutton were well connected. They were excellent door openers – to schooling, training places, work, even into university which for impoverished 'enemy aliens' without the means to pay obligatory fees, let alone living costs, was usually a barrier too high to climb. The Cambridge Refugee Committee (CRC) with its formidable women like Wood-Legh, Hartree, Hutton, Burkill and others, had a direct line to college tutors, school teachers, local employers and a complex web of decent foster families, who were readily cajoled into providing a home for these German - or Czech-speaking youngsters.

Lore's entry into the County High School for Girls was probably predicated on Mrs Hutton's personal contact with Joyce Field, the headmistress who wrote a personal letter to Sybil: '[...] am now hoping to be able to invite your refugee visitor here as soon as the first few days of term are over. It will be very pleasant to meet her.'

Sybil proved to be a brisk, efficient, not particularly warm, but caring house mother for Lore who was not alone at Chaucer Road. The Huttons looked after at least two other refugees in the house and employed a Jewish maid who had come on a domestic permit from Germany. The maid's younger brother, Fritz Lustig, also moved in with the Huttons. Robert and Sybil found work for the young man (not easy as strictly speaking refugees did not have the status to be employed) on a building site. Later in life Fritz talked proudly of the bungalow he helped to build in the village of Great Abington just outside Cambridge. Professor Hutton later found Fritz work in a boarding school and it was here that the young 'enemy alien' was arrested and taken to internment camps after the 'collar the lot' injunction from Winston Churchill during the invasion scares of May 1940. Eventually interned on the Isle of Man, Fritz continued to write to the Huttons and they did their utmost to urge the authorities to release the Jewish refugee, who was as far from being a supporter of the Nazis as one could possibly imagine. (Fritz Lustig was soon released from the Isle of Man, joined the Pioneer Corps' army band as cellist and was recruited into British Intelligence).

Lore flourished at her school and as de facto parent, Sybil pored over her progress reports with great care and dealt with the minutiae of daily life in wartime Cambridge. A restriction on aliens having bicycles (presumably to prevent them from joining a two-wheeled Blitzkrieg Korps) irritated Sybil, as Lore had been granted permission to cycle the two miles to school, but not for any other reason. Hutton wrote to the local constabulary, 'It makes it very difficult for her to go into the town on foot as it takes so much time and her only opportunity of getting into town is after school hours'. Mrs Hutton was also concerned that a lack of bicycle inhibited Lore from going to lectures at the refugee social club in Hills Road. There was also here an issue of personal safety, '[...] now that there are so many soldiers about I would prefer her to bicycle if this were allowed.' Sybil of course got her way.

When a child like Lore completed her schooling (with, say, a School Certificate) it was normally the job of the local refugee committee to help find a job or further training. Despite the fact that in 1940 the British government had yielded to pressure from Bloomsbury House to pay a small allowance to each refugee child in care, money was always a concern for foster families. It was generally understood that a child would leave school at the required minimum leaving age of 14 and then work to pay their way. Only if a young person was educationally gifted and fees could be found beyond 'elementary education', then they might be permitted to leave school at 16 or 18. In Lore's case, she passed her School Cert exams in July 1941 and Mrs Hutton immediately stepped in to help find her a job, '[...] she is looking for a post in a library as this is the kind of work that she would like to undertake. If a job does not materialise, the Children's Refugee Committee intend giving her training in secretarial work.' Though this job did not materialise, Mrs Hutton continued to seek a post for Lore whom she described as 'an intelligent girl [...] she has been living with me since she is in Cambridge (sic). I feel sure you will find her English perfect as she has always been top of this subject in her school.'

With the Huttons' continued support, a place for Lore was eventually found as a trainee nurse at Hillingdon County Hospital in Middlesex, an opportunity which was to become her lifelong vocation. After the war, Lore heard the news she had been dreading: her mother had died in Bergen Belsen, but her father who was eking out an existence in Holland, albeit half starved and riven by typhus, had survived and was keen to visit. Robert Hutton stepped in to organise a visa for her father and doubtless subsidised his trip to England. When it became clear that her father needed rest and recuperation, it was, of course, the Huttons who came forward with help. They offered their home to Lore and Walter's father for convalescence, but sadly he succumbed to the privations of persecution and terror and died shortly thereafter.

The close relationship between Lore (now with an English husband) and the Huttons continued for decades after the war. Looking back over her life with the Hutton family, Lore's memories are nothing but warm and positive:

'The Huttons [...] were kind, generous and a wonderful replacement for my parents who were caught in Holland on their way to the USA and sadly sent to Bergen Belsen. Professor Hutton took great trouble to arrange for my father who survived typhus to come to England, and father stayed briefly at Chaucer Road to

recuperate [...]. They were incredibly kind to me and several other
refugee children [...] to our children they were granny and grandpa.'

Lore's case was by no means the only one that took up much
of Sybil Hutton's time. As Case Secretary, Sybil Hutton carried
a huge burden of caring for the children under the wing of the
CRC. A few children such as Renata and Marianne Friedenthal,
had their parents with them but troubles were never far away.
In May 1940, under Churchill's order, most 'enemy aliens'
including Jews and non-Christian Aryans were interned. In the
Friedenthals' case, both mother and father were interned on the
Isle of Man in separate camps. Sybil, concerned that the children
were missing their mother, went to great lengths to have the girls
reunited with her. Prior to this move Sybil had been fighting
hard to provide a happy billet for the girls, one of whom was
being boarded in Bishop's Stortford. Though school places were
an issue, the main concern was to find financial guarantors for
each of the children. Sybil's role was to find private donors and
ensure that their payments were made regularly. In many cases,
the financial supporters of the children would find it impossible
to continue and new donors had to be found.

In 1941 Sybil stepped down from the CRC to focus her
attention on working for the Red Cross which had a station
a mile or two from her house. She could be seen (and heard)
tootling along in a little motor scooter to run the night shift.
Though her work with the CRC receded a little (only to be
fully rejuvenated a year or two later) Sybil's commitment to the
victims of Nazism in her house never weakened.

Sybil's actions may have been outstanding, but she was not
alone in working hard in support of refugees from Nazi Europe.
Before the war broke out, her husband Robert Hutton mounted

a one-man campaign to bring out fellow metallurgists with a Jewish or 'non Aryan' background from Germany and Austria. In the winter of 1938-39 Hutton flew out to Germany to make contact with the small but well-connected community of metal scientists who had been thrown out of their positions by Nazi decree. Visas could be obtained but only if a job was guaranteed back in the UK. Robert returned to Cambridge and began a furious campaign of letter writing to anyone he knew in the metals world (and he knew pretty much everyone – he was far from being an ivory tower type of don). Professor Hutton possessed the double advantage of being experienced in industry and knowing Germany well. He was also fluent in the language and had built up a considerable network of colleagues across continental Europe.

A cache of his letters, currently housed in Churchill College Archive Centre, Cambridge, reveal the tenacious side of his gentle character. He would write copious letters to potential employers in labs or industrial works around Great Britain. A recommendation from the esteemed professor was a potent weapon but the correspondence reflects how few British companies were able to oblige with offers of posts, however lowly – thus consigning the German industrial scientists to a dreadful fate in the Holocaust era, which began in earnest in 1941. Once war was declared, the gates to immigration were shut tight but Robert continued to recommend his European colleagues – at least those who made it out – to potential employers.

After the imposition of restrictions on 'enemy aliens' beginning in September 1939, Professor Hutton's work turned to providing character references to his German Jewish colleagues, insisting that they were utterly loyal to the British crown. In his memoir, Robert Hutton talks with humility about the scientists he helped out of Germany (probably at least 200), among them some of the finest minds of their time, but also his frustration that the British government, afraid of fifth-columnists, often objected to their employment. It genuinely hurt him to see such a waste of talent (some having to stay behind to face a deadly fate and others taken up by countries such as the USA).

Sybil died in 1988 without much fuss or public fanfare. There does, however, remain one report of the ageing Sybil: in 1977 when she was reported in the Cambridge Evening News as having attended a lunch given in her honour for years of service to the National Council for Women. She was described in the piece as formerly, 'a member of the Woman's Suffrage Movement in Manchester.'

Her final public words surely ring out across the decades from this unjustly forgotten figure. Speaking of Sybil Hutton the paper reported, 'She believes there is still a lot to fight for'.

Chapter 14

The Émigré
Greta Burkill

Portrait of Greta, Burkill, Image 20

'A forceful, outspoken character, she was capable of cajoling the most complacent men into charitable actions that they would never have otherwise contemplated.' This is how the Times obituary described Margareta (Greta) Burkill; one of the most active volunteers caring for the needs of refugees in Britain. According to one former Jewish refugee:

'Any German Jewish refugee who happened to start a new life in Britain was more than fortunate to do so in Cambridge. Greta Burkill, German by birth, married to a British mathematician, a young mother with three young children and a menagerie of animals

130

in the garden, opened her home to all of us, men and women as well as a large number of children and teenagers.'

Greta was the chief guiding light to the many refugees, adults and children, who found succour in the East of England. She held key posts on the Cambridge Children's Refugee Committee from 1938 until 1950 and was directly responsible for the welfare of at least 100 refugee children in the city. Many hundreds more could be found in the wider area of East Anglia at any one time, and these children also needed the care and attention of Greta and her colleagues once war was declared.

She busied herself with endless energy to ensure that 'her' refugee children were happy, well-cared for and above all, educated to their utmost potential. According to those that remember her, Greta's primary interest was with education, ensuring that the young refugees should be given every possible opportunity to go to the best schools and, if (in her estimation) they were gifted, be equipped for eventual university entrance.

She was a tireless networker and would knock on college doors to smooth the paths for refugee scholars who had been refused opportunities in their native Germany or Austria. She used her own friendship circles to make sure that the youngsters were given a fair hearing by the senior tutors at Cambridge who dealt with admissions. In one instance she persuaded the formidable head of Homerton Teaching College at Cambridge to take in a refugee girl who possessed neither qualifications, nor very much English. Yet Greta saw her potential and thanks to her efforts, the girl was put on the road to a lifetime in the teaching profession. She received a year's tuition at Homerton despite never being officially registered.

Later in life, visitors to Greta's retirement flat in Cambridge would enjoy her reeling off names of academics, scientists, researchers, doctors, senior nurses and many more who had passed through her hands and on to very successful academic and professional careers.

As the wife of Professor Charles Burkill, an eminent mathematician destined in 1968 to become Master of Peterhouse College, Cambridge, Greta was surrounded by a formidable network of influential people. Two of these, Sybil Hutton and Eva Hartree, made up the powerful triumvirate of unpaid officers who essentially ran the Cambridge Children's Refugee Committee. Hartree and Hutton, assisted Greta in finding suitable homes for the children. When none could be found, the three ladies opened their own homes as foster mothers. Greta and her husband went a step further by permanently caring for a young boy from Germany, Harry Greatz, who later changed his name to Burkill. They also fostered the son of Ernest Reuter, a prominent German Social Democrat and post-war mayor of Berlin.

Greta Burkill herself was an immigrant to Britain. Born Margareta Braun in Berlin in 1896, she was the youngest child of Adolph and Bertha Braun who were of Jewish origin. Her father was a left-wing journalist and her mother was born in the Russian Empire. The family were forced to leave Berlin as a result of Adolph's trade union activities.

After the break-up of her parents' marriage, Greta's mother remarried an Englishman and they moved to St Petersburg where Bertha founded a language school. Thrust into a world of Russian and French (the language of the educated people), Greta felt happier than she had ever been. This was not to last: her stepfather insisted that Greta should be educated in England and, at the age of around 15, she was sent to Harrogate

Ladies' College in Yorkshire. In 1913, her mother and stepfather moved to London and Greta was sent to a school in the capital run by suffragettes. But this was also destined not to last and she soon returned to Harrogate. A childhood forever on the move and having to contend with unfamiliar languages, may well have given Greta a particular empathy for the many displaced refugees she would care for in later life.

In 1917 Greta went up to Newnham College, Cambridge to read Modern Languages and switched to Economics. After a short, unsuccessful marriage to a fellow student, she met Charles Burkill and they were wed in 1928. They had three children and settled in Cambridge when Charles accepted a post at Peterhouse College.

Greta's involvement with refugees started as early as 1935, when she worked on an informal Cambridge committee aimed at helping Jewish and other students escape persecution in Germany. With the accession to power of Adolph Hitler, Jewish students were soon debarred from entering German universities and letters begging contacts in Britain to help them continue their studies soon landed in the pigeon holes of academics in Cambridge and other university towns. Those with a possible contact in Cambridge were passed on to Greta and her team, including some Jewish refugees who had already arrived in the city (after 1933). Getting students into British universities was no easy task; nor was there much conformity in the way they were accepted. In the 1930s some universities allowed refugee students to complete their unfinished German degrees; others insisted that they start their course over again. Greta enthusiastically took up the offer from the Head of The Leys, a well-respected private school, to provide some free places to Jewish boys ousted from schools in Germany. This offer, and others such as the Perse School and the Friends' School in Saffron Walden promised either free places or reduced fees. This enabled children to overcome visa hurdles imposed by a British government, who were nervous of public opinion and largely hostile to the idea of opening the doors to large-scale immigration.

This public mood changed overnight on the 9th of November 1938. The events of 'Kristallnacht' galvanised people like Greta into renewed energies. She later said that after Kristallnacht, the shock of the brutal attacks on Jews went through the whole of Britain like an electric current. 'In every town and village the cry went up, 'We must save the children'.' In late November 1938, that cry was answered in Cambridge with the establishment of a special committee to look after the needs of the many children expected to be allowed into Britain as part of the 'Kindertransport' scheme.

At first frustrated by the slow pace of German Jewish children arriving in the city, Greta and her team were unexpectedly faced with a sudden rush of arrivals from April 1939 (due in part to the Nazi occupation of Prague and surrounding territories in March of that year) up to the outbreak of war that September. In that time, just over 100 unaccompanied children arrived in the city. When the door closed on any further refugees, Greta Burkill's work consolidated into providing a huge range of welfare service for the children.

Although Greta succeeded in persuading Jesus College, Cambridge to offer a building at a reduced rent for the offices of her committee, the Burkill house at 20 Chaucer Road (a leafy middle class academic enclave) became the unofficial 'home from home' for many of the young refugees. Another stalwart member of the refugee committee, Mrs Sybil Hutton was a neighbour at 1 Chaucer Road.

The Burkill house was always filled with the aroma of Greta's delicious cooking and included an enormous range of delectable puddings. A former refugee remembers her home with huge affection:

'She was an extremely good listener who had time for us all. The front door of her house in Chaucer Road was never locked; we just entered and then heard her high-pitched voice from the kitchen or the nursery or the garden, 'Come in, I will be with you in a minute.' Then she was there, followed by a dog or two, with or without apron, chatting away to make us feel at ease: cups of tea, home-made cakes or biscuits and then FULL attention to whatever we had come to say. I was one of the teenage girls; when I told her that I was not happy with my foster parents, she found a new family for me. When I pleaded that I did not want to go to school but to try to earn my living as soon as possible, she got me accepted at a teacher training college – although I was too young, did not have the required School Certificate and at first knew no English. She comforted young women who were unhappy slaves in households; she took up their causes and never thought of herself'

During the war years, Greta and Sybil Hutton were given a small petrol ration and motored around East Anglia, visiting children fostered by hundreds of local people. She reassured herself that little Ilse, Lore, Heinz or Fritz were doing well at school, coping with their subjects and having their school fees paid.

She also sat on the wider regional committee, one of twelve such committees established to oversee the care of refugees in the civil defence areas, into which the country was divided after the outbreak of war. The Cambridge Regional Committee took in the eastern counties of Cambridgeshire, Essex, Norfolk, Suffolk, Bedfordshire and Hertfordshire. Over the whole war period it was responsible for up to 2,000 refugee children, many of whom had been evacuated from London's eastern and northern boroughs only a few weeks after arriving in England.

The pressures on Greta and her small committee of volunteers were immense as they sought to find suitable homes for hundreds of these, often traumatised, new arrivals, while also negotiating such challenges as dealing with religious issues. These often arose when children from orthodox Jewish homes in their home countries were fostered with non-Jewish or non-religious households. Chief Rabbi Hertz at the time became increasingly concerned by the threat of orthodox boys and girls losing their faith and culture. There were examples, of children in the region being taken away from their Christian foster homes and sent to Jewish families or hostels elsewhere. Greta took a strong line on removing children from otherwise caring and happy families. Talking of her experience sorting out the religious needs of Jewish children who had been evacuated to a school in Ely, a small town in the Fens, Greta noted:

'A lot of the children were evacuees from very orthodox orphanages in Czechoslovakia and had never met anyone but Jews. They would not drink the milk, they would not do this, they would not do that. It was a really heart-breaking job [...] We did have a very great deal of trouble with that school... Ely was a real cross to bear... Luckily it was near enough for us to interfere frequently.'

Where there were problems to do with the quality of care at home or financial issues, Greta and her committee would seek donations from local sponsors, or appeal to the central committees in London for help. She also busied herself being on the wider regional committee, responsible over the whole war year period for up to 2,000 refugee children (with constant comings and goings, there were around 800 child refugees in the region at any one time). Many of these had been evacuated from London's eastern and northern boroughs – for most a second major upheaval in just a few weeks. The pressures on her and the small committee of volunteers was immense; it wasn't only the challenge of finding suitable homes for hundreds of, often traumatised, children but also new pressures such as dealing with religious issues. As Greta said later about the committee:

'They had to deal with people belonging to a close religious community, who had not mixed with their fellows, who were bewildered and lost, in a way affecting them more deeply and distressingly than the normal British-tied citizen, though they also suffered from shock... The dossiers flooded in and we had to sort them.'

With the ending of the war in 1945, Greta's task was far from complete and she continued to work on the Children's Refugee Committee. She was concerned by all manner of post-war issues relating to the former refugees who were by now young adults. Many had been in the armed forces and were looking to continue their academic studies. Others were to be reunited with family who had survived the Holocaust and needed travel documents, money for tickets, clothes and emotional support – all this was provided by Greta and her team.

In one particularly poignant case, it was discovered that a Jewish father destined to be murdered by the Nazis, had left a large trunk full of his belongings to his only child now living in East Anglia with a foster family. Greta undertook to send emissaries to Paris where the trunk was discovered and to arrange for the opening of a sealed letter from the father to the daughter he would never see again. Greta was determined that the late father's wishes be respected and arranged for some of the contents (mostly his clothes) to be sold to raise money for the girl. Her trusted emissary, himself a former refugee, was given the task of opening the letter which contained US dollars. Greta made sure that this money was banked for the little girl and that it would eventually be used to help her make contact with her only living relatives.

After the war, one of the chief concerns of Greta's committee was naturalisation – the process whereby the German, Czech or Polish immigrants became British. Greta lobbied anyone she could think of - local MPs, cabinet ministers, high-ranking academics and distinguished scientists to work on behalf of the young people, now in her care, who longed to become fully British citizens. It wasn't always easy to succeed in obtaining naturalisation papers. One former refugee who had escaped from Poland in 1939 had volunteered for army service, been taken as a PoW by the Germans (although he escaped captivity) and had wanted to continue his studies as a British citizen – yet still had his naturalisation request refused. The Home Office dragged its feet because the young man was officially still a Polish citizen and not 'stateless'. He was thus subject to the many delays and obfuscations meted out by a British government keen not to upset its former ally Stalin, the leader of the Soviet Union. This ruling applied to those Jews born in Germany or Austria, the latter having been stripped of their citizenship by the Hitler regime.

After 1945, over 100,000 Polish troops who had fought with the allies were brought back to Britain from fighting in Italy and other theatres of war. All were deemed to have Polish citizenship and it was assumed they would return home. But as soldiers, airman and sailors loyal to Britain they were now seen by Stalin as potential enemies. These men and women were thus caught in a diplomatic no-man's-land; unable to return home, but not welcomed by Britain as fellow citizens. Greta launched herself into months of correspondence and meetings with government officials to address this confusing situation. It was only in 1947 that she managed to succeed and the Jewish refugee in question was given British citizenship.

The post-war years saw no sign of Greta's energies diminishing. She threw herself into supporting the cause of lonely graduates (by helping to set up the Cambridge University Graduate Centre), assisted in founding a college – New Hall – and fought for the rights of students who found themselves in Britain as refugees. Just days before her death in 1984, she was still writing persuasive letters to the British Home Office to call for the granting of extended visas to students from Iran who had been stranded in the country following the revolution in Teheran in 1979.

Looking back some 30 years after the events in Cambridge, Greta Burkill reflected on her work with the refugee children:

Justice to the child was paramount in my view. It created bitter argument, but I won through and all the gifted children got their opportunity... and they have proved their worth in this country, and the rest of the world... It was great work to be involved in.'

Nina Lieberman was the secretary to the Cambridge Refugee Committee from 1940. In her memoir she said of Greta Burkill:

'To have known Greta Burkill was a privilege [...] looking after these children, proved a tower of strength not only to her co-

Chapter 15

The Temperance Campaigner
Henry Carter

Henry Carter Image 21

Henry Carter was a pacifist, a Methodist leader and staunch temperance campaigner who devoted much of his life to working with refugees and displaced persons. The son of a basket maker, he was born in Plymouth in 1874 and brought up by a devout mother. In 1905 he was ordained as a minister and six years later appointed secretary to the Temperance Committee of the Wesleyan Methodist Church. Increasingly involved in social welfare matters throughout the 1930s, he helped found the National Peace Council and was a strong voice against antisemitism.

Henry Carter became aware of the refugee crisis in 1937

during a visit to Bled, in what was then Yugoslavia, with his old friend the veteran leader of the Labour party, George Lansbury. There he heard that an eminent cancer surgeon, a Jewish refugee from Germany, had been forced to flee for fear of being pursued by the Gestapo. 'In a flash the meaning of the Hitler persecution of the Jews stood revealed in its stark horror', he wrote years later. 'I have given nearly all my time to refugee work; it was that incident at Bled which illumined for me not only Hitler's brutality, but the meaning and no less black pages of European history.'

Returning from his travels in 1937, Carter set about warning his fellow Christians about the dangers he foresaw in the Nazi persecution of the Jews. He was quick to see that a key duty was to stamp out antisemitism in Britain:

Ill-will against Jews is being deliberately inflamed throughout our country. The evil policy of racial hatred directed against men and women and children of the Hebrew race and faith, which we have deplored in Germany, is now proclaimed in Britain. It has been our proud boast for centuries that Britain gave welcome to persecuted refugees from other lands.

Carter called for reconciliation between Jews and Christians – failure to do so, he claimed, would lead to 'disgraceful attacks on Jews and the growth of an enduring alienation.' E. C. Unwin, who worked with the Reverend Carter and later wrote a memoir of his fellow Methodist, recalled assisting in the migration of non-Aryan Christians. The two men were present when, on 6 October 1938, a Christian Council for Refugees from Germany and Central Europe was jointly established by Carter, Archbishop Lang, Cardinal Hinsley, the Moderators of the Church of Scotland and the Free Church Federal Council.

Carter took an active role in the Council from its inception, chairing its board of management and, in 1948, the Council itself. According to Unwin, "With the outbreak of war, he steadily withdrew from active participation in his Departmental office to give his energies to meet the demands which the care of refugees – and the help for Conscientious Objectors [...] He found himself a lodging with his books in Bloomsbury House."

Carter was appointed Joint Chairman of the Central Office for Refugees along with Anthony de Rothschild. Unwin talks of the 'immensity of labour' that Carter undertook in this role:

There were negotiations with Government authority [...] and of obtaining Government grants in aid. Above all, there were the personal problems of the refugees themselves – involving the most meticulous case-work – the care of the aged, the provision for children, and the integration, wherever possible, of refugees in positions where perchance they could earn a living.

Close to Carter's heart was the setting up of a hostel called Riversmead near Blackburn in Lancashire. On Carter's say-so, the National Children's Home Organisation (NCHO) agreed to look after the children of parents who had been put into German concentration camps, and offered Riversmead to a group of seventy refugee boys from Germany, Austria and Prague who had come over to England in the summer of 1939. They were non-Aryan Christians who had kept up their faith. The home remained open throughout the war years, staffed by English and German teachers. Older boys went to work in industry and younger ones were sent to Blackburn to complete their studies.

Carter visited the home many times to check on the welfare of the boys, some of whom were reunited with their families after the war and most of whom became British citizens. A few months after settling in, Carter recalled his first meeting with the boys at Riversmead, 'I saw them soon after arrival, an anxious, weary and almost silent company; probably many of them were thinking of those from whom they were parted and wondering what life in England would be like.' Several weeks later, Carter visited again and noted that the boys were much happier with a newly-forged strong sense of community. He was clearly pleased to note that they were 'well-liked in the community', had made friends locally, played football with neighbouring schools and gathered on Sunday in local churches 'maintaining Christian worship in their native language.'

Carter's experience with the refugee work led to his co-founding of the Council of Christians and Jews, whose aim was to combat racial and religious intolerance as well as to improve relations between faith members. After the war, Carter's energies turned to the vast refugee crisis emerging in continental Europe, where millions of displaced persons (DP) and survivors of the Nazi persecutions were in desperate need of help. In the summer of 1945, sponsored by the Inter-governmental Committee on Refugees, he paid an extended visit to the DP camps in Switzerland. His subsequent report pulled no punches in terms of the vast scale of relief necessary to prevent millions starving to death in the winter to come.

He was appointed first Chairman of the Ecumenical Refugee Commission of the World Council of Churches after the role was declined by Bishop George Bell. Now in his seventies, Carter threw himself into the whole issue, helping to organise international conferences in which aid and rescue were paramount issues. He personally raised finances to help secure the offices of the Commission in London and helped set up a series of relief field teams throughout Europe, focussing on priorities such as clothing, medicines and food. He liaised closely with the newly created United Nations Organisation for Relief and Rehabilitation Abroad (UNRRA) and set up what Unwin called 'a beneficent ministry [...] to the victims of the war's ravages in Central Europe'.

Carter's sympathies extended to the nine million ethnic Germans who had been expelled from parts of the former German Reich. In 1949, he raised the issue at an international conference and talked of the misery and destitution of these people. The result was a comprehensive plan involving resettlement, emigration, training and education, with Carter ensuring that there was full participation by the evolving German government and the occupying powers. In addition, he set up a Methodist Relief Fund to disburse aid to church agencies throughout Germany and Austria. In 1950 he published "The Refugee Problem in Europe and the Middle East".

Exhausted and increasingly frail, Henry Carter died in 1951. An obituary said of him, 'He gave himself to the help of Christians and Jewish victims of Hitlerite oppression [...] His crowning work was for the care of refugees and displaced persons in Central Europe.'

Chapter 16

The Homemaker
Mary Hughes

Mary Hughes, Image 22

Mary Hughes was a quiet but determined rescuer who not only found homes for many children but also took into her own family in York, two young, very unhappy refugees and their desperate mother.

Mary was born into a middle-class Anglican family in 1886, the daughter of a civil engineer, Donald Stuart. As a young man, Donald had helped his father build railways in India and Argentina and when Mary came into the world, he became secretary to the contractor for the railway tunnel under the River Severn (completed in the year of Mary's birth) and a commercial agent for the Manchester Ship Canal. When the latter was formally opened by Queen Victoria in May 1894, the Stuart family shared a boat on the canal with former Prime Minister, William Gladstone, who affectionately patted the eight year-old Mary's head. Mary attended private schools in Ealing and Harrogate in North Yorkshire and later attended a so-called 'finishing school' in Belgium. A surviving report shows a model, all-round pupil.

Her marriage to the Reverend John Hughes in 1912 was a true meeting of minds and shared interests. John Hughes was the left-wing son of a coal miner from County Durham. A bright choral scholar, John had been financially supported by a wealthy local woman to take a place at Oxford University. From there he entered the clergy to become a country vicar and served as an army chaplain during World War One. Later he was offered the post of Vicar Choral at York Minster.

It was during his time in York that John Hughes developed a close friendship with Seebohm Rowntree, the eminent Quaker industrialist and social reformer. The combination of Rowntree's influence and a questioning of his own beliefs after his war experience, led John to turn towards Quakerism, and his future wife Mary followed at her own pace. John Hughes enjoyed acting and it was this interest that brought Mary into his life. She first spotted her future husband at a play rehearsal and noted in her diary, 'A Mr Hughes there, not bad.' It is not clear if she was referring to his acting skills or some other attraction.

Come 1920, John was offered the wardenship of the York Educational Settlement – a college supported by the Rowntree family to provide an education for working-class adults. Lessons were given free to the unemployed and included courses in history, art, French, literature and economics. In 1922, following his own passion and aptitude in the dramatic arts, John formed an amateur theatre company – The York Settlement Community Players – a company still active in the 21st century. For her part, as the warden's wife, Mary helped run women's groups and gave talks on poetry, a lifelong love. She was also fond of classical music and was an accomplished cellist. She delighted in the English countryside, especially the landscape of her beloved Yorkshire, and her gentle and empathetic character attracted a wide circle of friends.

Mary Hughes first answered the call to help refugees during the Spanish Civil War in 1937, when some Basque children came to York as part of the nationwide effort to provide a peaceful haven in Britain. She was instrumental in setting up a refugee committee and assisted these and other children in finding places at Bootham, the local school run by the Society of Friends. Later she would find a similar place for a young Jewish refugee from Vienna.

In the summer of 1938, her 19-year-old son David, soon to go up to Cambridge to read Geography, decided to take a cycling holiday through Western Europe, including Nazi Germany. Mary urged him to spend some time visiting Jewish families she knew in Germany, via her network of colleagues in the Society of Friends who were active there. She had no doubt that their lives were in peril and that it was important to do what she could to help them out of danger.

David visited families in Nuremberg and Berlin, where he stayed with a Dr and Mrs Deutschland to avoid the glare of the Gestapo. Dr Deutschland was a Jewish scientist and former colleague of Albert Einstein, and the couple shared their dismay and fears with David about the future of Jews in Germany. Their family had lived there for hundreds of years, fought for Germany in World War I and been honoured by a grateful nation. Yet now their lives were in peril simply for being Jewish. Thanks to Mary's efforts with the Jewish refugee organisations in Bloomsbury House, she managed to secure visas to allow them to leave Germany and enter the UK. They were joined by other families whose safe exit from the Reich was also facilitated by Mary.

After his cycling holiday in the summer of 1938, David travelled to Cambridge to begin life as a student, but a few weeks into his studies, the November Pogroms began in Germany and within days the first child refugees, part of the Kindertransport, docked at the port of Harwich. The first batch of 200 or so were housed in temporary accommodation at Dovercourt Holiday Camp.

Early in December that same year, Mary suggested to her son that as he was a relatively short distance (around 80 miles) from Dovercourt, a seaside resort near the port of Harwich, he could perhaps volunteer to spend his winter vacation helping the children. Mary knew that David spoke fluent German and had a kind heart. True to character he set off for Dovercourt as soon as term in Cambridge had ended.

At the Dovercourt Holiday Camp, David was given a key to his wooden chalet and settled into life at what had become a crowded refugee camp for children. He was soon given the vital task of running the camp post office, a hugely important job considering the children were desperate to hear from their parents and of course, to write back to tell them how they were doing in this strange country where something white and sticky called porridge and a strange fish called kippers were served for breakfast. The role of selling stamps, distributing letters and postcards, and sorting the mail put David at the very epicentre of operations at the holiday camp. It also helped him keep a *workers but also to the children whom she truly befriended. She was especially interested in those boys and girls who were intellectually gifted and managed to place a good number of them in public schools and later on, at the university. Many a physicist, mathematician or legal scholar owe their career opportunities to the tenacity of Greta Burkill. Indeed when thwarted by bureaucrats, she could be like a tigress fighting for her cubs [...] Truly, she continues to live on in the lives she influenced.*

close eye on the children.

Though most of the children David observed from his post office counter were cheerful, it was clear that two youngsters were far from happy. A foster family living in the Bristol area had provided a home for ten year-old Harry Baum and his sister Franzi, five years his senior. Franzi had been given a room, barely furnished, in a dusty attic. Neither was given any pocket money and when Franzi asked for stamps, paper and envelope to write home, it was refused. Somehow she managed to get hold of some stationery and sent a letter back to Mr Bush, the head person at Dovercourt representing the Refugee Children's Movement. She begged him to take her and Harry away from this misery and thankfully Mr Bush duly caught the next train down to the West Country and brought the children back to the holiday camp.

David Hughes could see how distressed they both were, so he picked up the telephone, called his mother and asked Mary if she would be prepared to take these siblings as foster children. Without a moment's hesitation, Mary simply replied, 'Yes' and the brother and sister were put on the next train to York to begin a new life with the Hughes family. Putting the phone down on that brief conversation with his mother, David ran off to tell the camp managers the good news. Mr Bush shook David's hand in tearful gratitude and told him, 'It's things like that which last – it will be remembered by the descendants of all these children for generations'– a prescient comment indeed in 1938.

Once the euphoria of Mary Hughes' generous offer had worn off, David began to reflect on some harsh realities. He wondered how his family would cope with the extra financial burden, but back in York, Mary's attitude was typically practical. In a letter to David's sister, she revealed not only the importance of what she had agreed to do but also an insight into the problems she faced:

'Did you know that we are to have two refugee children coming, maybe tomorrow? [...] I daren't think of what I shall do with them – 'sufficient unto the day' [...] I gather the parents have an affidavit for America, so I shall have to see about getting them over next. I have cases coming to me almost daily now and just can't find hospitality for. Oh that people would open their doors! I feel that every Quaker home should be ashamed if it hasn't had one refugee at least – but will they come forward? No! Some of course we can always rely on [...] I'm up to my eyes in refugees still: every day I wander off trying to arrange for hospitality etc. – interviewing folks and writing endless letters [...]'

Any misgivings held by Mary Hughes about her decision to foster two German Jewish children were soon swept away when they arrived on her doorstep. Also writing to her daughter:

'The increase in the family arrived yesterday and they're both darlings! Davy was right – I fell for them on sight [...] They were overwhelmed with tiredness though, and would eat nothing [...] and they went to bed at 6 30 and I believe slept soundly for the whole night which will do them no end of good'

She reiterated that her next priority would be to get the children's parents out of Germany. Even while settling in the young strangers, Mary was busy thinking of others in need. She had just attended a meeting to raise money for the refugees from Spain and, with her fellow Quakers, managed to raise the considerable sum of £100 for a food ship leaving Hull for Barcelona. Her husband John started the ball rolling with a donation of £5 (perhaps £300 today) which he raised by selling some shares owned by the family.

The seemingly endless responsibility towards those in danger was not one that fazed Mary Hughes. She acknowledged that it was hopeless to try to catch up on refugee work as new cases, and new challenges, were mounting as the months towards war advanced. This meant regular trips down to London to liaise with the central refugee organisations, together with outings to North Yorkshire to give talks on her work (with the aim of raising funds and finding more desperately needed host families). She had a telephone installed in her bedroom to handle incoming calls at all times of the day and night. She would wake up to deal with cablegrams from America asking for background information about specific refugees. Her morning postbag was enormous and included airmail missives from Jews in Germany desperate for her help. This would mean sending a telegram to her head office – the Germany Emergency Committee (G.E.C.), a Quaker body based in Bloomsbury House – to see what could be done for the benighted families. It could be exhausting work, but like so many who found themselves in the front line of refugee work, Mary began to realise that she possessed unsuspected reserves of energy and effective powers of persuasion. Despite all the challenges she faced she wrote in her diary, 'It's too much for me but I would rather die than not do this.'

A few weeks after arriving at the Hughes' household, Mary could report to her daughter that the two children had settled down and were 'good as gold and are happily part of our ménage now. They are very helpful and easy, good tempered and happy.' Harry was bought his first bike from a local shop which reduced the price by £1 when they heard that the boy was a refugee. Mary was also hard at work relieving the lot of older refugees from the Reich. She heard of a young man in nearby Leeds, who had been a prisoner in one of the Nazi concentration camps, before being released and ordered to get out of Germany. The lad's brother had fled to Czechoslovakia but had been threatened by the authorities (still in early 1939 nominally independent of Hitler's regime) to be sent back to Germany and into the hands of the Gestapo.

Mary went to Leeds to meet the young man and the chair of the local refugee committee. A plan was devised whereby a guarantee would be sought for the brother in peril. Though the Hughes' had run out of their own funds, Mary remained determined to raise money for such cases and appealed to some wealthy Jews in New York for financial assistance. In the meantime, she paid another visit to Leeds to see a Jewish benefactor (unnamed in her diary) there who promised to help in any way he could. He told Mary he was amazed that Christians should be doing so much for the Jewish victims of Nazi persecution. John Hughes is reported to have responded, 'There is neither Jew nor Christian in all this – but something above and beyond to which we all belong.'

Mary's work seemed to grow exponentially as 1939 progressed. She started up a scheme for a refugee hostel, which was opened by March, and lobbied influential people including Archbishop Temple to help support the new venture. She also managed to get the children's mother (but not their father) out of Germany and up to the Hughes' house in York on a domestic permit. She was registered as a maid to the Hughes household, but in fact not expected to do anything other than learn English in preparation for a more permanent post. In the meantime she slept in David's room while he was studying in Cambridge. Mary noticed that Mrs Baum, though grateful for her rescue by the Hughes' was pale and anxious about the fate of her husband.

War brought a new set of challenges for volunteers such as Mary Hughes. With no prospect of helping any new refugees, she threw herself into ensuring that the refugees already in York were either being educated or gainfully employed, and doing the rounds of hospital visiting when they were ill. When, within weeks of the outbreak of hostilities, the government began a programme to assess all citizens, or former citizens of Germany and Austria, to establish whether they posed a security threat, Mary also made it her business to accompany each of 'her' refugees to the local tribunal so that she could speak up for them. She would often spend all day in the law courts, but her advocacy ensured that none were interned in those first months of what became known as 'the Phoney War'.

This phase ended abruptly with Hitler's invasion of the Low Countries and France, and the introduction of internment for thousands of 'enemy aliens'. From May 1940 some of the older refugees in York were arrested and sent off to internment in Canada, Australia or closer to home in England, including in specially isolated camps on the Isle of Man. Furious about the policy of locking up people persecuted by the Nazis and throwing them into camps where they would come face to face with their enemies, Mary wrote to the Manchester Guardian:

'It is surely the refinement of cruelty to ask a poor Jewish girl to share the bed of her tormentor, a Nazi girl. We who have been working for these poor refugees so long can tell which are true friends of this country, but we are the last people to be consulted.'

In May 1940 Mary wrote to her son David:

'I can see myself toiling on with refugees of every nationality until we are all refugees to Canada! All our men have been interned [...] and we shall have to help the wives all we can now to keep cheerful.

I see that as our main task [...] to keep up the morale of the country generally. There will be lots of sadness and much utter despair – once we lose heart, we are done – so let's never.'

Mary Hughes continued to work tirelessly for the welfare of the refugees until her husband John died following an operation in June 1942. 'Her' refugees rallied round helping her tend the garden and other duties, but sadly her health began to deteriorate and she gradually gave up her work. Those she had helped never forgot her selfless devotion and became lifelong friends and supporters. After the war she developed heart trouble, and a stroke in 1947 confined her life to a wheelchair. Mary died in 1955.

Years after her death, Harry Baum who had received the MBE for his services to industry, looked back at the part played by the Hughes family in his life. He thought of his sister Franzi who had become a nurse and emigrated to the USA, and his mother who ended her days in England. In a letter to David Hughes, Baum said:

'No words can express the enormous debt of gratitude I owe you and your late, truly sainted parents for all that you have done for Franzi, my late mother and I [...] Of all the Kindertransportees who shared similar experiences, we must certainly have been by far the most favoured and the most fortunate.'

He ended his tribute with a fond memory of Mary Hughes. For her he wrote:

'[...] nothing was too small or too difficult and (she) knew the best way of tackling every problem: if she didn't, she built it as she tussled with it.'

Mary's spirit of compassionate action was inherited by her son David. A conscientious objector during the war, David volunteered to drive trucks and ambulances. After VE day in the autumn of 1945, he was asked to drive a lorry to Holland full of relief supplies for the war-devastated area around Arnhem and Nijmegen. He was shocked at the destruction of whole cities and towns and the abject state of the children of collaborators left starving in displaced persons camps. Later he worked to provide relief for the destitute refugees living in war-ravaged Germany. Back in Britain, he became a teacher and in retirement published books on Shakespeare and the moral teachings of Jesus.

For the rest of his life, even into his late nineties, David Hughes carried in his pocket a treasured object as a constant reminder of those terrible days in 1938-39 when the needs of refugee children were so great. It was a key fob marked 'H13' – the number of his chalet at Dovercourt camp.

Chapter 17

The Rose Grower
Hilda Murrell

Hilda Murrell, Image 23

Kindertransport rescuer and murder victim, Hilda Murrell was born in Shrewsbury in 1906 and hailed from a family of well-established horticulturalists who ran a successful nurseries business.

Studious and strong-minded, Hilda went up to Newnham College, Cambridge in 1924 to read English and Modern Languages. After graduating from Cambridge, she settled into managing the family rose-growing business.

In 1939, as war loomed large on the near horizon, Hilda's energy, hatred of injustice and can-do attitude saw her becoming the Honorary Secretary of the Shrewsbury Committee for

Jewish Refugee Children. Her shrewd business skills and hard-working, persuasive persona were immediately put to very good use in raising funds to help look after the welfare of incoming child refugees. Her role was to find suitable foster families for the boys and girls who made the long journey from Germany, Austria and Czechoslovakia.

Hilda was instrumental in bringing together a diverse group of activists from many backgrounds: Roman Catholics, Quakers, Unitarians and Rotarians. She helped to find and encourage a long list of local subscribers – people committed to underwriting the children's financial needs and to raise funds through events and concerts. Famous classical performers of the day, such as Dame Myra Hess, Adila Fachiri and the violinist Jelly d'Aranyi were all persuaded by Hilda to play without fee. Thanks to Hilda's efforts, the committee raised the considerable sum of £1,745 (the equivalent of £70,000 today). At least 90 per cent of this funding was used for the maintenance of 14 refugee children and young people under her care. Hilda's committee worked tirelessly to find free places for their young refugee charges at local schools, bearing in mind those children who wanted to stay on at school beyond the leaving age of 14 had to pay fees for their education.

One of these refugees was Hana Bandler who arrived from Prague at the age of 16. Hana's early years flourished within a liberal Jewish family, who lived in Czechoslovakia but whose first language was German. Her father owned a small men's outfitters shop in the village where they lived. By 1939, the Bandlers had moved to Prague and Hana was enrolled as the only Jewish girl in her school. A keen chemist and biologist, Hana had dreams of becoming something in medicine or science. This would be a dream fulfilled many years later in her new home in England.

Young Hana came as part of the Czech Kindertransport organised by Sir Nicholas Winton and Trevor Chadwick, and arrived in England in July 1939. Like so many others, she had waved farewell to her parents at the Wilson Station in Prague and set out for a journey to London. She could only carry a small suitcase and her Girl Guide's rucksack with enough food for the two-day journey, and 10 German marks, which was the maximum allowed by the Nazi authorities. She promised her parents that she would stay clean and tidy for the journey and hoped they would meet soon; they never did, as her mother, father and most of the extended family were murdered in the Holocaust.

On arrival at Liverpool Street Station, Hana and others were actually met by Sir Nicholas and put on another train to foster families in Shropshire. Hana's was a familiar story of separation, loneliness and a coming to terms with a completely new life in a strange country. Some time in the first weeks of 1940, Hana was invited to tea with Hilda Murrell, no doubt a very enjoyable experience, which became a regular feature for the Shrewsbury children. As Hana was of working age, Hilda soon found her a job in a local shop which paid five shillings a week, half of which went to her foster parents for her keep.

Hana was found a foster home with a Mr and Mrs Barrie. She was happy enough there but Mr Barrie became registered as a conscientious objector. This might of course have led to his imprisonment in wartime Britain, so he decided to leave the house, buy a smallholding and grow his own vegetables to ensure that his family was self-sufficient should he be sent away. Unfortunately, Hana was not part of this plan and so Hilda had to find her a new foster home.

This she did with her cousins, Mr and Mrs Johnson. He,

according to Hana, "Was a very nice clergyman," but Hana's happiness in her new home was short-lived. The clergyman joined the navy and his family moved out with him. Once more, the onus was back on Hilda Murrell to find yet another home for Hana. Luckily, the Johnsons had other cousins with a spare room in their house in Shrewsbury and took in Hana partly through Hilda's encouragement but also because the alternative was to take in an evacuee. They chose the young Czech woman over a child from the English inner cities which seems to have been a fairly common choice, especially in middle-class households; a well-educated, well-mannered German or Czech child often being seen as preferable to a poor, possibly rather rambunctious boy or girl from the East End slums.

Hilda's choice of new home for Hana was a very good one, as she was able to live with a girl of her own age, the granddaughter of the house owner. Phyllis Johnson became Hana's lifelong friend and a network of English companions grew as a result of her contacts. These included Phyllis' friend, Lucy Lunt, who went on to be a school friend of Hana's at Shrewsbury High.

One day when Hilda was visiting her cousins, Hana enquired if she could possibly find some work in a laboratory. Hana took a keen interest in the sciences, but Hilda decided it was better for Hana to continue her general education and found a place for her at the Priory School for Girls in Shrewsbury. On behalf of the Shrewsbury Refugee Committee, Hilda negotiated funding for this fee-paying school with the Czech Trust Fund, a body set up to disperse funds raised by the British Government as part of its compensation for the flawed agreement with Hitler and Mussolini in Munich, in September 1938. Hana actually only spent a year at this school before moving to the Czech State School housed in Hinton Hall, near Whitchurch, in Shropshire.

A report written for the Committee in 1944 reflects Hilda Murrell's concerns for the children's future as the war entered its final phase and some kind of peace began to seem at least imaginable:

As for the future – it is wrapped in obscurity. Many of the children's parents have not been heard of for several years. Will this country take the generous course and allow these young people to be naturalised – and if so, what sort of deal will they get afterwards? We do not know, and can only do our best to influence public opinion, but meanwhile to make some provision for the uncomfortable gaps in employment which are almost bound to occur.

These words were somewhat prophetic for young people like Hana. She was allowed to become naturalised and public opinion did not stand in the way of her chosen career path to work in hospitals. After the war, Hana took the School Certificate to enable her to go on to become a qualified laboratory assistant. She eventually became Head of Haematology at a hospital in Kent and retired at the age of 65. Following a long and active retirement devoted to gardening and charitable work for the blind, Hana died peacefully at home in 2012.

Minutes of the Mayor of Shrewsbury's Jewish Refugee Committee show that Hilda remained active as Hon. Sec. until at least the end of the war. She reports on the welfare of the children: one has failed her school examination but an alternative job has been found. Another, she reports has joined the R.A.F. and thanks were given for the fundraising concerts she organised in the town. The committee was finally wound up in July 1948 – a balance remained in the accounts for £140 and the decision, doubtless influenced by Hilda, was to hand over the whole sum for the training in domestic science for one of the former refugee girls.

Hilda continued her work in horticulture for the rest of her career. However, her life came to a tragic end just over thirty years later in a grimly mysterious coda to a career of activism and social engagement. By then a feisty campaigner against the nuclear industry, she had remained friends with several of the fourteen refugee children for whose care she had been responsible, including Hana Bandler who had seen her regularly throughout the previous four decades.

On 22 March 1984 Hana and her old school friend, Lucy Lunt, paid a visit to Hilda's house in Shrewsbury. They rang the bell but there was no answer. The house was locked up but the upstairs windows were open. It seemed strange perhaps with hindsight, but Hana and Lucy thought nothing of it and left.

A few days later, Lucy's son, a policeman, came round to tell his mother that Hilda's body had been found in the nearby woods. She had been sexually assaulted and stabbed to death.

There have been many conspiracy theories about the motives behind the murder of this famous rose grower. Many, though, still remember Hilda for the work she did with the Shrewsbury Refugee Committee and the hope she gave to Hana and many other refugee children from Nazi-occupied Europe. She is also remembered for something rather special; that she gave her name to a beautiful blossom: the Hilda Murrell Rose.

Chapter 18

The Youth Leader
Henry Fair

Henry Fair, Image 24

Henry Fair was a wanted man: in the early 1940s he even appeared on a Nazi hit list as someone to be shot if caught. In later life he said that he considered it something of an honour to have been wanted by the Gestapo, since one of his 'crimes' was saving Czech teenagers, many of them Jewish, by ensuring their escape to Britain.

Henry Fair, a Londoner, was one of the founders of the Woodcraft Folk, an organisation established in 1925 to offer young people an alternative to the more militaristic model set by the Scouts and Girl Guides Movement. Known to his young members as 'Koodoo', for many years he was also leader of the Woodcraft Folk which had, and still has, strong links to the Labour Party and the Co-operative Movement. With the rise of fascism in Europe, Fair's organisation took a strong stand against Oswald Mosley and was involved in the so-called 'Battle of Cable Street' in October 1936 – an attempt to prevent a march by fascist supporters through a largely Jewish area of London's East End.

The Spanish Civil War mobilised support across left-wing groups throughout the UK and the Woodcraft Folk were no exception. They raised money for medical aid in Spain and Henry Fair invited a group of youngsters from Valencia to one of the children's camps. They arrived in 1937 soon after the bombing of Guernica and Fair recalled the day that an aeroplane from a nearby airfield passed overhead and how the instinctive reaction of the Spanish children was to fall flat on their faces. The camp held at Peacehaven, near Brighton, was the Folk's first international gathering and of the 2,000 or so participants, 250 teenagers had come over from Czechoslovakia. Henry recalled the youngsters' arrival at Brighton Station, how they unfurled red flags and marched down the seafront to the camp. 'It was the time of the Public Order Act and one newspaper talked about an invasion of foreign Jews waving red flags. They asked, why can they do this when our patriotic British aren't allowed to wear black shirts and march with Moseley?' The fascist newspaper, Action, followed this up with a caricature of Fair with a stereotypically semitic nose; he was labelled, 'a foreign Jew' (Fair had no Jewish roots whatsoever).

One of the party from Czechoslovakia was Susanne Bernstein (later Medas), the fourteen-year-old daughter of the political editor of Vorwärts, the German Social Democratic Party newspaper, who had taken the family to Prague for their safety. Susanne was a member of the Social Democrats' youth movement, the Red Falcons, a sister organisation to the Woodcraft Folk. Their two weeks in England cemented long-term friendships between the Czech children and the Woodcraft Folk members. Thus, when the Nazis occupied the Sudetenland in October 1938, Fair was quick to call on his members to come to the aid of the Red Falcons. 'Your pals, boys and girls of that sad country [Czechoslovakia], need our help,' he wrote in the organisation's magazine. 'They are co-operative and socialist children. So are you. We'll get together and help each other [...] Don't forget, I'm waiting for those halfpennies, the price of a lollipop from you.'

As National Organiser of the Woodcraft Folk, Fair also urged members throughout the country to take in Czech children at risk of persecution, writing in a national circular to the organisation's volunteers in November 1938: 'Now, comrades, here is our chance to show our solidarity with our Czech comrades. Can you take a boy or girl or perhaps two boys or girls? Talk this over immediately, ask for copies of this circular for giving to Pioneers' [ten to twelve-year-old members] parents.' The Woodcraft Folk's own finances were, he acknowledged, 'precarious and we need cash ourselves, but this is a period of sacrifice by the workers for the workers' – a clear expression of his primarily socialist, anti-fascist view that these youngsters were as much in danger for their politics as for their racial status.

Helped by Nicholas Winton with whom he seems to have dealt indirectly through the Quakers, Fair managed to receive a group of twenty teenagers who came as a part of a larger Kindertransport in July 1939. One of them was the aforementioned Susanne Bernstein, who subsequently spent her life in Britain. Another was Sue Pearson, who never forgot the impact of Fair's welcome on the new arrivals: 'I well remember Koodoo meeting us, a bewildered little group, at Liverpool Street Station. His broad and winning smile – which remained with him to the end of his life – and his pure cockney voice were reassuring, even if not always understood by us.' Fair persuaded families in London, most of them rather poor, to take in the youngsters. Sue Pearson was fostered by a leading Woodcraft Folk leader in Sheffield and, while adjusting to English life (including strange foods such as custard) was not easy, children like Sue quickly made friends with others at the camps in Derbyshire and Epping Forest.

In addition to this transport, Henry Fair was instrumental in smuggling out of Continental Europe a pair of twins, whose father, a prominent anti-fascist, was being sought by the Gestapo. The two boys were part of a much larger group of Red Falcon children who had been sent to relative safety in Liege, Belgium after the occupation of the Sudetenland. Fair heard that they were in danger of being kidnapped and held hostage by the Nazis. During the following summer an international camp was organised in Belgium and was attended by 700 British youngsters under Fair's leadership. He decided to take the risk of hiding the twins among the British delegation and, despite their lack of passports, somehow succeeded in spiriting them into the country, where he took them into his own family in Balham, South London, as foster children. When war broke out shortly afterwards, Fair confessed what he had done to the Foreign Office – they needed their ration books and had to become 'official'. Possibly on Foreign Office advice, he sent the boys back to Belgium for a few days, only to bring them out again officially (as Kindertransportees).

With war imminent, Fair registered, as did many others in his organisation, as a conscientious objector. His case heard at a Bristol tribunal was dealt with sympathetically and he was allowed to carry on organising camps for the youngsters; others were not so lucky and were sent to jail. Henry was often called upon to visit imprisoned Woodcrafters to help them with their appeals and recalled in most cases that they were released to work in agriculture.

After VE Day, Henry helped to re-energise the Woodcraft Folk with the development of new branches and held international peace camps with children from Eastern Europe and the former German Reich. Koodoo left the Woodcraft Folk in 1954 to give his growing family some financial security and became cultural organiser for the Cooperative Movement. At the Labour Party's National Conference in 1984, Neil Kinnock awarded him the party's Certificate of Merit in recognition of half a century's service.

Henry Fair died in 1999 at the age of ninety-one. Eight years earlier he had attended a reunion in Prague of the former Red Falcon refugees, several of whom, including Sue Pearson, had remained in touch with him throughout the intervening decades. When they visited the Theresienstadt camp together, one of the group had put her arm round his neck with the words, 'If it wasn't for you, I'd have been in there'. He later said that hearing those words was the greatest reward of his life.

Chapter 19

The Theologian
J. Ernest Davey

Portrait of J. Ernest Davey, Image 25

Refugee champion and accused heretic, J. Ernest Davey was the rarest of men. Born in Northern Ireland he became an outstanding scholar and was ordained as a minister of the Presbyterian church just before the end of the First World War.

Davey first courted controversy in the early 1920s, with a series of publications and lectures in which he questioned some of the principles of Christian belief and practice. These views caused alarm among some sections of the Ulster Presbyterians, and in 1926, five charges of heresy were levelled against Reverend Davey. Among the accusations were his apparent denial of the literal truth of the Bible and the perfection of

Christ, arguing that the doctrine of the Trinity was not rooted in Holy Scriptures. The trial took place in 1927; Davey's considerable scholarly and determined defence won the day and he was acquitted of all charges. This led to the breakaway Irish Evangelical church but Davey's position within mainstream Presbyterianism was undimmed and Davey remains a divisive figure within Northern Irish politics to this day.

Davey became part of an extraordinarily, multi-denominational committee set up in the wake of the November Pogroms. Representing the Congregational Union, he was joined on the Belfast Refugee Committee by Rabbi J. Schachter (effectively the Chief Rabbi of Northern Ireland), Thomas Allen of the Methodist Conference, Bishop John Down, A.A. Harding of the Society of Friends, and a group of secular representatives, including academics, trades union, business and Rotary Club members. Peggy Loewenthal served as its first Honorary Secretary and at the first meeting chaired by Davey, they discussed finding temporary homes for refugees 'in transit', agricultural training on farms in Ulster, placing children in schools and finding university places for students. Appealing to the general public in Northern Ireland, a statement (probably penned by Davey), urged that:

'In the name of common humanity we must succour those who are in such distress and we must remember that very many of them are suffering for principles we hold dear [...] Adequate funds are essential for the promotion of any of these schemes.'

The genesis of the Belfast committee was described to me by Peggy Loewenthal (later Fink), by then in her nineties. As a Jewish resident of Belfast, she had heard about the plight of incoming refugees from her sister Helen who lived in London.

Peggy arranged a meeting at her parents' home to talk about how the people of Northern Ireland could help. She and her old school friends decided to form a committee under the umbrella of the Joint Christian Churches and she became secretary of the Belfast Committee for Refugees from Germany and Austria. This was separate from the one already set in operation by the Belfast Jewish community.

Loewenthal's committee chaired by Professor Davey focussed on getting work and domestic permits, financial guarantees, the fostering of children and payments of small allowances to the destitute incomers. Two weeks after war was declared, a letter written to a local newspaper by Davey urged the people of Northern Ireland to continue to welcome the refugees and cast aside suspicions. Davey assured readers that:

'Character and circumstances have in every case been closely investigated before entry into this country and we believe we are right to assure these refugees that the traditional Irish hospitality which they have already tasted will not be withdrawn from them in these trying days.

Davey appealed to readers for offers of hospitality, temporary or otherwise. He cited a boy who had been offered free tuition in a Belfast secondary school but who needed board and lodging in or near the city. He went on to add:

'Another type of case requires a money grant. We have a small family, for example, who have been given free use of a house pending immigration, but have no money for food [...] We should add that evacuation in England makes it probable that we shall be asked to find positions for a number of trained refugee domestics, and we should be glad to hear from friends who could place them.

Peggy Fink later recalled her work with refugees in Belfast:

'I often met these anxious and weary travellers as they got off the boat in the early morning in Belfast. Frequently I brought them home for breakfast and explained a little of their new life in Ireland, where they would live, something about their jobs and so on.'

She remembered a mother and two small children carrying a birdcage with a canary and a psychiatrist from Vienna who, as an older man, found it difficult adjusting to his new life. He often came to Peggy's house for baths as his 'digs' were short of hot water. She remembered how humiliated he felt being offered an envelope of money in the street as financial support.

Fink claimed that at the outbreak of war, the Belfast committee had enjoyed a close relationship with the local police, Northern Ireland government and Home Office. It was said at the time that 'Peggy was well in with the local police.' Thanks to this, she and Margaret McNeill, a Quaker member of the committee, attended the local tribunals and were largely successful in keeping most of the refugees out of internment camps or prison. The chairman of the tribunal, however, was particularly ignorant of the refugees' situation and asked why the children were living in Belfast without their parents and seemed to have little understanding about the fate of Jews in Germany. He was duly put straight by Peggy and Margaret during one notable tribunal hearing.

Despite their vigilance, the tribunal did send some of the refugees to the Isle of Man and a few to Canada or Australia. Fink recalls, 'We saw each of them off with a sleeping bag and a food parcel.' Only one person was placed in 'Category A' (the most dangerous), a young German boy who had been teaching at the local school of languages. The authorities were sorry to have to send him to prison and keen to ensure he had kosher food in his cell. McNeill was drafted to become a welfare worker for the women in 'Category B' who had been sent to Armagh women's jail.

Norah Douglas was another of Davey's colleagues who sat on the refugee committee. The eldest child of Quaker parents, Norah was born in Northern Ireland and from 1929 ran the Friends' School in Lisburn with her husband. Stirred by the events of 1938, Norah opened the school to several refugee children from Germany and worked tirelessly to raise awareness of the plight of Jews and non-Aryan Christians. As she wrote when taking in her first refugee child, '[...] we have shared in efforts to get public opinion stirred up locally. We have one boy among our pupils and he is getting on well but here too the magnitude of the problem laughs at our puny efforts.' This was something of an understatement – Norah personally helped at least five or six children and used a precious petrol ration to travel all around the province to visit the refugees to ensure their welfare.

While busy supporting the refugees who found themselves in Northern Ireland, Davey didn't forget about those left behind in the Reich. In early 1940, Davey conducted a service in German at the Presbyterian College Chapel in Belfast. It was attended by many of the refugees in the city and his message was to reach out to the many Germans and Austrians living under Hitler's regime, but in particular to provide moral support to, 'Millions of Germans imprisoned within the Reich who dare not raise their voice in protest.' He added, 'For the pitiful refugees in our midst, there is only sympathy, coupled with as much practical help as possible.'

By the summer of 1940, the Belfast Refugee Committee had 80 refugees under its care, 25 of whom were children. By then, some had gone to England, while others had been caught up in the internment round-ups. The situation created considerable indignation amongst the people of Northern Ireland. Writing in the Belfast Newsletter on 2 August 1940, Moya Woodside (probably a refugee committee member) cited several instances where she believed injustices had occurred. 'These people, our guests, have been deprived by the Nazis of their homes, possessions and occupations […]' She outlined how a university student had been imprisoned in a Belfast jail and been deported to Australia, 'He is entirely without means, and, when interned, was only given time to pack a small suitcase.' She talked about summary arrests and the subsequent destitution of refugee families living in the Province. In one case, she cited the predicament of a refugee businessman's wife who had suffered a stroke as a result of her husband's internment. Woodside's angry letter prompted a supportive response from Anne Calvert, who wrote: 'The citizens of Ulster have been most generous and warm-hearted towards the refugees from Nazi oppression who have found a home here.' She reported that many internees were desperately asking for food parcels and urged that the government free them and allow as many as possible to join the Pioneer Corps.

As Davey's committee worked through the war years, a parallel organisation run by Belfast's Jewish committee put its energies into running a refugee training farm at Millisle in County Down. It was organised by the Bachad Fellowship, a religious Zionist movement, and a lease on 70 acres of arable land was negotiated by Barney Hurwitz, the president of the Belfast Hebrew Congregation. Financial support came from the Jewish community in Dublin, together with the Agricultural Committee in Bloomsbury House, and among the first arrivals were a small group of young refugees who had gone to Dublin. The farm was in operation from 1939 right up to its closure in 1948. After the war Peggy volunteered to work at the former Bergen-Belsen concentration camp now operating as a hospital and rehabilitation centre. She helped innumerable survivors unite with missing relatives.

Ernest Davey died from cancer in 1960. His old friend, Rabbi Schachter, wrote from Jerusalem, 'Ulster has lost a great son and the Jewish people a great friend.' Later Rabbi Schachter described Davey as, 'an illustrious scholar and great humanist.' His biographer, Austin Fulton, said of Davey, 'He was a man of penetrating insight, clear understanding and broad sympathies [...] He was also the embodiment of courageous conviction.' Fighting off heresy charges and standing up for refugees was certainly testament to his courage and staunch principles.

Chapter 20

The Rabbi

Rabbi Dr Solomon Schonfeld

Rabbi Dr Solomon Schonfeld, Image 26

If ever the epithet of a 'one person British rescuer' applied to the pantheon of helpers during the 1930s refugee crisis, it was Rabbi Dr Solomon Schonfeld. Eschewing the bureaucracy of committees and the niceties of diplomacy, he was driven by one overriding passion: to save as many of his fellow Jews as possible and in the quickest possible way. He risked his life many times by travelling to Nazi Germany and Austria, firstly to secure the escape of orthodox rabbis and scholars, and then to organise what was effectively his own 'Schonfeld Kindertransport' for hundreds of children. His efforts did not diminish during the war and some of his plans were truly audacious, not least his purchase of a Caribbean island as a potential refuge.

It is said, although no definitive number has ever been confirmed, that he personally arranged safe havens for over 1,000 Jewish refugees from orthodox communities in Europe. From the November Pogroms until the end of the war (and beyond), Schonfeld was driven to save children not only from the Nazi clutches but also what he saw as the perils of assimilation in Britain. He spearheaded a vigorous campaign against Jewish children being sent to live in Christian homes, whether or not the motivation of the hosts was a missionary one, and was vocal in his condemnation of sending children from Jewish homes in Germany, Poland and Czech lands to Christian families.

Something of a verbal street fighter, the battling rabbi often took on what he dismissed as 'the Jewish establishment' led by people like Otto Schiff. He was dismayed that in his view the Refugee Children's Movement (RCM) and Schiff's committee paid little heed to the fostering of Jewish children in non-Jewish homes. This was somewhat unfair as the Jewish Refugees Committee and the Refugee Children's Movement were concerned that Jewish education be continued in even the furthest flung homes. Later in the war, Schonfeld raised the hackles of Schiff and others by characterising the work of the RCM as a 'children's estrangement movement'. Nor did he sympathise with liberal and reform clergy such as Rabbi van der Zyl, who sat on the JRC as a religious pastor to many of the Jewish refugee children who did not identify as orthodox Jews. He felt that such people should call themselves by the title of 'father' and not 'rabbi'. Solomon Schonfeld may have known how to make enemies but he certainly influenced people.

Known to his friends and congregants as Solly, the rabbi was born in London in 1912. He was the son of an orthodox rabbi with a passion for Jewish education. Solly, a tall, blue-eyed, strikingly handsome six-footer, charismatic, full of energy, irresistibly persuasive yet self-effacing and modest, was something of a prodigy. He earned his rabbinical title at the tender age of 21 and at the same time was awarded a doctorate from the University of Konigsberg. He took over from his father the headship of Britain's first Jewish Day School and in 1940 married the daughter of the Chief Rabbi, Joseph Hertz.

Alarmed by the indifference of Kindertransport pioneers to the religious needs of the children, Solly set up his own organisation, The Chief Rabbi's Religious Emergency Council (CRREC). Though it recruited several hundred volunteers, the CRREC was Schonfeld's baby. He ran the council with his customary flair, often relying on his innate chutzpah to get what he wanted – even from the labyrinthine Home Office – and cutting corners where necessary, telling a few white fibs if needed and setting himself a bar so high that it would have dizzied any other mortal.

A classic example of the Schonfeld approach to refugee rescue is seen in his housing of 300 orthodox children from Vienna who required landing permits to come to England. A Home Office official wanted to know where the children would be accommodated and Solly assured him that he had enough space to put up beds in the two empty school buildings for which he was responsible. The pupils had broken up for the Chanukah holidays but the official noted on his visit that in his opinion only 250 of the refugees could be housed. Schonfeld's response was typical – he had a large home and the extra 50 youngsters could easily be cared for by his family. Impressed by this tenacity, the official granted Schonfeld the right to bring the 300 desperate children out of danger. They came on two Kindertransports.

Housing the children in the schools could only be a temporary measure – what would happen after the winter holiday? One of the rabbi's volunteers recalled his solution to this problem. A team went from house to house in north London's Jewish community knocking on doors to ask if they would take in a 'frum' (orthodox) refugee boy or girl. The response was not all that positive – many said they had little or no room but in the end gave way to Schonfeld's dogged determination.

Schonfeld also managed to rescue around 200 Jewish scholars, rabbis and their families from brutal persecution in Vienna. To receive the required paperwork, the rabbi had to convince the Home Office that the essential jobs were available in the UK – ones that could not be filled by Britons. He persuaded the officials that there was a shortage of experts who could knot the fringes on Jewish prayer shawls and that only the men from Vienna could do this.

This was not all. It was said that he would often shave a year off the age of a 17-year-old to ensure they were eligible for a Kindertransport permit to land. He also dreamed up a helpful yeshiva plan. A yeshiva – a religious seminary – needed both students and teachers (the latter he would insist to Home Office officials were in short supply in Britain). He set up a 'paper yeshiva' whose notional existence gave the green light to rabbis and students alike. A future Chief Rabbi, Immanuel Jakobovits, was one of fifty yeshiva students brought over in one of Schonfeld's many transports.

He would stop at nothing to get the Jews out of danger. One 17-year-old refugee girl was desperate to bring her four siblings to Britain. She was not alone; this was the desire of most if not all of those who had made it to safety. The girl was advised to 'go to Dr Schonfeld'. He took up the case but told her that four children could not make up a kindertransport. 'We need more children! Get me more names of children in Vienna'. The girl wrote home and her father sent back a list of 25 children each of whom came on a Schonfeld Kindertransport. In the words of the refugee girl she described how she saw Schonfeld, 'send drivers to Oxford Street with hand-written instructions; they returned with truckloads of cots, beds, towels, blankets, and pillows [...] Soon Mrs. Schonfeld's beautiful parlour looked like the dormitory of a camp. What a joy it was when my sisters arrived in London on December 22, 1938!' Her brother aged ten, arrived three weeks later.

When the war began and the gates of freedom were shut tight, Rabbi Schonfeld turned his attention to the needs of orthodox boys and girls – including refugees – who had to be evacuated out of London. Fearing their dispersal to non-kosher homes, he set up a special school in the Bedfordshire village of Shefford. With the children boarded out to local families (there were no Jews here and most of the population had never met one before), Schonfeld set up classrooms in a series of hired halls including the village centre. According to the Jewish Chronicle:

'A kosher canteen has been instituted for lunches, and provides a full lunch daily and it is possible to have meat several times a week and always Sabbaths and Festivals. On the High Festivals, services [are] attended by 300 including 85 living in neighbouring villages'

One of the rabbi's first acts once the children were billeted in Shefford was to arrive in his car which was stuffed with boxes of kosher sausages.

There was no slackening in Schonfeld's activities to aid 'his' refugees during the war. He took a keen interest in the orthodox inmates of the internment camps and managed to secure the release of around 1,000 detainees.

When the horrors of the Nazi genocide against the Jews became public knowledge (from at least December 1942), the rabbi led a one-man campaign to find safe havens for those managing to escape the ghettos and camps. He lobbied Parliament and found a sympathetic ear in William Temple, the Archbishop of Canterbury and also Eleanor Rathbone MP. With their support he set up his own Council for Rescue from Nazi Massacres. His vision was to lobby the British government to offer safe havens for European Jewry in the colonies and dominions. His ambition was to persuade countries under Nazi influence but not yet occupation (Hungary for example) to give its Jews protection from deportation. Sadly the scheme came to nothing not least because of objections in Parliament. Schonfeld pressed on with ultimately fruitless plans to offer Ethiopia as a temporary haven. He even purchased an island in the Bahamas, Stranger's Key, in the hope that it would provide threatened Jews with a kind of protective British citizenship. Parliament rejected the bold idea. Unphased, Rabbi Schonfeld tried to open up Ethiopia as a place of at least temporary refuge. That too was turned down.

After the war, Solly's energy and burning passion to save the Jews never dimmed. He embarked on a courageous, one might say, foolhardy, mission to help the thousands of Jewish children who had survived the Holocaust in Poland, either in the camps or by being hidden with non-Jewish families. Most had been orphaned and had lost what Jewish heritage they had. Schonfeld wasted no time in going out to Poland. There is a photograph of Solly Schonfeld taken around this time. He is gazing at the camera under a smart military cap, a crisp uniform clearly visible. But Schonfeld held no rank and was not a member of the British army. He had in fact designed the uniform himself, the general of his own Schonfeld Army determined to bring the Polish-Jewish children back to the orthodox fold.

Throughout the winter of 1945 through to 1946, Poland faced turbulent times. An undeclared civil war between ethnic Poles and Ukrainians had caught the few surviving Polish Jews in the thick of violent disorder. Pre-war antisemitism had returned with a vengeance (there was a bloody pogrom in the city of Kielce in 1946) and a bearded English Jew seeking out foster children was not a welcome sight for many Poles. What might have made a difference was this seemingly high-ranking military officer who had the bearing (and the uniform) of an allied official looking like someone who should be listened to. Issuing orders (without in truth any authority apart from his own), the rabbi helped to set up soup kitchens, open up makeshift synagogues out of the ruins of those destroyed by the Nazi occupiers and where necessary offer bribes to prise Jewish children from Polish foster families reluctant to part with their charges. One of Schonfeld's most audacious acts of rescue was the chartering of a ship carrying 150 boys and girls from Gdansk to England. He even accompanied them on the journey teaching them English songs such as 'Daisy Daisy'. Between 1945 and 1947, Schonfeld made innumerable trips to Poland bringing out hundreds of Jewish orphans to be housed in orthodox families in Britain. All the arrangements were made by the rabbi and his team.

Schonfeld's fake uniform also stood him in good stead for his visits to the displaced persons' camps in Germany – where most of the rump of European Jewry now survived. Barking orders and using his considerable energy and guile, the faux officer brought kosher food, medical supplies and prayer shawls to the needy living in camps that had been places of torment, starvation and murder during the war. Rabbi Schonfeld's last rescue transport was a group of 150 children from Prague in 1948.

It is not clear how many Jews Rabbi Solomon Schonfeld managed to save – perhaps thousands. When once asked 'how many did you save?', his reply was typical, 'How many didn't I save?' Though a largely forgotten figure, Solomon Schonfeld's rescue achievements were finally recognised in 2013 when he was posthumously awarded the medal of 'British Hero of the Holocaust'.

PART III:
BEYOND THE KINDERTRANSPORT

Chapter 21

The Refugee
Anna Essinger

Anna Essinger, Image 27

For those child refugees sent from Germany to Bunce Court School in England, one figure stands out in their memory: a large, determinedly tough lady with thick round glasses (a consequence of her near blindness), a strict demeanour and, behind her brusque facade, a loving nature. Her name was Anna Essinger. Universally known by her pupils as 'Tante Anna' or 'TA', she was the founder and principal of the school, a boarding establishment in the Kentish village of Otterden, which provided a secure home for at least 400 refugee children, most of them Jewish.

Anna Essinger was born in the German city of Ulm in 1879,

one of nine children. At the age of twenty, she was invited by an aunt to study in the USA, where she attended the University of Wisconsin. Of Jewish descent, a non-Zionist and a progressive thinker, in America she became attracted to the social, though never the religious, principles of the Quakers, by whom she was sent in 1919 to Southern Germany to work in one of their famine relief centres.

Essinger's passion was for coeducational schooling and progressive education, ideas which were gaining support in post-war Weimar Germany; she was in close touch with other educational reformers such as A. S. Neill, the founder of Summerhill School in England. Anna's sister Klara was also passionate about these new ideas and, after founding a children's home in 1919, decided to build a new school at Herrlingen in the Swabian Jura mountains near Ulm. Anna was invited to become its first head teacher in 1926 and, assisted by other women, including Anna's sister Paula, the school soon flourished and gained a reputation for its Montessori-like approach to learning. This emphasised communal living and cooperation, mutual respect and collective responsibility. The school, which was non-denominational, focused on modern languages and physical exercise, and music, art and drama were essential elements in the education of the young people in its care.

In 1933, Essinger was quick to recognise the dangers posed by the Nazis to her Jewish pupils, her staff and herself. As she wrote ten years later: 'We had many friends in the village, but all that happened in Germany on 1 April, 1933, had its repercussions even in that out-of-the-way place.' She felt that Nazi Germany was no place to bring up children in honesty and freedom, and, having determined to set up another school, began to look for a suitable location. She investigated Switzerland first, then Holland, before settling on England, where she had a few friends. She paid a visit to London in June 1933 and began to make all the necessary arrangements, including getting permission from the Home Office.

Throughout the summer of 1933, Essinger informed the children and their parents of the intended move abroad. Meanwhile, her friends in England discovered Bunce Court, a large 17th century manor house in 25 acres of rural Kent. It featured attractive parkland and gardens, several outhouses, a cottage and, by the time the first group arrived, a large hut suitable for the older boys (built by members of the small committee her friends had formed to collect funds to buy beds and furniture).

The move out of Nazi Germany was not without its dangers; Anna did not want to alert the authorities to the fact that Jewish children were being evacuated to England. Accordingly, she arranged for the pupils to be sent abroad in groups led by one or two adults and to depart from different towns in Germany. The groups would then reunite in Dover and make their way by buses to Bunce Court. Anna herself took one group of children on an 'educational trip' to the Netherlands but in fact stayed on the train until they reached England; her sister Paula did likewise via Switzerland. According to one of her former pupils, Leslie Brent, 'This mass emigration thus escaped the notice of the Nazi authorities who otherwise might have created difficulties and possibly imposed financial sanctions'. The school building she left behind was given to Field Marshall Rommel as his country home and it was here in 1944, that he decide to take his own life after being implicated in the attempted assassination of Hitler.

The first group of sixty-five children arrived in Kent on 5 October 1933 and school started the next day. That first winter had its problems: there were outbreaks of diphtheria and scarlet fever, as well as worries about whether the remaining children would arrive safely from Germany. Pressure for more places was already growing. As Essinger recalled, 'There were more applications than we could accept [...] By 1934, many parents had made up their minds to emigrate themselves, and they wanted their children taken care of whilst they were preparing to leave.'

Essinger immediately faced the challenge of finding English teachers and support staff who would be empathetic to the needs of her German-speaking charges. Few seemed able to fully comprehend the plight of young people fleeing from racial persecution. Despite the problems, however, she was ultimately successful in staffing the school with a highly dedicated, enthusiastic team and, in most cases, unusually for that time, child-centred teachers who shared her educational philosophy.

Daily lessons were held in small groups and from the outset Essinger was determined to take in a proportion of English and non-Jewish pupils. One of these was the young Londoner, Harold Jackson, later the Washington correspondent and columnist for 'The Guardian' newspaper. In later years he recalled 'TA' and the school regime with great affection and noted lessons were taught in a strange mash up of English and German. Working in the school kitchen, the lad allowed a saucepan to almost boil dry. The cook, Gretl Heidt, screamed at him to 'shit some water in' – mistakenly drawing on the German verb 'schütten' meaning 'to pour'.

The curriculum at Bunce Hall was largely humanities based – there were no resources for science labs – though an Englishman, Dennis Brind, taught biology. Thanks to Brind's scholarly influence, his pupil Leslie Brent went on to become a distinguished professor of immunology, one of many who owed their career successes to Bunce Court. Essinger's teachers comprised a mixture of British staff and former refugees such as Lotte Kalischer, who taught violin and gave classical recitals on the school grand piano; Hilde Oppenheimer, who taught French; and their fellow German Jewish exiles Hanna Barges (who would also assist Anna for a while at Dovercourt camp) and Essinger's sisters, Klara and Paula.

The emphasis on music, art and drama perhaps goes some way to explaining the prominence of creative figures among the Bunce Court alumni. One of the most famous of these ex-pupils was the artist Frank Auerbach. A business partner of Auerbach's uncle was a friend of the American writer, Iris Origo, who was based in Italy. Origo, who had also started her own school and been in correspondence with Essinger, arranged for Frank and two other children to be accepted at Bunce Court. In April 1939 Frank boarded the SS Washington from Hamburg, bound for the USA via Southampton, from where he and the other children travelled to London by train and were met by a representative of Bunce Court. The regime at the school would suit Auerbach's personality and he was very happy there. Another pupil inspired by the Bunce Court arts curriculum – in this case its rich theatrical life – was Frank Marcus, who fled to Britain with his parents in 1939 and whose play The Killing of Sister George won international plaudits in the 1960s. Music, art and theatre would also influence the career of one of the school's more eccentric pupils, Gerard Hoffnung. The celebrated humourist, musician, artist and cartoonist attended Bunce Court after coming to Britain just before the war. His premature death at the age of thirty-four would shock admirers of his offbeat drawings, monologues and concerts such as his Concerto For

Orchestra and Vacuum Cleaners.

Shortly after Auerbach arrived at the school, the younger children were moved into their own accommodation, Dane Court, about ten miles from Bunce Court. Their young house teacher, Gwynne Badsworth, resembled a kindly mother figure to the small children, reading bedtime stories to them and giving them baths. Auerbach recalled: 'She didn't have any of this nonsense about not speaking English, so within three or four weeks we all were able to communicate in English. We were enrolled as Wolf Cubs or Brownies and did country dancing in the hall.'

Essinger's role as headteacher was principally to set the tone of the school – she demanded high standards of everyone, though she could be seen by many as a rather dour, often distant character. Her primary responsibility was raising finances for the school, an essential task as money was a constant concern, especially during the war years. She was successful in attracting wealthy donors and made many influential friends such as Norman Bentwich, who described her as 'a refugee teacher of strong personality'.

It was Essinger who insisted that the language spoken in Bunce Court was English. Leslie Brent remembers that it would be a brave pupil who continued to speak German in her presence. He recalls her sitting at the top table at meal times and whenever the noise of chatter got too loud, she would bring the dining room to heel with her cry of 'silence, please' – always stretching out that second word. On one of her birthdays, the Bunce Court staff gave her a small silver bell inscribed with the characters 'pleeeaaase!!!'.

Essinger was keen to ensure that the refugee children could meet English families, partly to learn the language and culture of their host nation, but also to provide them with a holiday break. Leslie Brent, for example, was introduced to a Mr Baulch, a railway worker, and his wife, who lived in Basingstoke. They invited him to their house for tea and took him on trips to the seaside in their little Austin 7 car. In the summer of 1939, they offered to adopt Leslie and discussed it with Essinger who told them that the decision had to be made by the boy himself. Leslie didn't have to think too hard – as far as he was concerned he was not an orphan and to have agreed to the wishes of the Baulchs would have been an act of disloyalty to his living parents.

As the situation for Jews in Germany deteriorated, the applications for places grew beyond the financial capacity of the school, especially as it took in ten to twelve boarders whose parents or family were unable to pay any fees. To compound this challenge, there was a very high turnover of pupils and from October 1933 to December 1938, 319 children were enrolled and 195 left. In the pre-war months, the numbers entering and leaving were almost identical and many children were placed in the school while they awaited more permanent homes with British foster families.

December 1938 saw Anna Essinger taking charge of the temporary refugee camp at Dovercourt in Essex for a few weeks. Through private gifts, the school was able to accommodate some of the unaccompanied children from Dovercourt who were housed in two annexes, one being a former hospital in Faversham which was offered rent-free by the Town Council. Thirty of the youngest children were housed at an old farmhouse in Chilham.

Just before war was declared, the supporters of Bunce Court raised a mortgage to buy the land from the leaseholders and many of the children were able to live on site rather than in the annexes. However, being close to the Channel coast, in June 1940, Essinger was given a week's notice to quit Bunce Court when the district was declared out of bounds for 'enemy aliens'. She immediately began to search for suitable alternative premises and soon found Trench Hall in Shropshire through her network of friends and contacts. Some of her pupils were temporarily housed in Stoatley Rough, a school in Haslemere, Surrey.

The logistical challenge to move an entire school within a matter of days was considerable. She saw the house on 8 June, signed a lease the day after and within 24 hours the German teachers at Bunce Court, along with all pupils over 16 years of age had left Kent for the journey to Shropshire, complete with sheets, blankets, 120 mattresses and enough food for two days. Beds and cooking facilities soon followed in a fleet of hired lorries, but to Anna's regret they had to leave the school's large library behind.

Anna Essinger's move to Shropshire presented real challenges – even for her. Trench Hall was only one fifth of the size of the Bunce Court estate; the house had been left empty for years, the water supply was inadequate, the roof leaked and the plumbing was bad. The 125 children plus staff who relocated there had to work hard to make it habitable. As Essinger recalled, 'Walls had to be distempered, schoolrooms prepared, bedrooms made out of garages and stables, a nearby grazing field rented and ploughed up in order to feed us'.

Despite all this, TA's vision and optimism came to the fore: 'The park shows signs of past splendour which we may restore. There is an overgrown rose garden which can be adapted to serve as an open air theatre.' She and her depleted team managed to feed the children from the land for the first year, and they seemed to thrive on it: the top form sat for their School Certificate examination only one month after they arrived, and all of them passed. As children left the school, many were not replaced due to pressure on space. The facilities at Trench Hall could only comfortably accommodate eighty children, around a quarter of whom were English. Despite this, local youths would occasionally scream 'dirty Jerries' at the pupils (though in general relations with neighbours were good, there were occasional tensions). In 1945, for instance, TA would not allow the children to attend the local cinema (to see Olivier's 'Henry V'). She had heard that the programme included a newsreel report of the liberation of Bergen-Belsen concentration camp and, with its shocking footage of emaciated prisoners and corpses, would stir up local youths to take it out on the pupils.

One of TA's first tasks at Trench Hall was to try to discover the fate of many of the parents left behind in Nazi-controlled Europe. She quickly came to a bleak conclusion writing in August 1940 that, '[...] for a very large number we have no assurance that their parents are still alive [...] I have tried to investigate through the Red Cross.'

Most of the children at Trench Hall were housed in the main building, but the older boys slept in dormitories in a group of converted stables. At night time, although there were the usual youthful high jinks, the news that TA was on her way to inspect the 'dorms' meant that the lights-out rules were quickly applied. She was a stickler for good manners and correct posture. Leslie Brent remembered an incident when TA was passing the lavatory block. Seeing one of the doors unlocked, she pushed against it only to see a boy sitting on the toilet. Unphased by this discovery she barked at the lad, 'Sit up straight!'

At Trench Hall the older boys were encouraged to help out

the local farmer, thus gaining valuable skills in agriculture in the process. Essinger also encouraged all pupils to take an interest in the progress of the war and posted extracts from the Manchester Guardian and the New Statesman on a wall in the building. As in Kent, drama played an important role in the children's development. Frank Auerbach took on various acting roles, including Fabian in Twelfth Night, which was directed by Wilhelm Marckwald, the school's gardener and boilerman who, prior to 1933, had been a distinguished actor, director and producer in Germany. After the war Auerbach helped paint the scenery for theatrical productions mounted by his old school friend, Frank Marcus.

At both Bunce Court and Trench Hall, Anna expected her pupils to help out with daily tasks such as washing up, gardening and carpentry, and each week a list of duties was posted so that the children could indicate a preference. As we have seen, the kitchen was dominated by Gretl Heidt, a German non-Jewish émigré. She was legendary among former pupils as an excellent cook, who was sorely missed when she was interned as an enemy alien on the Isle of Man in 1940.

All the refugee men and boys over sixteen were also interned, along with three older girls. Hans Meyer, a married teacher, became another victim of Churchill's order to 'collar the lot'. He had come to England in 1934 as a Jewish refugee unable to continue his medical studies. Meyer helped teach in the carpentry workshop at Bunce Court and also supervised the early morning open-air gymnastics – an activity that did not meet with universal approval by the pupils, despite his having an outstanding relationship with them. Meyer's role at the school came to an abrupt end when he was arrested and transported on SS Dunera to be interned in Australia. The ship became notorious for the brutal treatment of internees on board by the British crew. Meyer survived the experience and eventually returned to England in 1944 where he rejoined the school. At the end of the war Essinger took several youngsters into the school, who had survived the concentration camps in Germany, or had been in hiding in Poland. As victims at Auschwitz-Birkenau concentration camp, each had had tattoos given to them; at first none of them spoke English but they soon settled down with remarkable speed.

In 1946 Anna supervised the return of the school to its premises at Bunce Court. What she found there was a very run-down and badly maintained set of buildings that had been commandeered by the army. She set about restoring the school and stayed on in charge until it finally closed in 1948. This for her was not an easy decision but one forced by financial pressures, her advancing blindness and a reluctance to hand the school over to others. There was also a suggestion that TA was getting tired, '[...] one cannot expect people to be pioneers all their lives.' After the school closed Anna and her sisters lived out their lives in the grounds of their beloved Bunce Court. Many former pupils came to visit the old lady and regular reunions of 'Old Bunce Courtians' continued to be held for many decades.

The impact of Bunce Court on those who were educated there cannot be overstated. According to Veronica Gillespie, who worked at Bloomsbury House during the war, 'I always knew a Bunce Court child when they walked into my office. They were confident, well spoken, and courteous. Most of the Kindertransport children were timid and mumbled in their effort not to offend anyone.'

Anna Essinger died in1960. Former pupil, Leslie Brent, said of her in his eulogy:

She devoted herself single-mindedly to the cause of education and the saving of young lives from the persecution of Nazi Germany, and in this she was sustained by an unshakeable faith in the idea of human progress [...] She was quite incapable of hating. I should be tempted to describe her as a perfect example of scientific humanism [...] Above all she had the courage of her convictions [...] Our grief at her passing may be tempered by the knowledge that Anna Essinger has truly had the satisfaction of realising the fulfilment of her life's work.

In the hot summer of 2018, a small group of surviving former pupils and their families gathered at the elegant country house in the Kentish countryside that once was home to Bunce Court School and its refugee teachers and pupils. They admired the old school bell now displayed in the front gardens, but their main purpose was to witness the unveiling of a plaque on the gateway presented by the Association for Jewish Refugees. There were moist eyes as the words of the plaque were read out loud:

'Anna Essinger 'Tante Anna' 1879-1960 Founder and Headmistress Bunce Court School 1933-1948 who gave a home and a sound education to hundreds of refugee children, mainly Jewish, during that time. Remembered with affection by so many for her great foresight, progressive educational endeavour, wisdom and compassion.'

Chapter 22

The Society Lady
Rachel Alexander

Portrait of Rachel Alexander, Image 28

Rachel Alexander was one of six daughters from a wealthy, influential banking family with Anglican and Quaker roots. In later life Rachel's concern for the less fortunate would have a profound effect on the life of a young Jewish refugee, Josef Meller.

In 1873 Rachel's father had bought Aubrey House, a grand eighteenth-century residence in London's leafy suburb of North Kensington, where Rachel was born two years later. For the Alexander children life was comfortable and well-connected: one sister, Cecily, was painted by Whistler and Rachel herself was sketched as a child by Ruskin.

While three of her sisters left home to be married, Rachel, together with her other sisters, Jean and Mary, continued to live at Aubrey House where they devoted their lives to philanthropic works. Rachel's instincts to help others surfaced dramatically during World War One.

In 1916, she accompanied a group of Quakers to the battlefields of France to work at the Friends' Mission in Lorraine. Its role was to house, clothe, feed and support the thousands of French people displaced by war. Showing great personal courage, Rachel drove supply lorries and took charge of finding work for the French refugee women. She ran a toy-making factory to employ young working-class girls and set up a successful embroidery business for French women which sustained their mental and physical wellbeing. She helped tend the wounded and saw at first hand the devastating effect of war on innocent civilians.

After the Armistice, the sisters returned to England and focused their efforts on providing decent and affordable accommodation for local families, buying and renovating flats for the poor of the borough who were living in squalid conditions in vermin-infested slums. Mary lobbied for improvements in the conditions of workhouses, a legacy of the nineteenth-century New Poor Law which was still on the statute book in the years leading up to the Second World War. What motivated the sisters to their philanthropy? According to their great nephew:

A whole welfare state in miniature was contrived by these determined spinster sisters and at the end of their day's work, they would return to their fifty-room mansion on top of Campden Hill. With feelings of guilt? No, just that of duty done.

Given their range of concerns, it is perhaps not surprising that with the rise of fascism in the 1930s the sisters became involved in the rescue of victims of persecution. In particular, Rachel's experience of the grim conditions endured by French refugees from German bombardment in Lorraine during the First World War, helped shape her determination to assist a whole new cohort of displaced persons and refugees in the lead-up to the Second. At the same time, her close ties with the Society of Friends served to bring sharp focus to the work.

Encouraged by her Quaker contacts, Rachel's first act was to set up a hostel for refugees in Westbourne Road, in London's Paddington district. She rented the building and paid for everything herself. Meanwhile, at Aubrey House Rachel was starting to receive what would become a flood of letters from Jews desperate to leave Germany. Complete strangers, hearing about Rachel's work through the Quakers in Germany, would write to Rachel begging for financial help which would give them the all-important right of asylum in Britain or elsewhere. One of the letters sent to Rachel illustrates the desperate plight of the Jews in the Reich: '[…] I entreat you with all my heart to help us in our great distress. This is indeed a question of life or death for me'.

In response to the growing crisis, Rachel Alexander threw open a country property she owned through her family connections, Andridge Farm near High Wycombe, for the use of incoming refugees. The farm accommodated around 37 refugees, mostly Jewish exiles from the German Reich. Among this mix of middle-class Jews were a child psychologist, a journalist, teachers, shopkeepers and musicians. It also included Mendel Meller, his wife Liebe and 18-year-old son Josef. Mendel had been a successful owner of a perfumery in Vienna – that is until

Hitler's laws robbed him of a livelihood. Josef was a bookish and rather serious child whose personality may have verged on the anxious. He had hopes of becoming a writer but these and all other aspirations came to a crushing halt when German troops effortlessly marched into Austria in March 1938. In accordance with Germany's Nuremburg Laws, young Josef was forbidden to attend school and the family's business was abruptly confiscated.

Mendel and Liebe heard about Rachel Alexander through the Quakers in Vienna and wrote to her asking for help to obtain a visa to come to the UK. With Rachel's assistance and support as financial guarantor, the Meller family were issued with temporary visas and negotiated exit papers from their local Gestapo offices. They duly arrived in England on 28 March 1939 and were accommodated at Rachel's hostel in Paddington before moving on to Aldridge Farm in the summer of that year.

Once the family were settled at the farm the young Josef could start to think again about his future. After having abandoned his original ambition to become a writer, he now planned to become an architect and go to college. But even these aspirations were dashed with the outbreak of war in September 1939, and with the decision to move him to Richborough near Sandwich in Kent.

It was here that Jewish refugee committees in London had set up a special refugee camp for up to 4,000 young Jews fleeing from the German Reich. The rows of wooden huts, previously a disused army facility, were known as the 'Kitchener Camp'. It was not in any sense a prison or internment camp: the young chaps were allowed to visit the nearby town, spend rest time in local cafés, flirt with the waitresses and marvel at a concoction totally unknown in their former homes: tea with milk.

Many made friends with locals and some inevitable romances

blossomed between the Jewish men and Kentish girls. The Kitchener Camp was designed to be a training ground for Jewish men who could learn new and employable skills such as carpentry, plumbing and building. The aim was to help these refugees become self-sufficient as quickly as possible so that they would not become a 'drain on the Exchequer'.

For Josef, the harsh, almost military, discipline of a camp whose function was to create robust trade and craftsmen was not for him. Nor were the temptations of local girls who took a shine to the exotic foreign men at the camp. During his brief time at the hostel in London, Josef encountered a young Jewish woman, Ilse Epstein at a left-wing society meeting. Born in Vienna in 1918, she had left the Reich to go first to Paris and then to London in June 1938. Josef and Ilse fell in love and later they would become man and wife.

Writing to Josef in the Kitchener Camp, from Andridge Farm in December 1939, Rachel told him that, 'To my great surprise nobody seems much to want to leave here – I thought that everybody would feel very dull so far from shops, concerts etc.' She went on to surmise that it was the cook's dishes that kept everyone down on the farm. It was probably also their sense of being safe and properly cared for, not to mention that there were very few other places they could go.

It was while at the Kitchener Camp that Josef began a regular correspondence with Rachel. He wrote to her, for instance, in his halting English, about his first Christmas, December 1939:

Dear Miss Alexander, the very next days will be Christmas and people all around the world will celebrate it. I never before celebrated Christmas as Jews generally do not. But this year the first time I shall do it in the camp as good as I can for there is a fierce desire of myself to have a feast this time.

Rachel's letters to Josef constantly ask about his welfare and assure him that she was struggling to get him sent back to Andridge Farm from his rather miserable bunk in the Kitchener Camp. On the 16th December 1939 she wrote: '..next week I do hope that you'll be safely back at Andridge. Everybody will be glad to see you back. You are to have a good rest and Mrs Kalisch (the cook), will fatten you up.'

This last remark is in response to a worrying piece of news heard by Josef's parents and Rachel. As Christmas approached, he had been ill, suffering from weakness and fainting fits. He had also developed several eye infections and the camp authorities thought him not well enough to stay in Richborough. Josef managed to write a New Year message to his benefactress that clearly showed his unhappiness:

'The camp life has its heaps of disadvantages and uncomfortable positions too.... The camp is just an institution, organised by a committee, there is no feeling of charity.'

Following the declaration of war on 3 September 1939, Josef was ordered to appear before a special tribunal to assess the degree of risk he posed to the British state. Josef was duly given a 'Category C' status which meant that, at least for the time being, he could continue at Richborough. Though not at all happy there – he found the conditions poor and was not cut out for robust physical work – at least he felt a sense of freedom; at least he was not in a German concentration camp like so many of his contemporaries who had not managed to get out in time.

All this changed in May 1940. With the fall of the Low Countries and France and the bitter defeat of the British army at Dunkirk, the threat of invasion became all the more pervasive and a warrant for Josef's arrest as an enemy alien was made. He was taken by a policeman from Richborough to a hastily enclosed camp in Huyton, a suburb of Liverpool. He was interned there from June to October 1940.

At Huyton, in effect a half-built council housing estate, conditions were poor (though not as bad as some camps, such as the rat-infested, crumbling former mill in Bury, Lancashire). The one bright spot in his rather bleak life was permission given to write to his girlfriend Ilse. Though opened by the official censor, Josef could at least inform his future wife that he was safe and well.

Huyton was always intended as a temporary solution to the 'enemy alien problem'. On the 10th October 1940, Josef and other inmates were sent by ship to a more permanent internment camp on the Isle of Man. This isolated UK territory, in the middle of the Irish Sea, had become the destination for up to 15,000 prisoners, at least 12,000 of whom were Jews who had fled from Nazi Europe. The term 'internment camp' may conjure up images of wooden huts, watch towers and barbed wire - and that last element was indeed a feature - but these Isle of Man camps were not purpose-built. They were often large houses, previously used as small hotels, which had been requisitioned and fenced off from the civilian public.

Josef was sent to the 'Mooragh Camp', a series of houses in the port of Ramsey. There on the island he joined a fellow 'Category C' enemy alien, his father Mendel. His mother Liebe was also an internee but in the special women's camp housed a few miles away in the former Falcon's Nest Hotel in Port Erin, on the south of the island.

As Josef languished in Mooragh Camp, he became somewhat

bored and frustrated that his plans for an architectural career were to be put on hold. Following his incarceration in Huyton and the Isle of Man, Rachel Alexander upped her game. She wrote to everyone she knew to try to get Josef released from internment. She wrote a string of hopeful letters to Josef, perhaps to raise his spirits more than to secure an actual chance of release. After release from the Isle of Man, she helped Josef find a place at architectural college and continued to be his financial supporter. She wrote reassuring letters to Ilse. One letter talks about how the Bishop of Liverpool had visited the camp and made friends with Josef. She offered advice about future re-emigration, urging the young couple not to leave England unless they really wanted to do so.

Among her many letters to Josef on the Isle of Man was this one sent in December 1940:

[...] how exceedingly sorry I am to hear that you can't leave the Isle of Man at present – I know how terribly hard it is for you to have nothing to do and not to be able to work – far worse for a clever man than for a stupid person.

Rachel tried to cheer Josef up with parcels of 'eatables' and hopes for a brighter future. Josef knew full well how much he owed his guarantor, who was also becoming a friend. On 3 April 1941, Josef was released from internment and married Ilse a few weeks later. Not long afterwards, with Rachel's help and continuing financial support Josef found a place at architectural college and was on his way to becoming a professional architect. He wrote to Miss Alexander recalling his first visit to her grand house in North Kensington and the sense of calm and order he found there after the turmoil of his immediate past in Vienna. It was the promise of a new life and he never forgot all she had done to help him fulfil it.

Among the many other people helped by Rachel Alexander was the former anti-Nazi journalist Edward Spiro, who had been another resident at Andridge Farm. Interned also on the Isle of Man, Spiro wrote to Rachel thanking her for helping his wife and son find refuge in Lledr Hall, a hostel in Wales run by a Christian charity: 'Now owing to your magnanimity, my family is in safety, and I like to thank you, Madam, for all your kindness and assistance which you have showed us once again.'

The Meller family kept in touch with Rachel Alexander for the rest of her life. When their second daughter was born, they named her after their benefactress. She, in turn, wrote to the Mellers saying how proud she was that the child was to be called Rachel. Sadly Ilse died in 1953 and Joseph remarried. His new wife, Ruth, and daughters Claudia, Sonia and Rachel, were often invited to charity garden parties at Aubrey House. Rachel Meller remembers receiving a postcard from her namesake offering good wishes for her tenth birthday. A year later in 1964, Rachel Alexander died aged 89.

Chapter 23

The Charity Worker
Leonard Montefiore

Leonard Montefiore, Image 29

'I have never conceived it my duty to follow blindly public opinion […] being hopelessly old fashioned.' Thus said Leonard Montefiore in a characteristically modest way. But it was this 'old fashioned' drive to stand above the crowd that helped save so many lives.

As the Second World War drew to an end, the horrific truth behind the Holocaust came into stark view. The news of the liberation of camps such as Belsen by the British, Buchenwald by the Americans and Theresienstadt by the Soviets soon reached Britain and voluntary agencies turned their attention to the rescue and rehabilitation of the survivors.

Among these were 732 teenagers - survivors of the camps - who were brought to Britain to recover and attempt to build new lives. The first arrivals were a group of 300 who were flown from Prague to Carlisle and housed in a hostel by Lake Windermere. The rest were dispersed in hostels around the UK. Among a group of British people who organised the rescue of the Jewish youngsters (all but 80 of them boys), was Leonard Montefiore, a member of an old Anglo-Jewish family. Montefiore was Chair of a rescue committee funded by the Central British Fund for German Jewry (CBF), the Committee for the Care of Children from the Concentration Camps, an organisation based at Bloomsbury House.

Montefiore was not a disciplined 'organisation' man, rather one who was willing to cut corners and do things his own way when necessary. Charming, scholarly, gentle but with a puckish sense of humour, he was filled with a sense of duty: a man who shunned the limelight but was tireless in his support of the less fortunate. He loved to portray himself as an old fossil – 'I must confess that whenever I go to Woburn House and pass the door of the Jewish Museum (which was based there at one time along with the CBF), I wonder whether my appropriate place is not there rather than anywhere else in the building.' In fact, he gave a lifetime of service to a variety of causes and always threw himself at them with full vigour. One of the most active founders of the CBF, he is credited with being a virtual guardian to scores of child refugees from the German Reich.

Leonard Nathaniel Goldsmid Montefiore (known as Robin by close friends and family) was born in London in 1889, the only child of Claude Montefiore, founder of Liberal Judaism in Britain, and Therese Schorstein. Italian in origin, the Montefiores had been in England since the mid-eighteenth century.

Tragically, Leonard's mother died in childbirth and he was raised by his grandmother, an experience that may well have determined his lifelong empathy with children in peril. After a period of home schooling, he was sent as a boarder to Clifton College in Bristol, where he eventually became Head of House; and in 1908 went up to Oxford to read History. Many visits to Germany ensured that he became fully fluent in German and it was said that he could recite whole passages of Goethe's Faust by heart. After graduating, Montefiore threw himself into social work as a resident of Toynbee Hall, a radical 'settlement' in the East End of London which aimed to bring education and welfare to the poor. He was on active service throughout the First World War as an officer with the 9th (Territorial) Battalion of the Hampshire Regiment, as well as serving in India and Northern Russia, and was awarded the OBE for his wartime services.

After demobilisation, Montefiore immersed himself in worthy Jewish causes, including the Jews' Temporary Shelter (whose president from 1922 to 1948 was the banker and philanthropist Otto Schiff who became a close friend). From 1926 to 1939, Montefiore established himself as a leading figure in the Anglo-Jewish Association. He was president of the Association when Hitler came to power, an event which filled him with dismay, not only as a Jew but because Germany was a country he had grown to love. Linking up with his old friend Neville Laski at the Board of Deputies of British Jews, Montefiore used his fluent German to painstakingly follow the rising tide of anti-Jewish actions in the Nazi state and to warn the British government of the increasing peril faced by Germany's Jews. He was closely involved with the creation of both the Jewish

Refugees Committee and the Central British Fund, the main fundraising body for Jewish refugees from Germany, in support of whom he helped raise millions of pounds as joint chairman of the CBF Appeal.

By 1945 Leonard Montefiore had become treasurer of the CBF and in the spring of that year, together with Otto Schiff, he set about obtaining permits from the Home Office for admitting up to 1,000 child survivors from the zones of occupation (though in the end, of those, only 732 were admitted); Bertha Bracey and her Germany Emergency Committee took responsibility for non-Jewish victims. Montefiore had been in Paris in May 1945 and had witnessed at first hand the physical state of many of the survivors of the concentration camps: 'I have never seen anything so ghastly in my life', he recalled. 'The people I saw were like corpses who walked.' He was under no illusion about the challenges that lay ahead, but he was equally clear-sighted about the qualities required to meet them. 'The orphans have no homes except the substitutes we can provide', he would later write. 'They have no one to care for them and no one to love them. I use the word "love" deliberately. After all, it is love that makes men into missionaries or sends others to work in leper colonies, yes, and in D.P. [displaced persons] camps.'

Under Montefiore's influence, in the year following VE Day, the CBF set aside some £300,000 (nearly £12 million at today's value) for the support of Jewish survivors. Just under half this sum was spent on orphaned youngsters brought to Britain. In August 1945, Montefiore was informed by representatives of the United Nations Relief and Rehabilitation Administration (UNRRA) that several hundred young Jewish people from Theresienstadt ghetto and other camps were gathered in Prague and fit to travel. They also reported that the RAF had room on ten Stirling aircraft which were due to fly back to England. Montefiore's team set about activating the permits allowed by the Home Office, which had ruled that orphaned children up to the age of sixteen could be admitted. However, the practical application of this ruling was immediately thrown into question, since few of the children possessed any official documents certifying their date of birth. Several arrived in Britain sporting beards and looking considerably older than their supposed ages. According to Norman Bentwich, who was also there to welcome the young people, the immigration officials were determined to turn a blind eye to the letter of the law: 'No questions were asked; and it may well be that no group of immigrants has ever entered this country with a more sympathetic welcome or with fewer formalities.'

So it was that on 14 August 1945 the first of 300 children arrived in the Lake District. The planes landed at Crosby-on-Eden airfield and their passengers were welcomed by two members of the Carlisle Women's Voluntary Service (WVS) and various officials including Montefiore, Bentwich and Joan Stiebel, executive director of the CBF. Stiebel, who for many years had been secretary to Otto Schiff, later recalled: 'When they arrived, the children were not in a very good shape. The plane had come down en route and the travellers had been plied with chocolate and oranges – not a good combination in rather choppy conditions!' She remembered seeing one of the boys throw up over an official who had come to welcome the group on the runway.

Their first home in England was to be on the Calgarth Estate at Troutbeck Bridge, Windermere – a wartime housing scheme built for workers producing the Sunderland Flying Boats. It was an extensive site with bungalows, shops, dining room and entertainment hall, and the young people were driven there in buses. Leonard Montefiore and others got to work to ensure that, after the group had been welcomed with cocoa and biscuits and their first full meal, they were issued with clothes that fitted and given thorough medical examinations. One of the helpers, Berish Lerner, himself a former refugee, had been working on preparing the accommodation for weeks. When he heard the news of the children's impending arrival there was great excitement among his fellow volunteers:

During the waiting period, we had many discussions and numerous questions were raised: how would we be able to cope with these traumatised youngsters who had been subjected to almost five years of persecution and witnessed wholesale murder, most of whom had lost their families? We asked ourselves whether we could succeed at all in bringing back to them some semblance of what was considered 'normal'.

Lerner and his colleagues also mused over what religious instruction the children would require and pondered their reactions to such exposure given their experiences. Would Jewish learning be welcome, or would they resent such influences?

The psychological wellbeing of the youngsters was delegated to Oscar Friedmann, a psychoanalyst and social worker, who had been involved in the planning of the programme since it was first mooted. Something of a pioneer in the treatment of troubled adolescents, Friedmann seems to have made the welfare of children his life's work.

Though conditions in Windermere were somewhat spartan, what the youngsters found was beyond their imaginations: a real bed, clean sheets, a room to themselves. A local dentist calling in to check their dental health observed that most of the boys had not cleaned their teeth in five years. After their medical examination, some of the children were sent to recover in an isolation ward in a hospital near Ashford, while those with more serious ailments were cared for at another hospital. This side of their care was arranged by Lola Hahn-Warburg. As the person called upon to deal with troubled and difficult youngsters who appeared at Bloomsbury House, Hahn-Warburg had established herself as 'the reigning expert on children who were at odds with their foster parents or teachers or employers, or simply with themselves' and was a dedicated hospital visitor for those former refugees who had been taken ill. A mother of two, she kept a close eye on the new arrivals in the Lake District.

Another member of the Windermere team was Alice Goldberger, a forty-eight-year-old former refugee who had been appointed to look after the younger incomers. Goldberger's ability to provide professional loving care for the children derived in part from her background running a centre for underprivileged children in Berlin. It was also a by-product of a fortuitous friendship with Anna Freud. Alice was a much-loved figure whose reputation was given national exposure when her former charges and assistants paid tribute to her in a 1979 edition of the popular TV programme of the day, This is Your Life.

Looking after the teenagers in the Lake District was no easy task; they had learned to survive by whatever means they could. There were fights over clothes and shoes, and Joan Stiebel observed that some of the children 'stole' bread – a habit retained from their brutal treatment in the camps. Indeed, one lad remarked to Elaine Laski that the reason he was still alive was that 'I was strong enough to take a piece of bread from someone too weak to eat it'. Leonard Montefiore displayed a modest sanguinity and patience in the face of these challenges:

They have been in contact with every kind of vice and wickedness the mind can conceive. For them, during the whole of their childhood, honesty was the very worst policy. It led immediately to destruction. How can they be expected to learn, in a short while, the reverse of the maxim taught to them by bitter experience?

Montefiore and his team ensured that the youngsters were given a thorough basic education. He organised lessons not only in the English language – compulsory English classes were given each day – but in science and maths. Jewish history was considered an important element in the curriculum, and a rabbi, who also played football with the youngsters, was on hand to teach it. Berish Lerner recalled:

I was astonished and delighted to find that most of the boys had such a lively interest in many subjects; they seemed to have an insatiable thirst for knowledge. It was obvious that, having missed most of their formal schooling throughout much of the war, they were eagerly mopping up any knowledge that might come their way.

However, it was not all serious learning at Windermere. There were bicycling excursions into the Lakeland countryside, and the boys were treated to films in the large dining hall, which was equipped with a projector and screen. Lerner providing a live simultaneous translation into Yiddish, the dominant language of the group, for classics such as The Hunchback of Notre Dame. Nor were athletics neglected: the group included Sir Ben Helfgott, who went on to become a weightlifting Olympian representing Great Britain, his adopted country.

In October 1945 it was decided that the younger children would be better cared for separately. Six of the youngest, aged three and four, were taken to a house in West Hoathly, Sussex, donated by Lady Clarke, wife of the local MP. Gertrud and

Sophie Dann, refugee sisters who had been state registered nurses in Germany, were charged with minding the children.

The camp for the older children in Windermere was closed at the end of 1945. 'The Boys', as they came to be known (although the group also included some 40 girls), were dispersed to hostels in London, Manchester and other large cities; some emigrated to America or Palestine. Lola Hahn-Warburg remembered how she and Leonard Montefiore took stewardship of (and regularly shuttled between) twenty-seven hostels around the country and faced the growing need to find teachers and youth leaders.

Looking back at the support given to these children of the camps, Leonard Montefiore noted: 'The task was not always easy. Some experts made gloomy predictions. These young people, they said, had witnessed scenes of unimaginable horror [...] Of the vast majority, of 95 per cent, one may say, their gloomy prophesies proved false.' He attributed this great success to the work, among others, of Oscar Friedmann: 'We voluntary workers learned much from studying his methods; and he saved us from making many mistakes.'

A few months after they left Windermere, Montefiore wrote about his charges in a way that reveals his deep empathy with those troubled adolescents:

They are boys and girls at the most difficult age, rapidly growing into manhood and womanhood, at an age when those of you who have sons and daughters of your own, know it is impossible to issue orders. One can only argue, persuade, attempt to convince. Nor can they be satisfied with the simple pleasures of childhood, a tea-party or a conjuror.

They want things more difficult and more expensive to provide. They want opportunities [...] These 700 are in our own country,

213

they are living within a few miles of our own homes [...] [I]f we do not help them, there is no one else, who will.

One of the boys that Montefiore helped bring out of the camps was Jerzy Herszberg. Herszberg recalled that Montefiore always took a personal interest in the survivors and often brought the boys presents such as a radio set or drawing equipment to assist those aspiring to become architects or draughtsmen. He helped some, like Herszberg himself, eventually to get a university education and for the less academic to set up in trades. Perhaps above all, he provided the environment which enabled them, for many decades after they first arrived in Britain, to cohere as a tight-knit band of friends, akin to the family that most had lost. Indeed, surviving members still work together today under the aegis of the '45 Aid Society, a charitable organisation founded by 'The Boys' in 1963.

The last word goes to Montefiore's friend and colleague Lola Hahn-Warburg. Recalling his rescue of the more than 700 child survivors of the camps in a tribute written after his death in 1961, she paints a picture of Montefiore's irrepressible humanity all the more touching for its hint of affectionate exasperation:

In this work he could give expression to his great qualities. I know of nobody who had a warmer heart, he knew every individual child by name and all their troubles [...] How well do I remember having talks with adolescent boys and girls and having to be rather firm when they were making demands; invariably Robin listened in with his whimsical smile and I could tell from his expression that he felt I was too hard. When the boy or girl left the room he would slip out and more often than not open his wallet and give the sums they had asked for.

In 2020, a film was released for the BBC called, 'The

Windermere Children'. Directed by Michael Samuels with the aid of The Lake District Holocaust Project, the outstanding docudrama provides a vivid account of the children and their carers at Calgarth. Some of 'the boys', now old men, are seen paying tribute to the British people who brought them out of the concentration camps to health and rejuvenation in the idyllic landscape of the Lake District. One figure is seen played by the actor Tim McInnerny. He is a tall, balding, rather reserved English gentleman with a reassuring smile, a calm and gentle manner putting the traumatised children at ease, and an unmissable sense of rugged compassion for his young charges: it is Leonard Montefiore.

APPENDIX

The Kindertransport
Who, How and Where

'We told them who we wanted and they sent us the children.'

This, according to Lady Stella Reading, one of the prime movers, was how the Kindertransport was organised. It was of course a vast over-simplification. The mechanics behind bringing 10,000 children to safety were highly complex and depended on a whole swathe of people, expertise and contacts. Though records of the German end of the Kindertransport planning have not survived, those from Vienna have done and one can piece together how the children were brought out with recourse to memoirs and scattered records here and there. According to Lady Reading, the Movement for the Care of Children from Germany (MCCG) would inform their opposite numbers in Berlin and Vienna of the kinds of foster homes available – essentially a wish list of the types of children desired by British families. The Jewish men and woman at the Austro-German end would do their best to comply and put on the list of possible émigrés the children who could pass muster.

Following the announcement by Home Secretary, Sir Samuel Hoare, to ease entry criteria for Jewish children, the indefatigable Otto Schiff made representations to the Home Office to simplify travel documents for the children. He was a trusted figure in the corridors of governmental power and was among the first to persuade the British authorities that Jewish refugees would not be a 'burden' on the UK taxpayer and that the local community would find ways to foot the bill. A London-based stockbroker of German Jewish background, Schiff had been instrumental in setting up the Jewish Refugee Committee in March 1933 when he and others had the foresight to know that Jews from Hitler's Germany would need help and assistance to get out.

With its sister organisation, the Central British Fund (CBF) as the main fundraising arm, Schiff put together a powerful team of Anglo-Jewry's great and good including members of the Rothschild family who had a long tradition of philanthropy. The new committees also attracted women with huge experience in child welfare and community affairs – Cissie Laski, Alice Model and Anna Schwab amongst them. Many were active in the nationwide Jewish fraternal body, B'nai Brith, which inaugurated a hospitality committee to help find homes for the refugees and even a social club for their use in London. Schiff himself had a long history of helping poor Jews in London and experience of assisting Belgian refugees during the First World War. Always attentive to the threat of antisemitism and the very sensitive issues of Jewish immigration to Palestine, Schiff was good at walking diplomatic tightropes. Some say that he was often over-cautious in his dealings with government and certainly never one to advocate Britain as a haven for mass rescue from the Nazis. But with all these caveats in mind, Otto Schiff was the key driving force behind the acceptance into the UK of at least 70,000 Jewish immigrants, most of whom would surely have been put to death had they stayed in Berlin, Vienna or Prague.

The result of Schiff's lobbying in late November 1938 meant that the Home Office waived the need for children to require formal visas. Instead, they introduced a new system – a kind of collective passport, essentially two cards with the child's name and photograph, a few other details and a space for a stamp by immigration officials at the arrival port (mainly Harwich). All this was to facilitate the speediest exit for the Kinder and certainly in the first few weeks of the programme, it worked well. In the first ten days of the scheme, over 700 children were brought out of danger from Germany and Austria, the vanguard of 9,000 more who arrived in Britain over the next nine months – a remarkable effort in so short a time. I am often asked how was it possible to get the children to Britain so quickly? The answer is simple: already in place by November '38 were well established networks of movers and shakers who could obtain the correct paperwork, arrange transports, oversee arrangements for arrival in foreign countries. In effect much of the groundwork for the mass rescue of children had already been done.

It is time now to look at how this, the largest rescue mission of its kind, was put into action at both the German (and here also read Austrian) side of the programme. I will reveal who set up the Kindertransport programme and also show the composition of the British end of the rescue, unveiling key players who worked night and day to help the children in flight. They are largely forgotten names.

Not only were the German Jewish organisations geared up to the flight of children in late 1938, but there were precedents for the rescue of unaccompanied children to Britain. From 1933 and with the help of the Quakers, children had been brought over from Germany to live and study in a school called Bunce Court in Kent run by the refugee teacher Anna Essinger (see Chapter 21, The Refugee). A similar programme was established in 1934 with the help of leading Quaker, Bertha Bracey, at a newly established school for refugees at Stoatley Rough in Surrey (see Chapter 9, The Quaker). Within weeks of Hitler's accession, higher education students and academics were being helped by the Academic Assistance Council (AAC); academics and students were brought over to British universities and institutions right up to the outbreak of war.

As early as 1935, the AAC's leader, Walter Adams, discussed with social worker, Francis Bendit, the formation of a central organisation to assist and coordinate efforts to rescue child refugees from Nazi Germany. A special conference was held in London in March 1936 to bring all those concerned with refugee children from Germany – both Jewish and Christian – and the meeting included many of the great and the good of refugee rescue: Otto Schiff and Anna Schwab of the Jewish Refugee Committee (JRC), Francis Bendit and Gladys Skelton of Save the Children Fund, representatives of Bunce Court and Stoatley Rough schools and several other Jewish, Quaker and non-Jewish bodies.

The chairman of this seminal committee was Brigadier-General Sir Wyndham Deedes, a passionate Anglican Zionist who had worked at the highest level in British mandated Palestine. Skelton, a remarkable polymath, social historian and fighter of causes, not least the role of women in society, had been one of the founders of the Save the Children Fund. She was also a published poet, novelist, playwright, and biographer (including a study of Wyndham Deedes). Usually writing under her nom de plume, John Presland, she also penned in 1944 a somewhat rose-tinted spectacles view of the history of the children's rescue movement, 'A Great Adventure'. Few biographical details of Glady Skelton survive; she died in 1975, a forgotten lynchpin in the child refugee story.

For all its good intentions, the IACG only managed to bring in a fairly low number of children. In its first year of operation, hospitality had been arranged for 124 children, approximately half of whom were Christian, the rest Jewish. By late 1938, the committee had helped to bring to Britain just under 500 children. Part of the reason for this slow response was a shortage of funds; response to appeals up and down the land in a period before the great crises of 1938, was sluggish. A fillip to the cause of child refugees came in late 1937 with the establishment of the Church of England Committee for 'Non Aryan' Christians founded by Bishop George Bell (see Chapter 8, The Bishop). Working with Quakers in Berlin, attempts were made to find suitable 'non Aryan' youngsters who were in danger. Monies raised by Bell's committee would be earmarked for Christian children of Jewish extraction (as defined by the Nazis) as there was a feeling that Jewish fundraisers adequately catered for the needs of their brethren in Germany. That said, Jewish funds, as raised and distributed by the CBF (the Central British Fund) did not discriminate against non-Jewish victims of Nazism.

Though it effectively disbanded in November 1938, the Inter-Aid Committee under the chairmanship of Sir Wyndham Deedes provided the solid foundations on which the larger Kindertransport programme was built. It shared office space at Woburn House in London's Bloomsbury district and thus was at the heart of the refugee rescue committees also based in that building. The small committee had already engaged with organisations in Berlin and had set up the first foster family networks, often drawing on church or other groups in Britain. Led in its day-to-day work by Skelton, the committee was allowed to bring the children over to Britain as school students – not as asylum seekers. They were to be funded solely by the committee and not out of taxpayers' funds, and were to be returned once their schooling had been completed. Many of the key features of the subsequent Kindertransport programme: self finance and a commitment to leave Britain, were therefore in place.

Inter-Aid also laid down another key foundation stone in the Kindertransport rescue. Gladys Skelton and her committee had a part to play, albeit a small one, in the escape of nearly 4,000 unaccompanied children from the Basque region of northern Spain. The youngsters were refugees fleeing from the Spanish Civil War which, by 1937, had reached beyond the boundaries of that mountainous area. With General Franco's fascist army moving in towards the Basque capital of Bilbao, a valiant group of Britons led by Leah Manning (see Chapter 3, The Trade Unionist and the Duchess) set up camp in the port city and arranged the exodus of 3,800 children known as niños who, with their chaperones, were crammed on to a leaky old ship named the S.S. Habana. The arrival in the port of Southampton of this huge single cohort of Spanish children on the 21 May 1937 was itself a miracle of organisation. Again the Spanish programme led by Leah Manning, the Duchess of Atholl and others established protocols that would also become central to the Kindertransport rescue. The Duchess' prodigious organisational skills ensured that by the time the Basque children arrived, a central, well-funded body was in place, along with a series of provincial committees charged with finding accommodation for the youngsters. All served by volunteers, these committees such as the ones in Cambridge, Manchester, Glasgow, Cardiff, Margate and others took on parental responsibilities for the children. They raised local funds to run hostels, canteens, schooling and even day trips and longer holidays for the niños. The pressure on the British government to allow in these 4,000 Spanish exiles was kept up by a relentless campaign in Parliament by concerned MPs, most notably Eleanor Rathbone, who was dubbed (by her enemies) as 'The MP for Refugees'. As an independent, Rathbone was supported across the political spectrum by the leading Liberal MP, Wilfred Roberts, Labour's Philip Noel-Baker and Josiah Wedgwood, in addition to the Conservative Colonel Victor Cazalet. Thanks to them and others, Spain and the plight of its children became a nationally recognised cause célèbre. The Basque children and their transport to Britain was a model that did not go unnoticed by those keen to help Jewish victims of the Nazis. Some of those involved in the children's welfare effortlessly transferred their time and energy to the Jewish refugees arriving a year later. One such was Eva Hartree, a former president of the National Union of Women, who was Chairman of the Cambridge Spanish Aid Committee and also a senior figure in the Cambridge Children's Refugee Committee that looked after Jewish émigré children in the city.

Effectively armed with the lessons of that first 'Kindertransport' from Spain, after Kristallnacht, Gladys Skelton and her team agreed to merge the functions of the Inter-Aid Committee with that of a broader based, better funded organisation: the Movement for the Care of Children from Germany (MCCG). By the summer of 1939, the committee would be renamed 'The Refugee Children's Movement' (RCM), the title by which it was most commonly known throughout the war years and beyond.

How this children's committee was set up and whose idea it was is something of a mystery. There are two or three competing narratives. First, the Kindertransport programme was the brainchild of Wilfrid Israel, the Berlin-based de facto leader of the German Jewish community at the time. One theory is that he came up with the plan and communicated it to the Movement in London via a team of British Quakers who had sent out a fact-finding team immediately following the November Pogroms.

Another account has the plan forming in the mind of Helen Bentwich, the founder and leading light of the MCCG once the 'keys' to child rescue from Germany had been handed over by Gladys Skelton's committee. It is likely that Helen Bentwich's husband, Sir Norman, also had a hand in the plan. The rescue idea, it is said, was partly that of the Bentwiches but also of the publisher, Dennis Myer Cohen, who was well placed to conceive the scheme as the head of the emigration policy for the Jewish committees. Something of a dandy, Cohen had served in Palestine in the 1920s and was well-acquainted with the Bentwiches, Viscount Samuel and Wyndham Deedes. Cohen's wife Kathryn was also a key player in the RCM. A warm person, she often greeted the children at the port of Harwich making them feel welcome in their new country and escorting them to their foster parents, hostels or even her own home (a modernist building designed by two Jewish refugee architects from Berlin) in fashionable Chelsea.

Yet a third genesis of the Kindertransport places the idea in the head of Bertha Bracey and her Quaker colleagues in London and Berlin. Bracey's emissaries to Germany, such as the splendidly named Apollonia Rissik, undeniably reported that post-Kristallnacht, the only way to help the Jews was to get their children out and that they, the Quakers, would be instrumental in doing this. Rissik's report from Germany (a compelling insight from an eye witness to the assault on the Jews there) shows that she personally accompanied at least one group of Jewish children from Germany to London.

So whose idea was the Kindertransport? Wilfrid Israel or Helen Bentwich and Dennis Cohen? Bertha Bracey and the Quakers? Where does the truth lie? I suspect that the truth lies somewhere in the middle (as it usually does). As I have already said, the concept of unaccompanied child rescue was not new and the machinery for doing so was already in place both in Germany/Austria and Britain. This is not a story of heroic individuals but heroism on a collective scale. The British end of the Kindertransport could not have happened without the dogged organisation of the desperate, but cool-headed Jews and 'non Aryans' in Berlin, Hamburg and Vienna. It was unthinkable without the efforts, networks and quiet interventions of the Quakers in Germany. And of course, the children collected on to trains and ferries leaving for Harwich (or ships to Southampton) would have nowhere to go (and no official entry permission) without the almost superhuman efforts of the British refugee committees soon collectively to be dubbed 'Bloomsbury House' (because of its address on Bloomsbury Street in central London).

Let us now take a close look at the people involved both at the German/Austrian end of the rescue and the British side. With the almost certain destruction of records in Germany, the work of the rescuers there has become obscure. Forgotten names are plentiful. Research, where it has been done, is mostly in German.

If Bloomsbury House became synonymous with the Kindertransport children, the equivalent in Germany was Number 158, Kantstraße (Berlin). By November '38, this office building housed three key organisations working towards the emigration of Jewish men, women and children from Germany. First among equals was the Reichsvertretung der Juden in Deutschland or 'RV' (Representation of the Jews in Germany), by 1938 an official body which had been representing Jewish interests for years; with the rise of Hitler, its fundamental role was to prepare the Jews of Germany for emigration. The other two organisations under that sheltering roof at Kantstrasse 158, were the Jüdischer Frauenbund (JFB, Jewish Women's League) and the Hilfsverein der Juden in Deutschland (HV, Benefit Association of Jews in Germany). This last organisation was the main self-help group providing much-needed welfare support to the harassed Jews of the new Germany.

Yet another body was the Palästina-Amt (Palestine Office) which prepared young Jewish Germans for a new life in 'Eretz Yisrael' (the land of Israel). Following the Pogroms, the Nazis closed down most of the organisations and insisted that they were all subsumed into the RV. Later, membership of the Reichsvertretung (which by then had undergone a change of name) was to become compulsory for all German Jews and by 1943, the emasculated body was forced to comply with Nazi roundups and be party to the forced transportations of men, women and children to murder in occupied Poland, the Baltic states and Ukraine.

In 1938 the Reichvertretung's senior executives included the leading Liberal rabbi in Germany, Rabbi Leo Baeck, Otto Hirsch and the head of Germany's most prestigious department store chain, the Anglo-German Wilfrid Israel. These august gentlemen played a key role in dealing with the Nazis and liaising with countries that might take the children: the Netherlands, Belgium, France, Switzerland and Sweden. By the time war started, the largest number found safety in the UK.

The Reichsvertretung was divided into many departments, by and large run with great efficiency by a phalanx of German Jewish women many of whose names have been lost to public awareness. The day-to-day workings of these departments are elusive – the records have not largely survived. What we do know is that the head of the children's emigration section was the formidable Käte Rosenheim, a former social worker who in pre-Hitler times worked for the Berlin police. She kept in close almost daily touch with Lola Hahn-Warburg, in London by November 1938, and helped the escape of several thousand children to Palestine and other destinations.

Her secretary was a lively lady called Herta Souhami, a progressive educationalist who fled the Nazi regime just before all doors closed and ended up during the war years running the Jewish refugee hostel in Cambridge. Another key figure was Ottilie Schönewald who had close links with the Dutch Jewish women's organisations. Before the invasion of the Netherlands in May 1940, Holland was seen as a convenient destination for Germany's Jews. Famously, the family of Anne Frank took this very route to what they thought would be freedom from Nazi oppression but ending up in that iconic hiding place in Amsterdam. Ottilie Schönewald also escaped the Nazis and, like Souhani, spent the war years working for the refugee committee in Cambridge.

Other key players in the reconstituted Reichsvertretung were Jewish women who took leadership roles in the welfare of their contemporaries in Nazi times. Prominent among them was Hannah Karminski. She received an entry permit to Britain but decided to stay on in Berlin to take care of her community in Germany. This decision proved to be a fatal one. In 1942 she was transported to Auschwitz and murdered there along with most of her Jewish colleagues, including Professor Cora Berliner. During the Kindertransport period, Hannah Karminski became a familiar figure on the railway journeys out of danger. Formerly a leading figure in the Jewish Women's League, she would often accompany the frightened children as chaperone, calming their fears. As they approached the Dutch border, a signal for aggressive SS men to board the train and scare the youngsters with their shouting, orders to open suitcases for inspections and threats to put them off at the last German station. Hannah Karminski stayed with the children on many journeys to London and though enjoined to stay, always returned to the lion's den of Nazi Germany to help more children. When war closed all gates, Hannah and her lover Paula Fürst worked tirelessly against increasing Nazi harassment, arbitrary arrests and enforced closures. Looking back on her work, a former colleague wrote of Hannah Karminski: 'Hannah was endowed with a strong sense of self-discipline which was sometimes – wrongly – considered as detachment. She drew her indefatigable strength for her deep religiosity and her compassion for her fellow men.'

The Reichsvertretung and the Hilfsverein in particular were closely entwined with other leadership figures such as Wilfrid Israel, Max Warburg, the Hamburg banker and his daughter Lola Hahn-Warburg who later came to join the Movement (see below). The Hilfsverein had been helping Jews to leave Germany since 1933 and worked closely with the American 'Joint' – a well-funded Jewish welfare body – to try to set up schemes to let unaccompanied children into the USA. With offices in Berlin, Hamburg, Bremen and Stuttgart, by 1935 the Hilfsverein had facilitated the emigration of Jewish children in the low hundreds to American schools.

With a powerful team now assembled, the scene was set to get the children out of Germany following the dreadful events in mid November. Wilfrid Israel had long enjoyed good connections with British Quakers and knew their head,

Bertha Bracey, well. Israel asked Bracey to send a delegation to Germany to help identify parents who were willing, given the desperate circumstances, to send their children off with strangers on a journey to far off lands. The Quaker team consisted of the aforementioned Apollonia Rissik, together with Joan Clapham, William Hughes and Ben Greene (cousin of the author Graham Greene). Meeting at the Quaker office in Berlin, the foursome discussed the situation with Hannah Karminski and Wilfrid Israel. Other sympathetic church leaders were there along with Laura Livingstone (see the chapter on Bishop Bell). Israel and Karminski furnished the Quaker quartet with contacts in the Jewish Women's League all over Germany and, in a military-style operation, the four Quakers spread out to cover as much of the country as they could: Rissik to Bavaria, Clapham to East Prussia (the German enclave surrounded then by Poland), Hughes to Saxony and Greene to Western Germany. Their role was twofold: to witness the suffering of German Jews in these regions and report on their condition – and to work with the local Jewish welfare groups in gathering the names of children whose parents came forward to put their offspring on a Kindertransport to Britain. Word got around very quickly that a new escape route – but only for the children – was now in play. In most cases it was mothers who added their child's name to the list; fathers were often in hiding, or were being terrorised and beaten in the Nazi concentration camps of Dachau, Sachsenhausen and Buchenwald.

Lists of names and photos of the children chosen to be considered for a transport to Harwich and beyond were sent by the local Frauenbund and Quaker team to Berlin to be processed there. As Norbert Wollheim, a volunteer at the Berlin based RV, testified many years later, the negotiations to expedite the departure of the children was no easy matter. The Gestapo and other Nazi organisations did all they could to ensure that every pfennig through arbitrary taxes and charges was squeezed out of the Jewish families before the children were allowed to leave. The bureaucratic obstacles were formidable and laced with the ever present danger of arrest or arbitrary rejection. The Nazi officials just couldn't understand why anyone, including the British, should want to take in these young Jews. This was a time when all feelings of compassion among Nazi sympathisers and collaborators had evaporated to a harsh world view that Jewish children were the enemy of the future. Their blood was 'tainted blood' – a clear and present 'danger' to Aryan 'mastery'. Neither pity nor shame was an option for these fanatics; duty to the Fuehrer meant that the Jews, young and old, had to go. Later they would go in only one direction. To the East. To death.

Following the annexation of Austria in March 1938 and the brutal scenes witnessed against Jews in Vienna, the IKG prepared papers for hundreds of older children thought to be at special risk of persecution. As stated earlier, the Jewish organisation had already put in place a scheme for unaccompanied children to seek sanctuary in Britain. By the time of the Pogrom, at least 500 had their papers in order from the Viennese end but only a few had been given permission to enter the UK. It was of course only after the announcement by the Home Secretary, Sir Samuel Hoare, of the new scheme for mass child immigration that numbers started to swell. As ever in this sad history, demand for foster homes far exceeded supply. Financial guarantees had to be found for each potential child immigrant and soon a crippling £50 deposit (equivalent to around £3,000 today) had to be pledged for each. This was initially suggested by Bloomsbury House as a means to secure funds for any future onward migration from Britain to a third country. One of the stipulations of the British government was that each child was only allowed into the country on three key criteria: they could come on a temporary basis until ready to 're-emigrate' at the age of 18, they would not work and take the jobs of British people and that they had financial support for all their time in the country plus the aforementioned £50 for moving on. In no sense was this a kind-hearted asylum policy but one so entrenched in tight restrictions that most children in Nazi Europe never managed to escape. That said, however mealy-mouthed, the British position was far more generous than that of other countries (not least the USA which refused point blank to increase its annual quota of immigrants).

Bureaucratic hurdles were not only a German obstacle. The British government insisted that each child had a medical certificate of good health. What was regarded as 'poor' health could mean anything from a disability as mild as a squint, or speech impediment, to a history of recent infectious disease. A child's mental health and personality was also taken into account. Later additional constraints were actually imposed by Bloomsbury House to ensure that the child was more suitable to be fostered in a stranger's home. Examples of rude or unruly behaviour on a school report, suspicions of a lazy or 'uncooperative' nature could be enough to bar a child. These barriers from the British side were less to do with accepting only the healthy idealised child (very young, blonde girls were especially favoured) but more to do with the lack of suitable homes for them in Britain.

Once a child had been accepted by both the German end of the operation and the Movement for the Care of Children from Germany in London, the lists and documents would be sent to the Home Office in London where a permit card would be stamped and a Movement number given. The stamped permit would then be sent by air to Germany. This would be collected by the Reichsvertretung to be handed to the leaders of each transport to England. These permits meant that the child could sidestep the lengthy and tortuous procedure of a visa and at least from the Home Office viewpoint, emigration formalities had certainly speeded up by the time the first transport of children docked at Harwich, Essex on 2 December 1938.

The situation for the Kindertransports from Vienna was very similar to the German side, except that the Jews of Austria were much more concentrated in the one area – the capital. The organisation of the child transports was carried out by the Israelitisches Kultusgemeinde (IKG, the Jewish Community). The leading light of the IKG was Rosa Schwarz who, like her German counterparts, worked closely with Quakers and some dissenting churchmen and women.

In a rare contemporary memoir written in Palestine in 1944, Schwarz detailed her work and that of her many colleagues at the IKG. Harassment, arrests, evictions and bullying began the very day of the arrival of Nazi troops in Vienna in March 1938. Rosa's work involved providing what welfare she could to the harassed families now under the capricious dictat of the Nazi regime. Her team's remit was to rehouse orphans kicked out of their homes – in one case an entire Jewish children's home had to be abandoned immediately to make way for a Nazi women's group. Babies and toddlers had to make way for adult followers of the Fuehrer. These summary evictions became ever more common; only an outbreak of scarlet fever in a children's home on the Jewish Day of Atonement persuaded the man in charge of Nazi policy towards Austrian Jews, to change the order to clear the building. That man was no less than Hauptsturmführer Adolph Eichmann. The man later to become the architect-in-chief of the transports to the gas chambers, was in 1938 Hitler's man in Vienna charged with the role of impoverishing and isolating the city's Jews.

Following the November Pogroms, the go ahead came to Rosa Schwarz to complete the first of many children's trains to Britain and the Netherlands. It was, she recalled, 'an organisational task that forced us to work days and nights without interruption'. Inundated with requests by parents to put their children on one of these trains, Schwarz and her team had to have the children medically tested, luggage checked and a complex maze of Nazi bureaucracy waded through before full permission to leave was granted. By 10 December 1938, around 700 children had been fully registered to leave. These included over 200 'non Aryan' Christians selected by the local Quaker and church offices. It is hard not to forget that these children, the first wave of the 10,000 Kindertransportees, had seen the destruction of synagogues, Jewish homes and their parents' businesses. They had been eye witnesses to the first mass attack on their defenceless and reviled community. That said, Rosa Schwartz claims that most of the children, despite saying farewell to their distraught mothers, seemed happy and content believing that mutti and papa would soon be joining them overseas.

In her vivid account, Rosa Schwarz pays tribute to a Dutch lady – non Jewish – who helped find the children foster homes. But this lady did far more than this. She was instrumental in getting 600 of the children out of Austria on one single transport, the largest such in the whole history of the Kindertransport. That woman was Geertruida Wijsmuller-Meijer, known by the children she saved simply as 'Truus' (see Chapter 12, The Dutch

Aunt).

If the German and Dutch end of the Kindertransport rescue was well-organised, particularly against the backdrop of Nazi brutality, what of the British end of the programme? The executive of the MCCG (known as 'The Movement') was dominated by a group of well-connected women who all knew each other in the higher echelons of Anglo-Jewish society. Leading the way in founding the body was Helen Bentwich, known to her friends and family as 'Mamie'. Helen was a niece of the leading figurehead of the British Jewish refugee organisation, Viscount Herbert Samuel. She was also a member of the London County Council's education committee. Setting up in makeshift offices, sitting on packing cases in the first days, the Movement quickly got into the swing of organising the arrival and placement of the children from Germany. Bentwich was ably supported by Major Geoffrey Langdon, a former First World War veteran. Langdon brought a sharp business brain to the proceedings and he was one of the first on board to greet the arrival of 200 German children on the SS Prague when it docked in Harwich on 2 December 1938. Langdon served as the Movement's secretary for its first few months and, according to his daughter Janet, the major also had the bright idea to buy in fresh oranges to give to the weary children as a treat for their first meal on English soil.

Assisting Helen Bentwich was Lola Hahn-Warburg, who had fled Germany in September 1938 when she found out that she was on a Gestapo blacklist. She came to London with her husband Wilfred and two small children. She was the daughter of the former head of the eponymous banking house from Hamburg and a recent arrival to British shores. Tall, imperious and forceful, she was also sister-in-law to Kurt Hahn, the founder of Gordonstoun in Scotland, famously the rigorous school attended by Prince Charles.

Lola brought with her a Prussian attention to detail and an impressive address book of Jewish movers and shakers still in Germany – Wilfrid Israel included. Lola had been a leading light in the Hilfsverein which, from 1935, took on the crucial role of taking care of Jewish children caught up in the Nazi onslaught. She was a driving force in Youth Aliyah, a body aimed at preparing youth to emigrate to Palestine.

Later Lola would employ her expertise in sifting through the thousands of applications by desperate parents in Germany and Austria for their children to be placed on a Kindertransport. A former lover (it is said) of Zionist leader Chaim Weizmann (later the first President of the new State of Israel) she accompanied him and others on that fateful delegation to see the Home Secretary on the morning of the 21 November '38 – the day Parliament was first told of the plan to allow thousands of unaccompanied Jewish children into Britain. She continued to work for child refugees throughout the war and into the late 1940s. Those who visited her offices in Bloomsbury House, knew she would do her best to help but that she always demonstrated a strong practical side – she knew when constrained by the shortage of families offering hospitality, it was inevitable to say 'no'.

After the first arrival of the 500 children from Vienna on 12 December 1938, Elaine Marks (later Blond) was having dinner with her brother Simon, the head of Marks and Spencer. According to Blond's memoir, they discussed the huge challenges needed to both rescue and then look after the children. 'Someone ought to do something', Elaine told her brother. He replied in his no nonsense business way, 'You're right. Why don't you do something?' She needed little encouragement to throw herself into the task of helping the young Jewish exiles; Elaine had a reputation as a fundraiser for Zionist causes and so she joined the Movement as Treasurer. Once she started volunteering for the Movement she discovered that job descriptions meant little. Everyone on the committee put their hand to whatever was needed and it seems a special working relationship developed between Lola and Elaine.

Finding money to support the children in Britain was a pressing concern for Elaine. She calculated that each child would cost the Movement around £45 per head per year, and when Elaine joined the committee in early 1939, naturally no one had any idea how many children would be eligible. No upper limit had been set by the British government as long as funds could be found for them, but at nearly £50 per head, multiplied by many thousands each year, the burden on the budget was going to be huge. It doesn't take a maths genius to calculate that the 10,000 Kinder who did make it to Britain would cost half a million pounds per year (approximately £30 million at today's values). And that is for just one year.

Elaine Blond's budgeting troubles were partially alleviated in the first months of the Kindertransport programme. A special film and radio appeal to raise funds for the refugees was launched in December 1938 by former prime minster, Stanley Baldwin (a master of the fireside chat) and money poured in from the sympathetic British public. Family silver was sold at auction, raffles and fetes were held, collecting tins shaken outside railway stations, cash donors listed in the columns of The Times and other newspapers. Within a few short weeks, an astonishing £500,000 was raised by The Baldwin Fund of which two-fifths was allocated to Elaine's committee. Other appeals included one launched by the Lord Mayor of London, special charity cinema showings and a particularly poignant Mother's Day Appeal. The Women's Appeal Committee for German and Austrian Jewish Women and Children (known colloquially as 'The Women's Appeal') had been in operation since 1933 and, by the end of 1938, it had raised almost £53,000 through London and provincial appeals. Large sums, including £23,000 in a single evening, were raised by the then popular American film star and comedian Eddie Cantor who donated the proceeds of his 16-day tour of Britain to a refugee appeal set up by the Zionist organisation, Youth Aliyah. By the end of his barnstorming song, dance and crazy comedy show tour, the star had raised around £100,000 for Jewish refugees. B'nai Brith, the Jewish service organisation with its Lodges throughout the world also played a huge part in the setting up of hostels and the provision of guarantees for the refugee children. British B'nai Brith maintained close contact with its German colleagues and helped secure homes and finance for hundreds of children. Its central committee and provincial lodges – for men and women – raised significant funds through increased subscription charges, sponsored individual children and set up hostels such as the ones in Hackney, Willesden in London and Cheetham Hill in Salford.

Despite these huge sums, the ever-increasing demands on the finances of the Movement soon reached breaking point. The numbers allowed into Britain dipped dramatically in the first few months of 1939 only to recover in late spring and summer. This was probably less to do with the amount raised by the Movement than with the increasing insistence that the Kindertransport children be fully 'guaranteed' by private individuals, or sponsoring bodies such as synagogue communities, churches, youth organisations, clubs and associations. With no government funding forthcoming before the war, children were only permitted to come to Britain if they had a financial sponsor and (from April 1939) a pledge to pay a £50 deposit to cover the costs of 're-emigration' to a third country once the child had reached the age of eighteen. Though the £50 sum could be given either as a bank transfer or a legally binding pledge, for the refugee organisations it proved a major disincentive in finding suitable homes for the young people. Happily, the £50 deposit rule was phased out within a few weeks of its introduction.

Assisting Helen Bentwich, Elaine Blond and Lola Hahn-Warburg were two aristocratic ladies: Stella Isaacs, Dowager Marchioness of Reading and her step daughter-in-law, Lady Eva Isaacs (née Mond). Eva's husband, Gerald (the 2nd Marquis of Reading) also took on a senior role in one of the main bodies supporting all Jewish victims of Nazism. The urge to help these unfortunate people clearly ran in families. Eva was active in the Movement (though Elaine Blond thought her rather imperious and condescending in her attitude towards the refugees). Gerald and Eva's daughter, Joan, also volunteered to help the child refugees in the reception camp at Dovercourt in Essex during the harsh winter of '38-'39. By late 1938, Stella had founded the Women's Voluntary Service (WVS), a post that made her a well-known name throughout the Second World War. It is through Stella, Lady Reading, that an early tie-in was created between the Jewish child refugees from Germany and the mass evacuation programme of British children during the Second World War. In January 1939, Stella's new organisation, the WVS, sent an inspector to report on the conditions in Dovercourt reception camp. The reasons were twofold: to check on the welfare of the refugee children, but also to assess whether former holiday camps such as those run by Butlins and Warners could accommodate evacuated children from British cities. The WVS assessment was that they could not. The conditions at Dovercourt were described as 'primitive' and therefore not suitable for the children from London, Manchester, Glasgow and the rest.

Stella, the Marchioness of Reading's first name, crops up time and time again on committees and fundraising appeals. Throughout 1938 and '39, there were endless appeals to which she lent her name and she would appear as the grandee at fundraising balls and dinners. Her name was associated with 'The Jewel Fund,' a series of auctions in which wealthy ladies were urged to sell their jewellery for the cause of refugees.

The high profile Movement team was further enhanced by Rebecca Sieff, the sister of Elaine Marks. She had been active in aiding Jewish refugees since 1933 when she founded the Women's Appeal Committee of the Central British Fund for German Jewry. A founder member of the 'Movement' in 1938, her true passion was Zionism and working to help get young Jews out from the Nazi clutches to Palestine. At the start of the war, Rebecca Sieff was instrumental in setting up the Jewish Agricultural War Committee whose aim was also to create a series of training farms in Britain for would-be pioneers in Palestine.

In a diverse group like the Movement there were bound to be personality clashes. One such came in the august figure of Rabbi Maurice Swift (an appointee of the Chief Rabbi) who was placed in something of a lion's den. Bentwich, Sieff, Blond, Reading and Hahn-Warburg represented a liberal Jewish thread in Anglo-Judaism; Swift, a staunch member of the Orthodox

Beth Din (rabbinical court) was antagonistic to this world of reform practice. It was a tension that would only rise in the coming years. Stella Reading in her autobiography, noted that one of the key issues for the Movement was where to place Jewish children – and the suitability of putting them in 'gentile homes'. In what was to be a constantly fractious issue, the liberal majority of the Movement took issue with the orthodox voices who were very much against placing Jewish children in Christian homes. For Stella Reading and others, the issue was the availability of homes where traditional Jewish life was observed. For people like Rabbis Swift and Schonfeld, they suspected a kind of reformist conspiracy to deny the refugee children access to what they saw as their rightful heritage. These were circles that simply could not be squared.

Supporting all these strong figures on the Movement executive was Grete Exiner, who like Hahn-Warburg, was a recent refugee from Nazi Germany. Exiner brought some incredibly useful skills to the executive: she had been working from 1933 to 1938 at the Palestine and Orient Lloyd travel bureau in Berlin. This crucial travel office had played its part in getting emigration tickets and papers for Jewish prisoners in concentration camps. This experience was to prove invaluable in arranging the flight of the 10,000 children to Britain. Exiner's work rate and great organisational skills surprised Helen Bentwich who remarked, 'I never thought I would have to work with Germans'.

With the transports from Germany under way, attention turned to the terrible plight of Jewish refugees in the Czech lands of Bohemia and Moravia. Some of these were children of families who had fled from the Czech German-speaking borderlands known as Sudetenland. Those lands had been occupied by Nazi troops after the Munich Agreement had given the green light for Hitler to act as he wanted with Czechoslovakia. Terrorised by the anti-Jewish laws and government-led persecution that they knew to be heading their way, thousands of families left their homes and headed for unoccupied Czech areas. Hastily created refugee camps were put in place around cities such as Prague and it is said that 200,000 refugees lived in these makeshift camps – some of them rat infested, crumbling, unheated castles. Conditions were primitive and outbreaks of disease common.

The desperate situation drew attention from both British left and liberal political wings and Prague became a hotbed for those wanting to help the outcasts – Jews and non-Jews alike. Principal among them was Doreen Warriner, a London-based academic who arrived in the city determined to help and armed with £150 from the Save the Children Fund. With the Czech government overwhelmed by the huge influx of families, it was clear that only international aid agencies and people like Warriner could help them. An inexhaustible worker and no mean networker drawing in Czech and British politicians with equal success, Warriner and others soon had a dynamic organisation in place. The British Committee for Refugees from Czechoslovakia (BCRC) helped hundreds of political exiles escape the clutches of the Nazis via an 'underground railway' route through Poland. Visas (but only in the 100s) were obtained for entry into Britain and Warriner gathered round her a team of British Quakers, including Tessa Rowntree and Mary Penman. It is said in Mary's family, that Mary Penman helped to hide refugees in her flat in central Prague. One day there was a heavy knock at Mary's door. A Jewish girl hiding in the flat was terrified. Penman told her not to hide but to calmly answer the door. The Gestapo men did not suspect so brazen a ruse, breezed in, looked around and left satisfied that no one was hiding there.

Warriner also mobilised the British end via her friends in the Labour Party and worked under the radar with sympathetic British official, Robert Stopford, who quietly helped hundreds if not thousands of political refugees get out of the Czech lands. Doreen Warriner lost no time in forming a very good relationship with Marie Schmolka, a prominent Prague Jewish activist who had her own Czechoslovak Refugee Committee. Schmolka's home in Prague Old Town became a veritable clearing house for refugee rescue. She was unrivalled in creating partnerships with organisations at home and abroad. Very sadly, however, the trauma of being arrested by the Nazis and being subjected to long interrogations, severely damaged her health and though she managed to escape to Britain, she died of a heart attack aged only 46. Neither Warriner, nor Schmolka could deal with the sheer volume of refugee children languishing in the camps or living in fear in Prague.

Here is where fate took an astonishing leap when Warriner met a young London stockbroker called Nicholas Winton who had been summoned to Prague by his friend Martin Blake. Abandoning plans for a skiing holiday, Winton flew out to Prague and met Warriner and the MP Eleanor Rathbone, who happened to be there on a fact-finding mission. Warriner immediately recognised that Winton was highly organised and passionate about helping the children. Between them they concocted a plan to create a special children's division of the Czech refugee committee. Winton was to lead the new team and work on finding foster homes in Britain for the children on what became known as the Czech Kindertransport or the 'Winton Trains'. The name of Nicholas (later Sir Nicholas) Winton has become synonymous with the whole Kindertransport programme, and ever since a remarkable appearance on BBC

TV ('That's Life') in 1988, his fame spread exponentially as 'Britain's Schindler'. He helped to find homes for over 660 Jewish children from Prague but he was part of a much larger team. While Winton made his base at home with his mother in London, his colleagues stayed in Prague to help organise the transports. As with Vienna and Berlin, they were inundated by parents anxious to get their children to safety. Names had to be recorded, health checks made, exit procedures carried out and after March 1939, Gestapo officials had to be cajoled or bribed.

All this work was carried out, under increasing threat from the Nazis, by a formidable team of volunteers. Chief among them was Trevor Chadwick, a schoolteacher from Dorset who had given up his job to take charge of the Prague end of the Kindertransport. By all accounts this former lifeboat crewman was highly personable, popular and determined. He was good at calming the fears of parents about to say long farewells to their children, and adept at manipulating local Nazi officials who liked him enough not to stand in his way, at least for the first few months after the occupation of Prague. Alongside him was an equally forceful young Canadian Beatrice Wellington, and a slightly mysterious figure, Bill Barzetti, who may or may not have had some espionage role but was certainly an active part of Chadwick's rescue team. Among the 669 Czech Kinder rescued by Chadwick, Winton and others were Lord Alf Dubs (a tireless campaigner for current refugee rescue) and little Suzie Spitzer who left her parents as a five year-old to start a new life in Cambridge.

Back in London and not involved in the Czech Kindertransport, the Movement set itself an enormous series of tasks. Not only was there the ongoing crisis of financing the refugee programme, but also the desperate search for hospitality.

Get the children out!

What began as a few volunteers led by Helen Bentwich sitting on packing cases in makeshift offices, became by the summer of 1939, a far more professional outfit. A non-Jewish Chairman, Lord Gorrell, formerly president of The National Council for the Unmarried Mother and her Child, was appointed (not without considerable opposition from the orthodox Jewish community who thought he would have too little regard for the religious needs of the children). Other non-Jewish leaders were appointed such as the Reverend W.W. Simpson (later co-founder of the Council of Christians and Jews) and Canon George Craven. The Movement also appointed its first full-time General Secretary, Dorothy Hardisty. More has been said about this powerhouse of child refugee welfare in Chapter 4. The presence of these non-Jews was to reassure the wider public that the rescue of children was not solely a cause for one minority group, but a moral issue for all.

The Kindertransport, then, was a massive logistical operation involving a raft of highly talented, frenetically energised humanitarians who recognised the perilous danger into which the Jews of Europe had been plunged. In an age before the Internet, astonishingly good communications were kept up between London, Berlin, Vienna, Amsterdam and elsewhere. Telephone lines buzzing, telegrams constantly toing and froing, visitors from Berlin to London arriving daily – the Kindertransport was, if nothing else, an awe-inspiring triumph of communication and international cooperation. But then it needed to be.

Images
Index and accreditation

We would like to express our gratitude to the many people who helped provide the images for this book.

Image 1, Page viii, The Chadwicks, kindly supplied by Ann Chadwick.

Image 2, Page xix, The Times Advertorial, licensed from News Licensing.

Image 3, Page 1, Frank Foley, generously supplied by Yad Vashem - The World Holocaust Remembrance Center, Israel, www.yadvashem. org.

Image 4, Page 1, Inge and Robert T. Smallbones, kindly supplied by Sandra Wellington.

Image 5, Page 15, Josiah Wedgwood, kindly supplied by Simon James Josiah Wedgwood.

Image 6, Page 22, Leah Manning, licensed from the National Portrait Gallery, UK, www.npg.org.uk.

Image 7, Page 22, Katharine Marjory Stewart-Murray (née Ramsay), Duchess of Atholl, licensed from the National Portrait Gallery, UK, www.npg.org.uk.

Image 8, Page 50, Dorothy Hardisty, kindly supplied by Sandra Galton.

Image 9, Page 51, Lord Alan Sainsbury, generously supplied by The Sainbury Archive, UK, www.sainsburyarchive.org.uk.

Image 10, Page 57, Truus Wijsmuller, made avaliable for use without licence by The Dutch National Archives, The Netherlands, www.nationaalarchief.nl.

Image 11, Page 65, Sir Wyndham Deedes, kindly supplied by Jeremy Deedes.

Image 12, Page 72, George Bell, licensed from Alamy, UK, www.alamy.com.

Image 13, Page 83, Bertha Bracey, generously supplied by The Library of the Society of Friends, UK, www.quaker.org.uk.

Image 14, Page 92, Frank Bond, kindly supplied by Mandy and Darren Netherwood.

Image 15, Page 105, Emily and Harry Moye, kindly supplied by Edward James.

Image 16, Page 105, Keith Lawson, kindly supplied by Ian Lawson.

Image 17, Page 110, Alan Overton, kindly supplied by Jane McKenzie.

Image 18 & 19, Page 116, Sybil and Robert Hutton, kindly supplied by Chris Wakefield.

Image 20, Page 130, Greta Burkill, kindly supplied by Julia Butler.

Image 21, Page 141, Henry Carter, generously supplied by Oxford Brookes University - Oxford Centre for Methodism and Church History.

Image 22, Page 146, Mary Hughes, gifted to the author by the late David Hughes.

Image 23, Page 157, Hilda Murrell, licensed from Alamy, UK, www.alamy.com.

Image 24, Page 163, Henry Fair, kindly supplied by Margaret Craig.

Image 25, Page 168, J. Ernest Davey, generously supplied by the artist Matthew Phinn, www.matthewphinn.com.

Image 26, Page 175, Rabbi Dr Solomon Schonfeld, kindly supplied by Jeremey Schonfeld.

Image 27, Page 184, Anna Essinger, we were unable to identify the owner of this image. If you have any information regarding the owner of this image please contact hello@lemonsoul.com.

Image 28, Page 196, Rachel Alexander, kindly supplied by Jeremy Musson.

Image 29, Page 205, Leonard Montefiore, kindly supplied by Claire Montefiore.

Selected Bibliography

Atholl, Katharine. Searchlight on Spain, Penguin, 1937.

Auspitz Labson, Gabriella. My Righteous Gentile: Lord Wedgwood and Other Memories, Ktav Publishing, 2004.

Barnett, Ruth. Person of No Nationality: a Story of Childhood Loss and Recovery, David Paul Press, 2010.

Barnett, Victoria. For the Soul of the People, Protestant Protest Against Hitler, Oxford University Press, 1992.

Baumel-Schwartz, Judith Tydor. Never Look Back: the Jewish Refugee Children in Great Britain, 1938–1945, Purdue University Press, 2012.

Baxter, Julie Renate. Ray's Story, Published Privately, 2017.

Bell, Adrian. Only for Three Months, Mousehold Press, 2007.

Bell, Bishop George. Humanity and Refugees, Jewish Historical Society of England, February 1939.

Benjamin, Natalia (ed). Recuerdos, The Basque Children Refugees in Great Britain, Mousehold Press, 2007.

Bentwich, Norman. They Found Refuge, Cresset Press, 1956.

Benz, Wolfgang, Curio, Claudia and Hammel, Andrea (eds). Die Kindertransporte 1938/39, Fischer, 2003.

Bergas, Hanna. Memoirs, Published Privately.

Berghahn, Marion. Continental Britons: German-Jewish Refugees from Nazi Germany, Berghahn Books, 2011.

Bermant, Chaim. The Cousinhood, Eyre and Spottiswoode, 1971

Bill, Ron and Newens, Stanley. Leah Manning, Muze UK, 1991

Blond, Elaine and Turner, Barry. Marks of Distinction, The Memoirs of Elaine Blond, Vallentine Mitchell, 1988

Baruch-Brent, Leslie. Sunday's Child, A Memoir, Bank House Books, 2009

Bolchover, Richard. British Jewry and the Holocaust Littman Library of Jewish Civilization, 2003

Brinson, Charmian. Please Tell the Bishop of Chichester, George Bell and the Internment Crisis of 1940 Kirchliche Zeitgeschichte, Vol. 21, No.2.

Burkill, Margareta (Greta). Memoir, Unpublished, The Burkill Papers, University of Cambridge Library

Chadwick, Ann. Suzie the Little Girl Who Changed Our Lives, Keystage Arts and Heritage, 2012

Chandler, Andrew (ed). The Church and Humanity: The Life and Work of George Bell, 1883-1958, Routledge, 2012

Cohen, Susan. Rescue the Perishing: Eleanor Rathbone and the Refugees, Vallentine Mitchell, 2010

Cohen, Susan. Voluntary Refugee Work in Britain, 1933-39. An Overview, Insight Into British Jewish Studies, PaRDeS Journal of the Association of Jewish Studies, 2012

Cooper Ray. Refugee Scholars, Moorland Books, 1992

Coupland, Philip. George Bell: Speaking for Germany and European Unity, 1939-1950, Kirchliche Zeitgeschichte, Vol. 21, No. 2

Craig-Norton, Jennifer. The Kindertransport, Contesting Memory, Indiana University Press, 2019

Curio, Claudia. 'Invisible' Children': the Selection and Integration Strategies of Relief Organizations, SHOFAR Vol. 23 No. 1 (2004)

David, Rob. A County of Refuge, Refugees in Cumbria 1933-1941, Cumberland and Westmoreland Antiquarian and Archaeological Society, 2020.

Dineley Francis. The Rich are Always With Us, Notes on the Use and Abuse of Money, Published Privately, 1994.

Drucker, Olga Levy. Kindertransport, Henry Holt, 1992.

Dubrovsky, Gertrude. Six from Leipzig, Vallentine Mitchell, 2004.

Dunlop, Margaret M. Goodbye Berlin, The Biography of Gerald Wiener, Birlinn, 2016.

Eliahm, Elanth (ed.). Memories of Sir Wyndham Deedes, Published Privately, 1958.

Ehret, Ulrike. Church, Nation and Race: Catholics and anti-Semitism in Germany and England, 1918-1945, Manchester University Press, 2012.

Fast, Vera R. Children's Exodus: A History of the Kindertransport, IB Tauris, 2011.

Fink, Margaret. Belfast to Belsen and Beyond, Penfolk Publishing, 2008.

Friedlaender, Sophie. Sophie & Hilde: Ein Gemeinsames Leben in Freundschaft und Beruf, (translated for the author by Kathrin Peters) Ed. Hentrich, 1996.

Fulton, A. J. Ernest Davey', Presbyterian Church in Ireland, Presbyterian Church in Ireland, 1970.

Frankl, Mike. Hana Bandler, A Less Ordinary Life, Published Privately, 2013.

Fry, Helen. Spymaster, The Man Who Saved MI6, Yale University Press, 2021.

Gershon, Karen. We Came as Children, Victor Gollancz, 1966.

Gilbert, Martin. The Boys, Triumph Over Adversity, Phoenix, 1996.

Gissing, Vera. Pearls of Childhood, Robson Books, 1988.

Göpfert, Rebekka. Kindertransport: History and Memory, SHOFAR Vol. 23 No. 1 (2004)

Gottlieb, Amy Zahl. Men of Vision: Anglo-Jewry's Aid to the Victims of the Nazi Regime, Weidenfeld & Nicolson, 1998)

Grenville, Anthony. Jewish Refugees from Germany and Austria in Britain, 1933–1970, Vallentine Mitchell, 2010)

Haber, Gilda Moss. Cockney Girl, Derby Books, 2012

Hammel, Andrea & Lewkowicz, Bea, eds. The Kindertransport to Britain 1938/39: New Perspectives, Vol 13 of The Yearbook of the Research Centre for German and Austrian Exile Studies, Institute of Germanic and Romance Studies, Univ. of London

Harris, Mark Jonathan & Oppenheimer, Deborah, eds. Into the Arms of Strangers: Stories of the Kindertransport: the British Scheme that Saved 10,000 Children from the Nazi Regime, Bloomsbury, 2000

Hill, Paula. Anglo-Jewry and the Refugee Children 1933-1945, Unpublished PhD thesis, University of London, 2001.

Holfter, Gisela. The Irish Context of Kristallnacht, Refugees and Helpers, Irish-German Studies 8, 2014

Homes,Rose. A Moral Business: British Quaker work with Refugees from Fascism, 1933-39, Unpublished PhD thesis, University of Sussex, 2013.

Hutton, Robert. Recollections of a Technologist, Pitman, 1964

Jasper, Ronald. George Bell, Bishop of Chichester, Oxford University Press, 1967

Josephs, Zoe. Survivors, Jewish Refugees in Birmingham 1933-1945, Meridian Books, 1988

Kranzler, David. Holocaust Hero: Solomon Schonfeld, Ktav Publishing House, 2004

Kranzler, David & Hirschler, Gertrude, (eds). Solomon Schonfeld: his page in history: recollections of individuals saved by an extraordinary Orthodox Jewish rescue hero during the Holocaust era, Judaica, 1982

Kaye, Lucie (ed). Burning for the Cause, Centenary Celebration of Lola Hahn-Warburg, Lola Hahn-Warburg Memoir Project, 2001.

Kotzin, Catherine. Christian Responses in Britain to Jewish Refugees from Europe, 1933–1939, unpublished. PhD thesis, Southampton University.

Kushner, Tony. Remembering Refugees: Then and Now, Manchester University Press, 2006.

Leverton, Bertha & Lowesohn, Shmuel. I Came Alone: Stories of the Kindertransport, Book Guild, 1990.

Lieberman, Nina. He Came to Cambridge: Rabbi David Samuel Margules, Ellisons' Editions, 1983.

London, Louise. Whitehall and the Jews, 1933–48: British Immigration Policy, Jewish Refugees and the Holocaust, Cambridge University Press, 2000.

Manning, Leah. A Life for Education, An Autobiography, Victor Gollancz, 1970.

Manning, Leah. What I Saw in Spain, Victor Gollancz, 1935.

Morrell-Norwood, Leslie, The Christadelphian Response to Nazi anti-Jewish policy of WWII.

Unpublished paper, Brandeis University, May 1996.

Mulvey, Paul. The Political Life of Josiah C. Wedgwood: Land, Liberty and Empire, 1872-1943, Royal Historical Society, 2010.

Musson, Jeremy. Aubrey House, Wheatsheaf Press, Cambridge, 2014.

Oldfield, Sybil. It is Usually She: the Role of British Women in the Rescue and Care of the Kindertransport Kinder, SHOFAR Vol. 23 No. 1 (2004).

Oldfield, Sybil. This Working-Day World, Women's Lives and Culture (s) in Britain 1914-1945, Taylor and Francis, 1994.

Overton, R., A. Report of the activities of the Rugby (Christadelphians) refugee committing the special reference to the two Jewish boys' hostels at Rugby July 1942, Reprinted in Leverton, B. and Lowensohn, S., I Came Alone, The Stories of the Kindertransport

Paldiel, Mordecai. Saving the Jews, Schreiber, 2000

Pattenden, Rosemary. Greta Burkill: Mother To Thousands, In Peterhouse Annual Record, 2012/2013

Presland, John (Gladys Bendit). A Great Adventure: the Story of the Refugee Children's Movement, Refugee Children's Movement,1944

Radcliffe, James. Bishop Bell of Chichester and non-Aryan Christians, Kirchliche Zeitgeschichte, Vol. 21, No. 2

Samuel, Viscount. Memoirs, Cresset Press, 1945

Schonfeld, Rabbi Dr. Solomon, Message to Jewry, Jewish Secondary Schools Movement

Segal, Lore. Other People's Houses, The Bodley Head, 1958

Sharples, Caroline. Reconstructing the Past: Refugee Writings on the Kindertransport, Holocaust Studies, Vol. 12 No. 3 (2006)

Shatzkes, Pamela, Holocaust and Rescue: Impotent or Indifferent? Anglo-Jewry 1938–1945, Palgrave, 2002

Shepherd, Naomi. Wilfrid Israel, Germany Jewry's Secret Ambassador, Weidenfeld & Nicolson, 1984

Sherman, A J. Island Refuge: Britain and the Refugees from the Third Reich 1933–1939, Frank Cass, 1994; orig. ed. 1973

Smallbones, Robert. Memoirs, Unpublished

Smith, Lyn. Heroes of the Holocaust, Ebury Press, 2013

Smith, Michael. Foley, The Spy Who Saved 10,000 Jews, Hodder and Stoughton, 2004

Stein, Joshua, S. Our Great Solicitor: Josiah C. Wedgwood and the Jews, Susquehanna University Press, 1992

Stein, L., and Aronsfeld, C.C. (eds). Leonard G. Montefiore 1889-1961: In Memoriam, Vallentine Mitchell, 1964

Stiebel, Joan. The Central British Fund, Jewish Historical Society of England Transactions, 1979.

Taylor, Derek. Solomon Schonfeld, A Purpose in Life, Vallentine Mitchell: 2009.

Tomlin, Chanan. Protest and Prayer: Rabbi Dr. Solomon Schonfeld and Orthodox Jewish responses in Britain to the Nazi persecution of Europe's Jews, 1942-1945, Peter Lang, 2006.

Turner, Barry. And the Policeman Smiled: 10,000 Children Escape from Nazi Europe, Bloomsbury, 1990.

Turner, Barry. The Long Horizon: 60 Years of CBF World Jewish Relief, CBF, 1993.

Ungerson, Clare. Four Thousand Lives, The Rescue of German Jewish Men to Britain, 1939, The History Press, 2014.

Urwin, E.C. Henry Carter, C.B.E., The Epworth Press, 1955.

Warner, Valerie, Langrish. A Warner Story, Seasons on the Sun, Evergreen Books, 2010.

Wasserstein, Bernard. Britain and the Jews of Europe 1939–1945, Oxford: OUP, 1979; Israel, Books International, 1999.

Wedgwood, J.C. Memoirs of a Fighting Life, Hutchinson, 1941.

Wedgwood, C.V. The Last of the Radicals, Jonathan Cape, 1951.

Wenbourne, Neil. 'A Desirable End': Vaughan Williams and the refugee relief effort of the 1930s and 1940s, Journal of the Ralph Vaughan Williams Society, October 2019.

Wijsmuller-Meijer, Truus. Geen Tijd Voor Tranen [No Time for Tears, The Wartime Memories of Truus Wijsmuller, (excerpt translated for the author by Sara Kirby) Van Kempen, 1961.

Williams, Bill. Jews and other Foreigners, Manchester University Press, 2011.

Williams, A. Susan. Ladies of Influence, Women of the Elite in Interwar Britain, Allen Lane, The Penguin Press, 2000

Williams, Frances. The Forgotten Kindertransportees, The Scottish Experience, Bloomsbury Academic, 2014

Wolfenden, Barbara. Little Holocaust Survivors and the English School That Saved Them, Greenwood World Publishing, 2008

Index

The plight of child refugees today
A message from Safe Passage

In 2015 a group of volunteers travelled to the makeshift refugee camp in Calais, France known to its residents as the 'Jungle'. They made the journey to see how they could help, but unlike others who delivered aid, they arrived with a simple question; why were thousands of children risking their lives trying to cross to Britain?

They didn't expect to hear such a simple and compelling reason – those in the camp had family in the UK who they were desperately trying to reach.

On their return, the volunteers learned that many of the refugees had a legal right to family reunion, but this safe route had never once been used to reunite a refugee child in France with their family in Britain.

This began a partnership between lawyers, community organisers and community leaders in the 'Jungle' camp, who were all determined to find a legal and safe way to help child refugees to reunite with their families.

After many hours of legal work, and painstaking work by refugee community leaders in the camp to document the children who were there, we won a landmark legal ruling at the Royal Courts of Justice, which opened a safe route to family reunion for children in Calais. Three children and one adult arrived safely in the UK days later.

And so, the story of Safe Passage International began.

Today our charity Safe Passage International works across Europe to provide safe passage to unaccompanied children and vulnerable people who are fleeing war and persecution. Many of these children are homeless, or living alone in camps, and have already made extraordinary journeys to try and reach safety and their loved ones.

Along the way we have had the privilege of meeting and campaigning alongside many of those who came to Britain on the Kindertransport over 70 years ago, as well as their children and grandchildren. Whilst the stories and context are very different, there is a common thread that connects them with child refugees today – the need for safe passage; resilience in the face of all that they experienced; the enduring love of family left behind and family joined.

These stories, old and new, must be heard and remembered. We are honoured to be connected to this book, and grateful to all those who continue to support the need for safe passage for child refugees today.

Beth Gardiner-Smith
Safe Passage International, CEO

£1 from the sale of this book will be donated to Safe Passage (charity number 1179608). Find out more about Safe Passage by visiting **www.safepassage.org.uk**

About the author

Mike Levy is a professional researcher for the UK Holocaust Memorial Foundation, the U.S. Holocaust Memorial Museum (contractor), educator, critic, playwright and journalist. Born in Leeds, Mike is married with two grown up children, a two year-old grandson and lives with his wife Sheila in Cambridge.

He holds a fellowship in Holocaust education from the Imperial War Museum and is a frequent educator on the 'Lessons from Auschwitz' programme. In 2012 Mike was awarded the In Memoria medal by the Polish government for his history play 'The Invisible Army'.

As one half of Keystage Arts and Heritage, Mike has researched projects as diverse as the British merchant navy in World War II, to the life of Samuel Pepys. He is a regular contributor to the arts magazine, 'The Cambridge Critique', and gives talks on a wide range of topics from Gershwin to Soviet jazz musicians.

However, it's for all subjects associated with Kindertransport history Mike is most in demand, contributing to the AJR podcasts on Kindertransport history as well as for the BBC World Service.

Mike is also chair of the Harwich Kindertransport Memorial appeal, which seeks to create a new sculpture in the port where most of the refugee children had a first sight of freedom.

Acknowledgements

This book has been a labour of love though at times the emphasis was on the word 'labour'. The concept behind this work began with a plan to write a collaborative book with friends in Cambridge – Debbie-Patterson Jones and Neil Wenborn. We worked on and off for a few years on the idea of forgotten rescuers but somehow life got in the way and it was not possible to finish the manuscript. What you have here is my own input with several additional chapters. I am deeply indebted to Neil who was stalwart in editing the chapters I had written for that original book. He has an amazing eye for detail and is a formidable researcher; any subsequent errors are entirely my own. Debbie too inspired me to look deeper into the subject and remains for me a deeply respected and knowledgeable colleague.

I must also thank my wife Sheila for putting up with strange requests for research visits and for providing a pin-sharp pair of eyes as a proof-reader. I can't thank enough my editor Sue Garfield for her tireless help and support, not to mention immense patience in dealing with my disorganised and mercurial mind. Any errors remaining in this book are entirely those of Mike Levy and I apologise in advance for any that are found.

Huge thanks are also due to the archivists at the Cambridge University Library (whose tearoom is a favourite haunt), the very helpful and friendly staff at Churchill College Archive Centre, The Wiener Holocaust Library, the Imperial War Museum and British Library. Again, I am so grateful to the families of many of the 'forgotten' who helped me with private papers, family photographs and stories. These include Jane Mackenzie, granddaughter of 'The Shopkeeper' Alan Overton; she shared with me many warm family memories of this remarkable man driven by a deep sense of 'doing the right thing'.

I was privileged to interview several people before they died – wonderful gentlemen such as Sir Nicholas Winton and the gracious foster father of Suzie Spitzer, Mr Aubrey Chadwick. We have got to know 'Chad's' family well especially Ann who has a huge private collection of letters and papers about her 'new' sister Suzie, not to mention a wealth of fond memories of the Kindertransport child which she so generously shared with me and the world through her book, 'Suzie, the Little Girl Who Changed Our Lives'.

I also pay tribute to the warm and witty Keith Lawson and his memories of the farming family that 'adopted' the German Jewish refugee. Much of my chapter on Henry Fair and Greta Burkill was sourced from the indomitable and much-missed former Kindertransportee and dogged researcher, Susanne Medas. I so wish she could have lived long enough to see this book (though no doubt she would be full of no-nonsense advice and helpful criticism). Even into her 90s, Susanne would answer any of my questions about events 80 years ago – and she would do so in long and cogent emails. I also cannot thank enough dear Lore Robinson who even in her mid 90s, was so helpful and kind in sharing her memories of Cambridge rescuers Professor and Mrs Hutton. Lore has become a dear friend and again it is an utter privilege to know her.

My several meetings with the nonagenarian David Hughes in his home town of Bishop's Castle were a true delight and I am so grateful to fate for allowing me to talk to him about his time helping at Dovercourt camp and the quiet heroism of his mother Mary. When David died at the age of 101, the world lost a true, quiet hero.

I would also like to thank Pete Doyle and his late mother for providing memories and the photograph of the former refugee child with Alan Sainsbury ('The Grocer'), not forgetting Camilla Woodward and the others in the Sainsbury family who helped me uncover the story of the hostel in Putney. I am indebted too to Mike Frankl for allowing me to share papers relating to his cousin Hana and the remarkable refugee committee lady, Hilda Murrell. Also, much thanks to Rachel Mellor for allowing me access to the private papers related to her father and Rachel Alexander. Jeremy Schonfeld was incredibly helpful in sharing memories and photographs of his late father Rabbi Dr. Solomon Schonfeld.

Mandy Wakefield has been a real stalwart supporter of my efforts to uncover the Dovercourt camp story. Her beloved grandpa and grandma were in charge of the camp in the late 1930s and besides many stories of Frank Bond, she was very generous in letting me see family photographs of that time. Three loud cheers also to the Hon Jeremy Deedes and his wife for their hospitality and access to private papers relating to the remarkable Sir Wyndham (again surely a full biography is long overdue).

Just as this book was reaching its concluding stages, I came across the 94 year-old Geoffrey Jago who gave me a spirited insight into the lifesaving part played by his Cornish parents in caring for two Jewish refugee siblings. Geoffrey wanted to dedicate his memories to his late father. Thanks too to Lawrence Collin for leading me to Geoffrey and allowing access to his interview with the late Harry Grenville, one of the children taken under the wing of the Jago family.

Being a lifelong non-linguist meant that many sources were not accessible for me. So, I am especially grateful to Sara Kirby for translating an extract from the memoirs in Dutch of Truus Wijsmuller (a rescuer surely deserving her own full biography in English) and Kathrin Peters for tackling those memories of Dovercourt camp and Bloomsbury House which were written in German.

I would also like to applaud Matthias Shirmer in Berlin and Professor Eva Thune at the University of Bologna for their help, advice, support and expertise on matters relating to the German side of the Kindertransport organisation. Thanks also to World Jewish Relief for granting access to some of their amazing digital records. Also, praise is much deserved by Carmen Kilner who runs the Basque Children's Association and is the font of all knowledge on the children's exodus from Spain to Britain in 1937. Similar thanks to our team which helped create the education website havenseast.org which tells the story of the Spanish 'Kindertransport'. Lesley Ford, my colleague at Keystage Arts and Heritage (keystage.org) has also been a helpful supporter.

There are so many others who have helped me research this book and I apologise for not naming each of them. Writing what amounts to a series of biographies carries great dangers of inaccuracies. I hope I have managed to spot all of them but if not I hope the reader can forgive and let me know what to put right.

Finally, I would like to thank my fellow team members of the Harwich Kindertransport Memorial and Learning Appeal. Our plan to have a new memorial to the Kindertransport in the port of Harwich were moving apace as writing this book moved to its conclusion. I hope in some small way that this work and the memorial will help stimulate new research and discoveries in the vast story that is the role of forgotten men and women who did their best to help save and care for child refugees in the 1930s and 1940s. As we say in Jewish prayer 'May their memory be a blessing'.

Mike Levy
Cambridge, 2021